Greatest Speeches of India

Greatest Speeches of India

Ram Kumar

PRABHAT
PAPERBACKS

Published by
PRABHAT PAPERBACKS
An imprint of Prabhat Prakashan Pvt. Ltd.
4/19 Asaf Ali Road,
New Delhi-110002 (INDIA)
e-mail: prabhatbooks@gmail.com

ISBN 978-93-5521-209-2
GREATEST SPEECHES OF INDIA
by Shri Ram Kumar

Edition
First, 2022

Price
₹ 500.00 (Rupees Five Hundred only)

Printed at
R-Tech Offset Printers, Delhi

Preface

In the beginning there was 'the word', which was the basis for creation. The power of words can tie the whole of humanity together. When these words come at the right juncture of time from some of the greatest personalities in our country, the effect it leaves behind is an indelible imprint in our hearts, minds and in time. Many of these personalities are men and women who have made invaluable contributions to our coming together as a nation of people and are the pride and honour of the country. These are people who have made a great impact on the lives around them and thus their words are the gems which had the power to evoke the courage and emotion in people and inspire them to make history. The power of a great speech, especially when everyone listens is something that sets the wheels of history in motion to many great events that changed the face of our known world.

We present here, a collection of 25 great speeches made by some of the tallest Indian personalities. We may or may not agree to all of their words but it is impossible to deny the power of these words that have emanated from their minds, which have given shape to a body of work by which they are defined. Some of these are from the era of the struggle for Indian independence from the colonial rule such as, Subhas Chandra Bose, Dr. B.R. Ambedkar, Mahatma Gandhi and Jawaharlal Nehru to mention a few. Polar contemporaries such as Nathuram Godse, Vinayak Damodar Savarkar also make an appearance in this collection to present a different perspective. In today's times, Ratan Tata, N.R. Narayana

Murthy, Kiran Bedi, Sachin Tendulkar are defining trailblazers in their own fields.

The quality of a great speech is not only the wisdom that comes from the experience of their unique lives but the timelessness of these words which work their magic anytime you hear or read it. It never fails to evoke the magnitude of honesty and the grit of their determination in their own times.

We hope this collection of 25 greatest speeches from some of India's unforgettable people always inspire to overcome all challenges and bring out the best of you, dear reader, in the face of all challenges.

Jai Hind!

Contents

My Vision for India

—A.P.J. Abdul Kalam

I have three visions for India. In 3,000 years of our history, people from all over the world have come and invaded us, captured our lands, conquered our minds. From Alexander onwards, the Greeks, the Turks, the Moguls, the Portuguese, the British, the French, the Dutch, all of them came and looted us, took over what was ours. Yet we have not done this to any other nation.

We have not conquered anyone. We have not grabbed their land, their culture and their history and tried to enforce our way of life on them. Why? Because we respect the freedom of others. That is why my FIRST VISION is that of FREEDOM. I believe that India got its first vision of this in 1857, when we started the war of Independence. It is this freedom that we must protect and nurture and build on. If we are not free, no one will respect us.

We have 10 percent growth rate in most areas. Our poverty levels are falling. Our achievements are being globally recognised today. Yet we lack the self-confidence to see ourselves as a developed nation, self-reliant and self-assured. Isn't this incorrect? MY SECOND VISION for India is DEVELOPMENT. For fifty years, we have been a developing nation. It is time we see ourselves as a developed nation. We are among the top five nations in the world in terms of GDP.

I have a THIRD VISION. India must stand up to the world. Because I believe that unless India stands up to the world, no one will respect us. Only strength respects strength. We must be strong not only as a military power, but also as an economic power. Both must go hand-in-hand. My good fortune was to have worked with three great minds. Dr. Vikram Sarabhai, of the Dept. of Space, Professor Satish Dhawan, who succeeded him and Dr. Brahm Prakash, father of nuclear material. I was lucky to have worked with all three of them closely and consider this the great opportunity of my life.

I was in Hyderabad giving this lecture, when a 14 year-old girl asked me for my autograph. I asked her what her goal in life is. She replied: I want to live in a developed India. For her, you and I will have to build this developed India. You must proclaim India is not an underdeveloped nation; it is a highly developed nation.

You say that our government is inefficient. You say that our laws are too old. You say that the municipality does not pick up the garbage. You say that the phones don't work, the railways are a joke, the airline is the worst in the world, and mails never reach their destination. You say that our country has been fed to the dogs and is the absolute pits. You say, say and say. What do you do about it?

Dear Indians, I am echoing J.F. Kennedy's words to his fellow Americans to relate to Indians……. "ASK WHAT WE CAN DO FOR INDIA AND DO WHAT HAS TO BE DONE TO MAKE INDIA WHAT AMERICA AND OTHER WESTERN COUNTRIES ARE TODAY."

□

China and Tibet*

—Atal Bihari Vajpayee

[Atal Bihari Vajpayee is an Indian statesman who was the eleventh Prime Minister of India, first for 13 days in 1996 and then from 1998 to 2004. A leader of the Bharatiya Janata Party (BJP), he is the first Prime Minister from outside the Indian National Congress party to serve a full five-year term.

A parliamentarian for over four decades, Vajpayee was elected to the Lok Sabha (the lower house of India's Parliament) nine times, and twice to the Rajya Sabha (upper house). Vajpayee was one amongst the founder members of erstwhile Bharatiya Jana Sangh, which he had also headed. He was also the Minister of External Affairs in the cabinet of Morarji Desai. When Janata government collapsed, Vajpayee restarted the Jana Sangh as the Bharatiya Janata Party in 1980.

On 25th December, 2014 the office of President of India announced the Bharat Ratna award, India's highest civilian honour, to Vajpayee. In a special gesture, President of India conferred Bharat Ratna to Atal Bihari Vajpayee in his residence on 27th March, 2015. His birthday, 25th December, was declared 'Good Governance Day'.

* *Lok Sabha, New Delhi, 8th May & 21st August, 1959*

Vajpayee was born to Krishna Devi and Krishna Bihari Vajpayee on 25th December, 1924 in a middle-class Brahmin family in Gwalior. His grandfather, Pandit Shyam Lal Vajpayee, had migrated to Morena, Gwalior from his ancestral village of Bateshwar, Uttar Pradesh. His father, Krishna Bihari Vajpayee, was a poet and a schoolmaster in his hometown. Vajpayee studied from the Saraswati Shishu Mandir, Gorkhi, Bara, Gwalior. Vajpayee attended Gwalior's Victoria College (now Laxmi Bai College) and graduated with distinction in Hindi, English and Sanskrit. He completed his post-graduation with an M.A. in Political Science from Dayanand Anglo-Vedic College, Kanpur, and was awarded a first-class degree.

His activism started with the Arya Kumar Sabha of Gwalior, the youth wing of the Arya Samaj, of which he became the General Secretary in 1944. He also joined the Rashtriya Swayamsevak Sangh (RSS) as a swayamsevak in 1939. Influenced by Babasaheb Apte, he attended the Officers Training Camp of the RSS during 1940-44 and became a "full-time worker" in 1947, technically a pracharak. He gave up studying law due to the partition riots. He was sent as a vistarak (probationary pracharak) to Uttar Pradesh and quickly began working for the newspapers of Deendayal Upadhyaya, Rashtradharma (a Hindi monthly), Panchjanya (a Hindi weekly) and the dailies Swadesh and Veer Arjun. Vajpayee never married and has remained a bachelor his entire life.

Vajpayee's first exposure to politics was in August 1942, when he and his elder brother Prem were arrested for 23 days during the Quit India movement, when he was released only after giving a written undertaking, expressly declaring not to participate in any of the anti-British struggle and naming the underground leaders, leading the 'Quit India Movement'.

In 1951, he was seconded by the RSS, along with Deendayal Upadhyaya, to work for the newly formed Bharatiya Jana Sangh, a Hindu right-wing political party associated with the RSS. He was appointed as a national secretary of the party in charge of the Northern region, based in Delhi. He soon became a follower and aide of party leader Syama Prasad Mookerjee. In 1954, Vajpayee was with Mookerjee when he went on a fast-unto-death in Kashmir to protest against perceived inferior treatment of non-Kashmiri Indian visitors to the state. Mookerjee died in prison during this strike. In 1957, Vajpayee was elected to the Lok Sabha, the lower house of India's Parliament, from Balrampur.

In 1959, China's military crackdown on rebels in Kham and Amdo led to the 'Lhasa Uprising.' Full-scale resistance spread throughout Tibet. Fearing capture of the Dalai Lama, unarmed Tibetans surrounded his residence, and the 14th Dalai Lama fled to India. The government of India accepted the Tibetan refugees. India designated land for the refugees in the mountainous region of Dharamsala, India, where on April 1959 the Dalai Lama formed the Central Tibetan Administration (CTA) which popularly referred as the Tibetan government-in-exile.

During these events Vajpayee raised the issue in the Lok Sabha. Here is his two most important speeches delivered on 8th May and 21st August, 1959.]

Mr. Deputy Speaker Sir, one cannot deny the fact that due to the events in Tibet, a tension has been created in the relations between India and China. But the responsibility for this tension is not India's. Since the beginning of the communist government in China, India, in spite of a great friendship with Chiang-Kai-Tchek, has welcomed the new China and we have tried more than anybody else so that China gets respect in the nations of the world... We have defended China because we thought that, although we differ on communism, if the people of China take to this road, it is their business, and India and China can remain friends in spite of differences in our ways of life.

But the first blow to this friendship was struck when the armies of China "liberated" Tibet. At that time, our Prime Minister had asked: from what it is that Tibet is liberated? Tibet was not under any domination. India is the closest neighbour of Tibet. In the history of the past, if we had wanted we could have tried to annex Tibet, but today the leaders of China who accuse India of being expansionist forget that we never tried to annex Tibet. Tibet is a small country. But we respected its distinct existence. We respected the independence of Tibet, and we hoped that China would do the same. But the ways of the Communists are different. Their use of words is different. When they want to enslave people, they say that they are going to liberate them. Today when they want to oppress people, they say that they are going to reform them. If reform is at all necessary, the inclination towards reform should come from those who have to make reforms. Reform can't be imposed from above.

But what is happening in Tibet is not reform. Following the agreement of 1950, China should have respected the autonomy of Tibet, but China has interfered in the internal affairs of Tibet. Lakhs of Chinese from China have been brought to Tibet so that the Tibetans may become a minority in their own country and so that in the future Tibet may become an inseparable part of China. From Tibet thousands of young people have been sent to China to get education in the new religion, but when they came back and Chinese leaders saw that it had had no effect on them, their Tibetan colour had not been erased, their separateness was firm and their enthusiasm for protecting their way of life was indelible, then they got alerted and they tried to erase the way of life of Tibet. The present struggle arose because of a big nation desiring to swallow a small nation.

Deputy Speaker Sir, my submission is that when we accepted the sovereignty of China on Tibet we made a big mistake. That day was a very unfortunate day. But the mistake has been made. Perhaps we thought that the matter would be solved, that there would be no more fight, and we did not want to give others the opportunity to take advantage of differences between us and China. But what was the result? Not only did China break the agreement with Tibet, but they also violated the agreement with India which was in the background of this agreement. Where has the Panchsheel agreement gone? Those who proclaim Panchsheel say that according to Panchsheel, democracy and dictatorship can live together. If for the communist imperialism, the peace-loving and religion-loving people of Tibet can't keep their way of life, then it is meaningless to say that in such a big world communism and democracy can co-exist. We don't want to interfere in the internal affairs of Tibet. But Tibet is not an internal affair of China. China is bound to respect the autonomy of Tibet, to refrain from interfering in the internal affairs of Tibet. But this agreement was broken and I believe that now India, the Indian government, should revise its position. Agreements have two sides, they are to be respected by both sides. If China violated the agreement, we have the right to reconsider our situation. What is the reason for the people of Tibet to be deprived of their freedom?

Why can't Tibet remain free? People say that it was not free before. Does it mean that a country which was not free before cannot have the right to be free? that where there was servitude before, servitude should remain? If we support the independence of Algeria, and if this support does not mean interfering in the internal affairs of France, then how can the support for Tibetan independence be an interference in the internal affairs of China? My friend Shri Khadilkar has just said that no party in the country supports the independence of Tibet. I beg to disagree. I represent a small party, but our party defends the independence of Tibet. Whether the cause of Tibet's independence is right or wrong cannot be decided by the number of people who raise their voices. The Chinese imperialism today may suppress by their brutality the cry of Tibetan independence, but the thirst for independence cannot be extinguished. In this movement the repression will act like a windstorm in a fire, and to-morrow, if not today, the people of Tibet will definitely get their freedom.

But the question is: what can we do for it? I have said that we made a mistake in 1950. Now we have to bear the consequences. But the time has come to repent, to recognise the mistake. I hope that on this occasion the Prime Minister will truly represent the crores of people of this country. Except a few of our friends, all India is unanimous on this question that what is happening in Tibet should not happen. But is it possible that Tibet can enjoy autonomy under the Chinese rule? It seems to me that the communist system and autonomy are two contradictory things.

Under communist rule, autonomy cannot exist. In 1930, Mao Zedong had said: we have made the constitution in such a way that if somebody wants to go out, he can. The Tibetans did not speak about going out. They wanted to keep their separate existence, but even this permission was not given to them.

He also said that they wanted to see a flower blossom which will have a thousand petals. Forget about thousand, even the soft bud of Tibet is being crushed. What the imperialists do in Tibet, they accuse us. We never tried to annex Tibet. We have advocated for a place be given to China in UN, we could advocate also for a place given to Tibet. Ukraine is a part of the Soviet Union, but it has a separate seat in the UN. So could not Tibet, even though being with China, have a distinct seat in UN? But we have not done this, because of our friendship with China. What have we received in return for this friendship?

We want friendship even today, but we should not build the palace of this friendship on the dead body of Tibet's independence. We can't close our eyes on injustice. It has been the tradition of India, and in this tradition the Prime Minister has conducted the foreign policy of this country, that wherever there is injustice, murder of humanity, tyranny, we raise our voice in protest, we speak the language of truth and we fearlessly protect the rights of those who are trampled upon. Today Tibet is the criterion of the policies of Nehruji, Tibet is the touchstone of the firmness of the Indian government, Tibet is the touchstone of the desirability of PanchSheel. It is not with the declarations of PanchSheel that the feeling of PanchSheel will be respected. The touchstone of PanchSheel is the behaviour. The Prime Minister may act with restrain, nevertheless if the problem of Tibet is not solved with it, we will have to recognize that it is necessary to bring a little firmness, a little activity into this policy.

Whether the Dalai Lama should remain in Tibet or should go is not a big question. The Tibetans will decide among themselves. But Tibet is the touchstone for big nations swallowing small nations. If small countries are swallowed in this fashion, world peace cannot be firmly established. In South-East Asia, there are many countries where Chinese people live in great number.

Because of Tibet, in all these countries a wave of apprehension has arisen. As far as India is concerned... in the maps of China a province of us is said to be theirs. The communists of China have expelled Tchang-kai-tchek but have kept his maps. If they had wanted they could have rejected also his maps. And our communist friends have not seen these maps. I don't believe what they are saying. But this is an indirect attack of China on India. China has occupied two places in Uttar Pradesh. These events point to the danger ahead. We don't have to be terrified but we have to adopt a strong policy.

I will make another submission. The Dalai Lama has come to India. He is a fighter for freedom, he fights for the freedom of his country, and as a result he had to leave his country and come to India. I would like that he be allowed to lead the fight for the independence of his country from India. Although the restrictions have been placed for security reasons, they should be relaxed. In the days of the British Raj, if our patriots could go to other countries and, from there, fight for Indian's independence and be objects of respect for us, there is no reason why the Dalai Lama should not be given this liberty.

If the Dalai Lama is successful in making a compromise with China, and our Prime Minister can be a mediator in this relation, nothing will make the people of this country happier. But if the leaders of China can't be brought to the right path, if they can't be persuaded by political or diplomatic pressure, if having awakened the public opinion in Burma, Lanka and Indonesia, organised it and making a strong demonstration, China cannot be influenced, then India will have no other option left except allow the Dalai Lama to fight for the freedom of his country.

The youth of India consider the independence of Tibet as something precious not because they have a close relationship with Tibet, but because we have lived in servitude, we know the suffering and pain of servitude, we know the price of freedom they should be given the liberty to act. If the people of Tibet fight for freedom, the people of India will be with them. We will give them our sympathy and we would expect China not to give imperialist talks. The days of imperialism are over. But this is a new imperialism. The danger is that it comes under the pretence of revolution, it comes disguised in the garb of revolution, it comes raising the slogan of a new order, but colonialism it is, imperialism it is. In the history of the past, we fought against the imperialism of the white people but now on the roof of the world appears the imperialism of the yellow people. We should face it also with determination. Thank you.

[21st August, 1959]

Sir, I would like to move the motion: "The opinion of this house is that the government should send the Tibetan issue to the UN. "Sir, the General Assembly of the UN will have a sitting on the 15th September, 1959. The Indian Government has decided to raise the question of the inclusion of China in the United Nations. By this motion, I would like the House to suggest to the government to also raise the Tibetan question. India is a strong supporter of the UN. It is the one ray of hope in this world living under the threat of a nuclear war. We have always said that the international quarrels should be solved by sitting at the negotiation table, that force should not be used and that all disagreements should be solved through talks.

In the international domain, we have adopted the policy of remaining free from the different groups quarrelling between themselves, because we believe that not only it is in the best interests of our country, but it is also the right policy in the interest of the world-peace. By this policy India has got some prestige. We are respected. When people of the world are in trouble, they turn towards our Prime Minister, not because we are powerful militarily speaking, not because we have weapons, but because we have adopted a policy based on a moral understanding. The moral power that India has acquired demands that whenever there is an invasion, we should support the just side. And in the past, whenever the freedom of a country was endangered, India did not remain silent. We supported the right and just side without fearing any power.

You know that the problem of Tibet was raised in the UN in 1950, when the Chinese army entered that country. On

25st October, 1950 the Chinese armies entered Tibet and the 7st November, 1950, the leaders of Tibet sent a protest to the UN against the Chinese invasion. The 18th November, 1950, the representative of El Salvador officially put a proposal to the UN asking the General Assembly that a special committee be formed to study which means the UN should adopt for helping Tibet against the unjustified attack by China. But when the General Committee of the UN met, the Indian representative asked the Committee to cancel the whole issue and gave assurance that the advancing Chinese armies had stopped and there was no need for the Committee to deliberate on these issues.

The Indian Government wanted China and Tibet to solve the problem by peaceful talks and the Prime Minister advised the Dalai Lama to consider the assurances of the Prime Minister of China, who had come to India at that time, and to arrive at a compromise. On our assurances, the Dalai Lama made an agreement, the 17 Point Agreement with China.

Now I don't need to go into history. What happened in Tibet is clear. It is clear that there has been a violation of the 1951 agreement between India and China. The Dalai Lama was obliged to leave his country and take refuge in India. With him, thousands of Tibetans have come to our country. Even then, the Indian Government hopes that the situation will calm down so that a satisfactory solution can be found, based on reason.

What is happening in Tibet is painful for all those who love freedom and who believe in the dignity of man. They are astonished at the fate of the Tibetans. Now the question of the independence or autonomy of Tibet is not there any more. The question has become: will the existence of Tibet continue? Will the distinct existence of Tibet continue or will the people of Tibet be annihilated? We know, and the Dalai Lama has confirmed it, that huge numbers of Chinese are settled in Tibet. They have already installed there 50 lakhs Chinese and are in the process of settling 40 lakhs more.

The whole intention of China is to make the Tibetans a minority in their own country; in this way, the Tibetan individuality will be destroyed. This is a new scene, this is a new kind of imperialism. Except for South Africa, the Western countries, I mean the imperialists, reduced other races in servitude but they never tried to make them a minority in their own country so that they are completely wiped out from the world map.

France has colonised Algeria but the French Government respect the distinct individuality of Algeria. But it seems that the people of Tibet will have to go the way of inner Mongolia. The exterior Mongolia, although not completely free, has something her own, but China has absorbed inner Mongolia in itself and its existence as a free entity has ended. This is what is happening in Tibet. China has taken part in the Bandung meeting in which the declaration of the human rights has been accepted and is amongst the countries who signed this declaration, but these same human rights are being violated in Tibet.

According to the International Commission of Jurists, the right of the people of Tibet to freedom, the right to life and safety have being violated and are still being violated. The Tibetan are made to work by force. They are treated in a cruel and inhuman way. The right to home and privacy is being violated. The right to travel inside the country, to go outside the country and come back is violated, marriages are forced on unwilling persons, right to property is being arbitrarily violated, and the liberty of worship is murdered in a planned manner. If the human rights are violated in this manner by a country which wants to be included in the United Nations, the world, and specially our country, cannot and should not remain a silent spectator. Along with the violation of human rights, the International Commission of Jurists has arrived at the conclusion, and they have proofs also, that prima facie there is a deliberate will to entirely or partly destroy Tibet as an independent country and put an end to the Tibetan interests. The commission called it prima facie a case of genocide according to the terms of the 1948 Convention. I will not go into these accusations. As long as a commission of free countries does not find out what is happening in Tibet by going there themselves, nothing can be said. Besides the Dalai Lama said that in the present movement 65000 people have disappeared and the people of Tibet are not given the right to build their future according to their ideals and principles.

Now it has been said that China is not a member of the UN, so to bring this affair to this organisation will not serve any purpose. May I say that India was among those countries who declared North Korea the aggressor, although North Korea was not a member of the UN. At that time, we did not say that "North Korea is not in UN, so we will not participate in the condemnation of North Korea as an aggressor". We want China to be part of UN because we have faith in the UN and we think that whatever the form of the government of the people of China, the government of China is a real government, therefore China should be made part of the UN. But it does not depend only on us. China is not there. But it does not mean that we should not bring the Tibetan problem to the UN.

People also argue that if we bring the Tibetan problem to the UN, the cold war will be accentuated. When British and French attacked Egypt, the whole world condemned this aggression and no country, including India, expressing fear or apprehension said: no, we should not criticise the French-British aggression because it will become a part of the Cold War. There is no relation between the Tibetan problem and the cold war. This is a question of human rights. The question is: will the small countries survive in this world or not? Or will they have to lose their existence, will they be erased? India has a moral responsibility towards the people of Tibet. There is the aspect of the security of India, and at the same time, considering our age-old relations with Tibet, how can India remain silent when before our very eyes the existence of the people of Tibet is being destroyed?

Let us suppose that India does not raise this issue in the UN. Some other country can raise it. I want to know that in this situation what will be our policy? We cannot prevent another country from raising the issue. What will be the policy of our government? All our efforts for peacefully resolving the Tibetan problem have failed. In spite of the good will of our Prime Minister, the Chinese communist leaders are not prepared to listen to the voice of justice and reason. On the contrary they call India and the people of India imperialists. India has abandoned the border rights obtained by the British government. Our Prime Minister has objected to calling the border India China the McMahon line, in fact he has opposed it; he said that that he did not like it because, I think, only the name of McMahon smells of British imperialism. As Shakespeare said, there is nothing in a name. But it shows how deep are our feelings against imperialism. Nevertheless the Chinese communists call us imperialists.

The Chinese make propaganda against India, against the people of India. A journalist has estimated that from 23rd April to 30th April, in seven days, in the governmental newspapers, press-conferences and through the radio, 77 articles commentaries and editorials, in all 44000 words against India, using a very uncontrolled language, have been published, distributed and spread. In Lhasa the police are still there in front of our embassy. The Indian currency has been declared illegal. The attack on an area of 30000 square miles of India by means of maps continues. No answer was given to our letter in which we had objected. Do we think that in the present circumstances China can be persuaded to accept the just rights of the Tibetan people?

The Dalai Lama has clearly stated that he and his followers are not against economic or social reforms in Tibet. But this is not the point anymore and I don't think that there is any other alternative for India but to prepare the world opinion against the Chinese aggression. Although China is not a member of UN, if the Indian Government raises this issue in the UN and we prepare the world opinion in favour of the Tibetan people, I believe that something good will come out of it. As a country who believes in the UN, this is the only way which is open to us.

When the Indian government, in spite of all that has been said and done against India by the Chinese communists, raised the issue of recognising and including China in the UN, it is only proper, I feel, that the Tibetan issue also be raised by our government in the next General Assembly of the United Nations.

The Government will gain by knowing the wishes of the House on this matter. I believe that my proposal will get an extensive support, that the Government will accept it and fulfil its moral responsibility towards the people of Tibet.

With these words, I move the motion. Thank you.

(The destruction of most of Tibet's more than 6,000 monasteries occurred between 1959 and 1961. In 1962 China and India fought a brief war over the disputed South Tibet and Aksai Chin regions. Although China won the war, Chinese troops withdrew north of the McMahon Line, effectively ceding South Tibet back to India. In 1965, the area that had been under the control of the Dalai Lama's government from the 1910s to 1959—Ü-Tsang and western Kham— was renamed the Tibet Autonomous Region or TAR.)

[There, his oratorial skills so impressed Prime Minister Jawaharlal Nehru that he predicted that Vajpayee would someday become India's Prime Minister. By virtue of his oratorical and organizational skills, he became the face of the Jana Sangh. After the death of Deendayal Upadhyaya, the mantle of the leadership of Jana Sangh fell on the shoulders of a young Vajpayee. He became the national president of the Jana Sangh in 1968 and, along with Nanaji Deshmukh, Balraj Madhok and L.K. Advani, led the Jana Sangh to national prominence.

From 1975 to 1977, Vajpayee was arrested along with several other opposition leaders during the Internal Emergency imposed by Prime Minister Indira Gandhi of the Indian National Congress party. In 1977, heeding the call of social reformer Jayaprakash Narayan for all the opposition parties to unite against the Congress Vajpayee merged the Jana Sangh into the newly formed grand-alliance, the Janata Party.

Following Janata's victory in the 1977 general elections, he became the Minister of External Affairs in Prime Minister Morarji Desai's cabinet. As foreign minister, that year Vajpayee became the first person to deliver a speech to the United Nations General Assembly in Hindi. By the time the Janata government crumbled in 1979, Vajpayee had established himself as an experienced statesman and a respected political leader.

The Janata Party was dissolved soon after Morarji Desai resigned as Prime Minister in 1979. The Jana Sangh had devoted its political organisation to sustain the coalition and was left exhausted by the internecine political wars within the Janata Party. Vajpayee joined many of his Bharatiya Jana Sangh and

Rashtriya Swayamsewak Sangh colleagues, particularly his long-time friends L.K. Advani and Bhairon Singh Shekhawat, to form the Bharatiya Janata Party (BJP) in 1980. He became the BJP's first President. He emerged as a strong critic of the Congress (I) government that followed the Janata government.

While the BJP opposed the Sikh militancy that was rising in the state of Punjab, it also blamed Prime Minister Indira Gandhi for her "divisive and corrupt politics that fostered such militancy at the expense of national unity and integrity." The BJP did not support Operation Blue Star and strongly protested against the violence towards Sikhs in Delhi that broke out in 1984 following the assassination of Indira Gandhi by two of her Sikh bodyguards. The BJP was left with only two parliamentary seats in the 1984 elections. During this period, Vajpayee remained at the centre-stage as party President and Leader of the Opposition in the Parliament.

The BJP became the political voice of the Ram Janmabhoomi Mandir Movement, which was led by activists of the Vishwa Hindu Parishad (VHP) and the RSS, and which sought to build a temple dedicated to Lord Rama in Ayodhya.

Victory in the assembly elections in Gujarat and Maharashtra in March 1995, and a good performance in the elections to the Karnataka assembly in December 1994, propelled the BJP to greater political prominence. During a BJP conference in Mumbai in November 1995, BJP President L.K. Advani declared that Vajpayee would become the Prime Minister of India. The BJP won in the May 1996 parliamentary elections. The BJP grew in strength in the early 1995s riding on pro nationalistic sentiments. In the 1996 general elections, the BJP emerged as the single largest party in the Lok Sabha. The then president Shankar Dayal Sharma invited Vajpayee to form the government. Vajpayee was sworn in as the 10th Prime Minister of India, but the BJP failed to muster enough support from other parties to obtain a majority. He resigned after 13 days, when it became clear that he could not garner a majority.

After the fall of the two United Front governments between 1996 and 1998, the Lok Sabha was dissolved and fresh elections were held. The 1998 general elections again put the BJP ahead of others. This time, a cohesive bloc of political parties joined the BJP to form the National Democratic Alliance (NDA), and Vajpayee was sworn in as the Prime Minister. The NDA proved its majority in the parliament. The government lasted 13 months until mid-1999 when the All India Anna Dravida Munnetra Kazhagam (AIADMK) under J. Jayalalitha withdrew its support to the government. The government lost the ensuing vote of confidence motion in the Lok Sabha by a single vote on 17th April, 1999. As the Opposition was unable to come up with the numbers to form the new government, the Lok Sabha was again dissolved and fresh elections were held. Vajpayee remaining the Prime Minister until the elections were held.

In the 1999 general elections, the BJP-led NDA won 303 seats out of the 543 seats in the Lok Sabha, in the aftermath of the Kargil operations, thereby securing a comfortable and stable majority. On 13rd October, 1999, Atal Bihari Vajpayee took oath as Prime Minister of India for the third time.

The NDA was widely expected to retain power after the 2004 general election. The 13th Lok Sabha had been dissolved before the completion of its term to capitalise on the perceived 'feel-good factor' and BJP's recent successes in the Assembly elections in Rajasthan, Madhya Pradesh and Chhattisgarh. The BJP hoped to capitalise on the slogan "India Shining" and released many ads touting the economic growth of the nation. However, the coalition lost almost half its seats, with several prominent cabinet ministers being defeated. The Indian National Congress, led by Sonia Gandhi, became the single largest party and, along with many minor parties, formed the United Progressive Alliance. With the conditional support of the leftist parties from the outside, the UPA formed a government under Dr. Manmohan Singh. Vajpayee resigned as Prime Minister and promised co-operation to the new government. Accepting moral responsibility for the defeat, he decided not to take up the position of the Leader of the Opposition and passed on the leadership mantle to Lal Krishna Advani. However, he retained his post as Chairman of the NDA.

In December 2005, Vajpayee announced his retirement from active politics, declaring that he would not contest in the next general election. Vajpayee was hospitalised at AIIMS for chest infection and fever on 6th February, 2009. He was put on ventilator support as his condition worsened but he eventually recuperated and was later discharged. Unable to participate in the campaign for the 2009 general election due to his poor health, he wrote a letter urging voters to back the BJP. His protege Lalji Tandon was able to retain the Lucknow seat even though the NDA suffered electoral reverses all over the country.]

□

Swarajya is My Birthright*

—Bal Gangadhar Tilak

[Bal Gangadhar Tilak had mellowed after his release on 16th June, 1914, because of having diabetes and also the ordeals faced in Mandalay prison. Tilak tried to convince Mohandas Gandhi to leave the idea of Total non-violence (Total Ahimsa) and try to get Self-rule (Swarajya) by all means. Gandhi, though respected him as his 'guru', did not change his mind. Later, Tilak re-united with his fellow nationalists and re-joined the Indian National Congress in 1916. When the World War-I was gradually approaching an end, Tilak helped found the All India Home Rule League in 1916–18.

He travelled from village to village for support from farmers and locals to join the movement towards self-rule. There were total of 1400 members in April 1916 and in 1917 there were approximately of about 32,000 members in the league. Tilak made his the most famous speech—SWARAJYA IS MAY BIRTHRIGHT—in May 1917 at Nasik (Maharashtra) during the first anniversary function his Home Rule League. He was speaking as an old man to the young and his words ware so impassioned that they become the clarion call of the national movement.

In coming years, League's further growth and

---

* *Home Rule League's First Aniversary, Nasik (Maharashtra), May 1917*

activity were stalled by the rise of Mohandas Gandhi and his Satyagraha art of revolution: non-violent, but mass-based civil disobedience. In 1920, the All India Home Rule League elected Mahatma Gandhi as its President. In a year, the body would merge into the Indian National Congress to form a united Indian political front. After Tilak's death his SWAJARYA speech gained more momentum. But, his demand could be incorporated in the Purna Swarajya (Full Self-rule) resolution of the Congress in 1929, about nine long years after his death.]

I am young in spirit though old in body. I do not wish to lose this privilege of youth. To deny the growing capacity to my thinking power is to admit that I have no right to speak on this resolution. Whatever I am going to speak today is eternally young. The body might grow old, descript and it might perish, but the soul is immortal. Similarly, if there might be apparent lull in our Home Rule activities, the freedom of the spirit behind it is eternal and indestructible, and it will secure liberty for us. The soul means Parmeshwar (Almighty God) and the mind will not get peace till it gets identified with Him. If one body is worn out the soul will take another; so assure the Gita. The philosophy is quiet old. Swarajya (Self rule or Freedom) is my birthright. So long as it is awake within me, I am not old. No weapon can cut this spirit, no fire can burn it, no water can wet it, and no wind can dry it. I say further that no CID can burn it. I declare the same principle to the Superintendent of Police who is sitting before me, to the Collector who has been invited to attend this meeting and to the government shorthand writer who is busy taking down notes of our speeches. The principle will not disappear even if it seems to be killed. We ask for Home Rule and we must get it. The science which ends the Home Rule is science of politics and not one which ends in slavery. The science of politics is the 'Vedas' of the country. You have a soul and I only want to wake it up. I want to tear off the blind that has been let down by ignorant, designing and selfish people. The science of politics consists of two parts. The first is divine and the second is demonic. The slavery of a nation comes into the letter part. There cannot be a moral justification for the demonic part of the science of politics. A nation which might justify this is guilty of sin in the sight of God. Some people have the courage to declare what is harmful to them and some have not the courage. The political and religious teachings consists in the giving the knowledge of the principle. Religious and political teachings are not separate, though they appear to be so on account of foreign rule. All philosophies are included in the science of politics.

Who does not know the meaning of Home Rule? Who does not want it? Would you like it, if I enter you house and take possession of your cooking department? I must have the right to manage the affairs in my own house. It is only lunatics and children who do not know how to manage their own affairs. The cardinal creed of the conferences is that a member must be above 21 years of age; do you not, therefore, think that you want your own right? Not being lunatics or children you understand your own business, your own rights and, therefore, you know Home Rule. We are told we are not fit for Home Rule. A century has passed away and the British Rule has not made us fit for Home Rule; now we will make our own efforts and fit ourselves for it. To other irrelevant excuses, to hold out any temptation and to make other offers will be putting a stigma on the English policy. England is trying to protect the small state of Belgium with the help of India; how can it then say that we should not have Home Rule? Those who find fault with us are avaricious people. But there are people who find fault even with the all-merciful God. We must work hard to save the soul of our nation without caring for anything. The good of our country consists in guarding this—our birthright. The Congress has passed this Home Rule resolution. The provincial conference is only a child of the Congress which submits to mandates of its father. We will follow Shri Ramchandra in obeying the order of our father in Congress. We are determined to make efforts to get this resolution enforced even if the effort leads us to the desert, compels us to live incognito, makes us suffer any hardship and even if it finally brings us to death. Shri Ramchandra did it. Do not pass this resolution by merely clapping your hands but by taking a solemn vow that you will work for it. We will work for it by every possible constitutional and law-abiding method to get Home Rule. Through the grace of God, England has changed its minds towards us. We feel our efforts will not be without success. England proudly thought that a tiny nation might be able to protect the empire by itself. This pride has gone down. England has now begun to feel that it must make changes in the Constitution of the Empire. Lloyd George has openly confessed that England cannot go on without the help of India. All nations about a nation of a thousand years old have to be changed. The English people have discovered that the wisdom of all their parties is not sufficient. The Indian soldiers have saved the lives of the British soldiers on the French battlefield and have showed their bravery. Those who considered us as slaves have begun now to call us brothers. God has brought about all those changes. We must push for demands while the notion of this brotherhood is existing in the minds of the English. We must inform them that we, thirty cores of the Indian people, are ready to lay down our lives for the empire; and that while we are with them none shall dare cast an evil glance at the Empire.

□

Closing Speech of The First Constituent Assembly of India*

—B.R. Ambedkar

[Bhimrao Ramji Ambedkar popularly known as Babasaheb, was a prolific student, earning a law degree and various doctorates from Columbia University and the London School of Economics, and gained a reputation as a scholar for his research in law, economics and political science. His later life was marked by his political activities, where he became involved in the negotiations for India's independence campaigning by publishing journals advocating political rights and social freedom for 'untouchables' and contributing significantly to the establishment of the state of India.

In 1936, Ambedkar founded the Independent Labour Party, which contested in the 1937 Bombay election to the Central Legislative Assembly for the 13 reserved and 4 general seats and securing 11 and 3 seats respectively. He published his book—Annihilation of Caste—in the same year. It strongly criticised Hindu orthodox religious leaders, the caste system in general. He oversaw the transformation of his political party into the Scheduled Castes Federation, although it performed poorly in the elections held in 1946 for the Constituent Assembly of India.

* *Constitution Hall, New Delhi, 25th November, 1949*

Upon India's Transfer of Power by British Government to leaders of High Cast on 15th August, 1947, the new Congress-led government invited Ambedkar to serve as the nation's first Law Minister, which he accepted. On 29th August, he was appointed Chairman of the Constitution Drafting Committee, charged by the Assembly to write India's new Constitution.

The text prepared by Ambedkar provided constitutional guarantees and protections for a wide range of civil liberties for individual citizens, including freedom of religion, the abolition of untouchability and the outlawing of all forms of discrimination. Ambedkar argued for extensive economic and social rights for women, and also won the Assembly's support for introducing a system of reservations of jobs in the civil services, schools and colleges for members of scheduled castes and scheduled tribes and Other Backward Class, a system akin to affirmative action. The Constitution was adopted on 26th November, 1949 by the Constituent Assembly.

But, a day before the assembly formally finished its work, Ambedkar made a memorable speech. In jubilant but somber and reflective tone, he actually warned the members against the popular protest, the blind following of charismatic leaders and the limitations of the political democracy. His speech perhaps retains more relevance today than in 1949.]

Sir, looking back on the work of the Constituent Assembly it will now be two years, eleven months and seventeen days since it first met on the 9th December, 1946. During this period the Constituent Assembly has altogether held eleven sessions. Out of these eleven sessions the first six were spent in passing the Objectives Resolution and the consideration of the Reports of Committees on Fundamental Rights, on Union Constitution, on Union Powers, on Provincial Constitution, on Minorities and on the Scheduled Areas and Scheduled Tribes. The seventh, eighth, ninth, tenth and the eleventh sessions were devoted to the consideration of the Draft Constitution. These eleven sessions of the Constituent Assembly have consumed 165 days. Out of these, the Assembly spent 114 days for the consideration of the Draft Constitution.

Coming to the Drafting Committee, it was elected by the Constituent Assembly on 29th August, 1947. It held its first meeting on 30th August. Since 30th August it sat for 141 days during which it was engaged in the preparation of the Draft Constitution. The Draft Constitution as prepared by the Constitutional Adviser as a text for the Draft Committee to work upon, consisted of 243 articles and 13 Schedules. The first Draft Constitution as presented by the Drafting Committee to the Constituent Assembly contained 315 articles and 8 Schedules. At the end of the consideration stage, the number of articles in the Draft Constitution increased to 386. In its final form, the Draft Constitution contains 395 articles and 8 Schedules. The total number of amendments to the Draft Constitution tabled was approximately 7,635. Of them, the total number of amendments actually moved in the House was 2,473.

I mention these facts because at one stage it was being said that the Assembly had taken too long a time to finish its work, that it was going on leisurely and wasting public money. It was said to be a case of Nero fiddling while Rome was burning. Is there any justification for this complaint? Let us note the time consumed by Constituent Assemblies in other countries appointed for framing their Constitutions. To take a few illustrations, the American Convention met on 25th May, 1787 and completed its work on 17th September, 1787 i.e., within four months. The Constitutional Convention of Canada met on the 10th October, 1864 and the Constitution was passed into law in March 1867 involving a period of two years and five months. The Australian Constitutional Convention assembled in March 1891 and the Constitution became law on the 9th July, 1900, consuming a period of nine years. The South African Convention met in October 1908 and the Constitution became law on the 20th September, 1909 involving one year's labour. It is true that we have taken more time than what the American or South African Conventions did. But we have not taken more time than the Canadian Convention and much less than the Australian Convention. In making comparisons on the basis of time consumed, two things must be remembered.

One is that the Constitutions of America, Canada, South Africa and Australia are much smaller than ours. Our Constitution as I said contains 395 articles while the American has just seven articles, the first four of which are divided into sections which total up to 21, the Canadian has 147, Australian 128 and South African 153 sections. The second thing to be remembered is that the makers of the Constitutions of America, Canada, Australia and South Africa did not have to face the problem of amendments. They were passed as moved. On the other hand, this Constituent Assembly had to deal with as many as 2,473 amendments. Having regard to these facts the charge of dilatoriness seems to me quite unfounded and this Assembly may well congratulate itself for having accomplished so formidable a task in so short a time.

Turning to the quality of the work done by the Drafting Committee, Mr. Naziruddin Ahmed felt it his duty to condemn it outright. In his opinion, the work done by the Drafting Committee is not only not worthy of commendation, but is positively below par. Everybody has a right to have his opinion about the work done by the Drafting Committee and Mr. Naziruddin is welcome to have his own. Mr. Naziruddin Ahmed thinks he is a man of greater talents than any member of the Drafting Committee. The Drafting Committee would have welcomed him in their midst if the Assembly had thought him worthy of being appointed to it. If he had no place in the making of the Constitution it is certainly not the fault of the Drafting Committee.

Mr. Naziruddin Ahmed has coined a new name for the Drafting Committee evidently to show his contempt for it. He calls it a Drafting committee. Mr. Naziruddin must no doubt be pleased with his hit. But he evidently does not know that there is a difference between drift without mastery and drift with mastery. If the Drafting Committee was drifting, it was never without mastery over the situation. It was not merely angling with the off chance of catching a fish. It was searching in known waters to find the fish it was after. To be in search of something better is not the same as drifting. Although Mr. Naziruddin Ahmed did not mean it as a compliment to the Drafting committee. I take it as a compliment to the Drafting Committee. The Drafting Committee would have been guilty of gross dereliction of duty and of a false sense of dignity if it had not shown the honesty and the courage to withdraw the amendments which it thought faulty and substitute what it thought was better. If it is a mistake, I am glad the Drafting Committee did not fight shy of admitting such mistakes and coming forward to correct them.

I am glad to find that with the exception of a solitary member, there is a general consensus of appreciation from the members of the Constituent Assembly of the work done by the Drafting Committee. I am sure the Drafting Committee feels happy to find this spontaneous recognition of its labours expressed in such generous terms. As to the compliments that have been showered upon me both by the members of the Assembly as well as by my colleagues of the Drafting Committee I feel so overwhelmed that I cannot find adequate words to express fully my gratitude to them. I came into the Constituent Assembly with no greater aspiration than to safeguard the interests of he Scheduled Castes. I had not the remotest idea that I would be called upon to undertake more responsible functions. I was therefore greatly surprised when the Assembly elected me to the Drafting Committee. I was more than surprised when the Drafting Committee elected me to be its Chairman. There were in the Drafting Committee men bigger, better and more competent than myself such as my friend Sir Alladi Krishnaswami Ayyar. I am grateful to the Constituent Assembly and the Drafting Committee for reposing in me so much trust and confidence and to have chosen me as their instrument and given me this opportunity of serving the country. (Cheers)

The credit that is given to me does not really belong to me. It belongs partly to Sir B.N. Rau, the Constitutional Adviser to the Constituent Assembly who prepared a rough draft of the Constitution for the consideration of the Drafting Committee. A part of the credit must go to the members of the Drafting Committee who, as I have said, have sat for 141 days and without whose ingenuity of devise new formulae and capacity to tolerate and to accommodate different points of view, the task of framing the Constitution could not have come to so successful a conclusion. Much greater, share of the credit must go to Mr. S.N. Mukherjee, the Chief Draftsman of the Constitution. His ability to put the most intricate proposals in the simplest and clearest legal form can rarely be equalled, nor his capacity for hard work. He has been as acquisition tot he Assembly. Without his help, this Assembly would have taken many more years to finalise the Constitution. I must not omit to mention the members of the staff working under Mr. Mukherjee. For, I know how hard they have worked and how long they have toiled sometimes even beyond midnight. I want to thank them all for their effort and their co-operation. (Cheers)

The task of the Drafting Committee would have been a very difficult one if this Constituent Assembly has been merely a motley crowd, a tasseleted pavement without cement, a black stone here and a white stone there is which each member or each group was a law unto itself. There would have been nothing but chaos. This possibility of chaos was reduced to nil by the existence of the Congress Party inside the Assembly which brought into its proceedings a sense of order and discipline. It is because of the discipline of the Congress Party that the Drafting Committee was able to pilot the Constitution in the Assembly with the sure knowledge as to the fate of each article and each amendment. The Congress Party is, therefore, entitled to all the credit for the smooth sailing of the Draft Constitution in the Assembly.

The proceedings of this Constituent Assembly would have been very dull if all members had yielded to the rule of party discipline. Party discipline, in all its rigidity, would have converted this Assembly into a gathering of yes' men. Fortunately, there were rebels. They were Mr. Kamath, Dr. P.S. Deshmukh, Mr. Sidhva, Prof. K.T. Shah and Pandit Hirday Nath Kunzru. The points they raised were mostly ideological. That I was not prepared to accept their suggestions, does not diminish the value of their suggestions nor lessen the service they have rendered to the Assembly in enlivening its proceedings. I am grateful to them. But for them, I would not have had the opportunity which I got for expounding the principles underlying the Constitution which was more important than the mere mechanical work of passing the Constitution.

Finally, I must thank you Mr. President for the way in which you have conducted the proceedings of this Assembly. The courtesy and the consideration which you have shown to the Members of the Assembly can never be forgotten by those who have taken part in the proceedings of this Assembly. There were occasions when the amendments of the Drafting Committee were sought to be barred on grounds purely technical in their nature. Those were very anxious moments for me. I am, therefore, specially grateful to you for not permitting legalism to defeat the work of Constitution-making.

As much defence as could be offered to the constitution has been offered by my friends Sir Alladi Krishnaswami Ayyar and Mr. T.T. Krishnamachari. I shall not therefore enter into the merits of the Constitution. Because I feel, however good a Constitution may be, it is sure to turn out bad because those who are called to work it, happen to be a bad lot. However had a Constitution may be, it may turn out to be good if those who are called to work it, happen to be a good lot. The working of a Constitution does not depend wholly upon the nature of the Constitution. The Constitution can provide only the organs of State such as the Legislature, the Executive and the Judiciary. The factors on which the working of those organs of the State depends are the people and the political parties they will set up as their instruments to carry out their wishes and their politics. Who can say how the people of India and their purposes or will they prefer revolutionary methods of achieving them? If they adopt the revolutionary methods, however good the Constitution may be, it requires no prophet to say that it will fail. It is, therefore, futile to pass any judgment upon the Constitution without reference to the part which the people and their parties are likely to play.

The condemnation of the Constitution largely comes from two quarters, the Communist Party and the Socialist Party. Why do they condemn the Constitution? Is it because it is really a bad Constitution? I venture to say 'no'. The Communist Party want a Constitution based upon the principle of the Dictatorship of the Proletariat. They condemn the Constitution because it is based upon parliamentary democracy. The Socialists want two things. The first thing they want is that if they come in power, the Constitution must give them the freedom to nationalize or socialize all private property without payment of compensation. The second thing that the Socialists want is that the Fundamental Rights mentioned in the Constitution must be absolute and without any limitations so that if their Party fails to come into power, they would have the unfettered freedom not merely to criticize, but also to overthrow the State.

These are the main grounds on which the Constitution is being condemned. I do not say that the principle of parliamentary democracy is the only ideal form of political democracy. I do not say that the principle of no acquisition of private property without compensation is so sacrosanct that there can be no departure from it. I do not say that Fundamental Rights can never be absolute and the limitations set upon them can never be lifted. What I do say is that the principles embodied in the Constitution are the views of the present generation or if you think this to be an over-statement, I say they are the views of the members of the Constituent Assembly. Why blame the Drafting Committee for embodying them in the Constitution? I say why blame even the Members of the Constituent Assembly? Jefferson, the great American statesman who played so great a part in the making of the American constitution, has expressed some very weighty views which makers of Constitution, can never afford to ignore. In one place he has said:

"We may consider each generation as a distinct nation, with a right, by the will of the majority, to bind themselves, but none to bind the succeeding generation, more than the inhabitants of another country."

In another place, he has said:

"The idea that institutions established for the use of the national cannot be touched or modified, even to make them answer their end, because of rights gratuitously supposed in those employed to manage them in the trust for the public, may perhaps be a salutary provision against the abuses of a monarch, but is most absurd against the nation itself. Yet our lawyers and priests generally inculcate this doctrine, and suppose that preceding generations held the earth more freely than we do; had a right to impose laws on us, unalterable by ourselves, and that we, in the like manner, can

make laws and impose burdens on future generations, which they will have no right to alter; in fine, that the earth belongs to the dead and not the living;"

I admit that what Jefferson has said is not merely true, but is absolutely true. There can be no question about it. Had the Constituent Assembly departed from this principle laid down by Jefferson it would certainly be liable to blame, even to condemnation. But I ask, has it? Quite the contrary. One has only to examine the provision relating to the amendment of the Constitution. The Assembly has not only refrained from putting a seal of finality and infallibility upon this Constitution as in Canada or by making the amendment of the Constitution subject tot he fulfilment of extraordinary terms and conditions as in America or Australia, but has provided a most facile procedure for amending the Constitution. I challenge any of the critics of the Constitution to prove that any Constituent Assembly anywhere in the world has, in the circumstances in which this country finds itself, provided such a facile procedure for the amendment of the Constitution. If those who are dissatisfied with the Constitution have only to obtain a 2/3 majority and if they cannot obtain even a two-thirds majority in the parliament elected on adult franchise in their favour, their dissatisfaction with the Constitution cannot be deemed to be shared by the general public.

There is only one point of constitutional import to which I propose to make a reference. A serious complaint is made on the ground that there is too much of centralization and that the States have been reduced to Municipalities. It is clear that this view is not only an exaggeration, but is also founded on a misunderstanding of what exactly the Constitution contrives to do. As to the relation between the Centre and the States, it is necessary to bear in mind the fundamental principle on which it rests. The basic principle of Federalism is that the Legislative and Executive authority is partitioned between the Centre and the States not by any law to be made by the Centre but by the Constitution itself. This is what Constitution does. The States under our Constitution are in no way dependent upon the Centre for their legislative or executive authority. The Centre and the States are co-equal in this matter. It is difficult to see how such a Constitution can be called centralism. It may be that the Constitution assigns to the Centre too large a field for the operation of its legislative and executive authority than is to be found in any other federal Constitution. It may be that the residuary powers are given to the Centre and not to the States. But these features do not form the essence of federalism. The chief mark of federalism as I said lies in the partition of the legislative and executive authority between the Centre and the Units by the Constitution. This is the principle embodied in our constitution. There can be no mistake about it. It is, therefore, wrong to say that the States have been placed under the Centre. Centre cannot by its own will alter the boundary of that partition. Nor can the Judiciary. For as has been well said:

"Courts may modify, they cannot replace. They can revise earlier interpretations as new arguments, new points of view are presented, they can shift the dividing line in marginal cases, but there are barriers they cannot pass, definite assignments of power they cannot reallocate. They can give a broadening construction of existing powers, but they cannot assign to one authority powers explicitly granted to another."

The first charge of centralization defeating federalism must therefore fall.

The second charge is that the Centre has been given the power to override the States. This charge must be admitted. But before condemning the Constitution for containing such overriding powers, certain considerations must be borne in mind. The first is that these overriding powers do not form the normal feature of the constitution. Their use and operation are expressly confined to emergencies only. The second consideration is : Could we avoid giving overriding powers to the Centre when an emergency has arisen? Those who do not admit the justification for such overriding powers to the Centre even in an emergency, do not seem to have a clear idea of the problem which lies at the root of the matter. The problem is so clearly set out by a writer in that well-known magazine "The Round Table" in its issue of December 1935 that I offer no apology for quoting the following extract from it. Says the writer:

"Political systems are a complex of rights and duties resting ultimately on the question, to whom, or to what authority, does the citizen owe allegiance. In normal affairs the question is not present, for the law works smoothly, and a man, goes about his business obeying one authority in this set of matters and another authority in that. But in a moment of crisis, a conflict of claims may arise, and it is then apparent that ultimate allegiance cannot be divided. The issue of allegiance cannot be determined in the last resort by a juristic interpretation of statutes. The law must conform to the facts or so much the worse for the law. When all formalism is stripped away, the bare question is, what authority commands the residual loyalty of the citizen. Is it the Centre or the Constituent State?"

The solution of this problem depends upon one's answer to this question which is the crux of the problem. There can be no doubt that in the opinion of the vast majority of the people, the residual loyalty of the citizen in an emergency must be to the Centre and not to the Constituent States. For it is only the Centre which can work for a common end and for the general interests of the country as a whole. Herein lies the justification for giving to all Centre certain overriding powers to be used in an emergency. And after all what is the obligation imposed upon the Constituent States by these emergency powers? No more than this–that in an emergency, they should take into consideration alongside their own local interests, the opinions and interests of the nation as a whole. Only those who have not understood the problem, can complain against it.

Here I could have ended. But my mind is so full of the future of our country that I feel I ought to take this occasion to give expression to some of my reflections thereon. On 26th January, 1950, India will be an independent country (Cheers). What would happen to her independence? Will she maintain her independence or will she lose it again? This is the first thought that comes to my mind. It is not that India was never an independent country. The point is that she once lost the independence she had. Will she lost it a second time? It is this thought which makes me most anxious for the future. What perturbs me greatly is the fact that not only India has once before lost her independence, but she lost it by the infidelity and treachery of some of her own people. In the invasion of Sind by Mahommed-Bin-Kasim, the military commanders of King Dahar accepted bribes from the agents of Mahommed-Bin-Kasim and refused to fight on the side of their King. It was Jaichand who invited Mahommed Gohri to invade India and fight against Prithvi Raj and promised him the help of himself and the Solanki Kings. When Shivaji was fighting for the liberation of Hindus, the other Maratha noblemen and the Rajput Kings were fighting the battle on the side of Moghul Emperors. When the British were trying to destroy the Sikh Rulers, Gulab Singh, their principal commander sat silent and did not help to save the Sikh Kingdom. In 1857, when a large part of India had declared a war of independence against the British, the Sikhs stood and watched the event as silent spectators.

Will history repeat itself? It is this thought which fills me with anxiety. This anxiety is deepened by the realization of the fact that in addition to our old enemies in the form of castes and creeds we are going to have many political parties with diverse and opposing political creeds. Will Indian place the country above their creed or will they place creed above country? I do not know. But this much is certain that if the parties place creed above country, our independence will be put in jeopardy a second time and probably be lost for ever. This eventuality we must all resolutely guard against. We must be determined to defend our independence with the last drop of our blood. (Cheers)

On the 26th January, 1950, India would be a democratic country in the sense that India from that day would have a government of the people, by the people and for the people. The same thought comes to my mind. What would happen to her democratic Constitution? Will she be able to maintain it or will she lost it again? This is the second thought that comes to my mind and makes me as anxious as the first.

It is not that India did not know what is Democracy. There was a time when India was studded with republics, and even where there were monarchies, they were either elected or limited. They were never absolute. It is not that India did not know Parliaments or Parliamentary Procedure. A study of the Buddhist Bhikshu

Sanghas discloses that not only there were Parliaments-for the Sanghas were nothing but Parliaments–but the Sanghas knew and observed all the rules of Parliamentary Procedure known to modern times. They had rules regarding seating arrangements, rules regarding Motions, Resolutions, Quorum, Whip, Counting of Votes, Voting by Ballot, Censure Motion, Regularization, Res Judicata, etc. Although these rules of Parliamentary Procedure were applied by the Buddha to the meetings of the Sanghas, he must have borrowed them from the rules of the Political Assemblies functioning in the country in his time.

This democratic system India lost. Will she lost it a second time? I do not know. But it is quite possible in a country like India–where democracy from its long disuse must be regarded as something quite new–there is danger of democracy giving place to dictatorship. It is quite possible for this new born democracy to retain its form but give place to dictatorship in fact. If there is a landslide, the danger of the second possibility becoming actuality is much greater.

If we wish to maintain democracy not merely in form, but also in fact, what must we do? The first thing in my judgement we must do is to hold fast to constitutional methods of achieving our social and economic objectives. It means we must abandon the bloody methods of revolution. It means that we must abandon the method of civil disobedience, non-cooperation and satyagraha. When there was no way left for constitutional methods for achieving economic and social objectives, there was a great deal of justification for unconstitutional methods. But where constitutional methods are open, there can be no justification for these unconstitutional methods. These methods are nothing but the Grammar of Anarchy and the sooner they are abandoned, the better for us.

The second thing we must do is to observe the caution which John Stuart Mill has given to all who are interested in the maintenance of democracy, namely, not "to lay their liberties at the feet of even a great man, or to trust him with power which enable him to subvert their institutions". There is nothing wrong in being grateful to great men who have rendered life-long services to the country. But there are limits to gratefulness. As has been well said by the Irish Patriot Daniel O'Connel, no man can be grateful at the cost of his honour, no woman can be grateful at the cost of her chastity and no nation can be grateful at the cost of its liberty. This caution is far more necessary in the case of India than in the case of any other country. For in India, Bhakti or what may be called the path of devotion or hero-worship, plays a part in its politics unequalled in magnitude by the part it plays in the politics of any other country in the world. Bhakti in religion may be a road to the salvation of the soul. But in politics, Bhakti or hero-worship is a sure road to degradation and to eventual dictatorship.

The third thing we must do is not to be content with mere political democracy. We must make our political democracy a social democracy as well. Political democracy cannot last unless there lies at the base of it social democracy. What does social democracy mean? It means a way of life which recognizes liberty, equality and fraternity as the principles of life. These principles of liberty, equality and fraternity as the principles of life. These principles of liberty, equality and fraternity are not to be treated as separate items in a trinity. They form a union of trinity in the sense that to divorce one from the other is to defeat the very purpose of democracy. Liberty cannot be divorced from equality, equality cannot be divorced from liberty. Nor can liberty and equality be divorced from fraternity. Without equality, liberty would produce the supremacy of the few over the many. Equality without liberty would kill individual initiative. Without fraternity, liberty would produce the supremacy of the few over the many. Equality without liberty would kill individual initiative. Without fraternity, liberty and equality could not become a natural course of things. It would require a constable to enforce them. We must begin by acknowledging the fact that there is complete absence of two things in Indian Society. One of these is equality. On the social plane, we have in India a society based on the principle of graded inequality which we have a society in which there are some who have immense wealth as against many who live in abject poverty. On the 26th January, 1950, we are going to enter into a life of contradictions. In politics we will have equality and in social and economic life we will have inequality. In politics we will be recognizing the principle of one man one vote and one vote one value. In our social and economic life, we shall, by reason of our social and economic structure, continue to deny the principle of one man one value. How long shall we continue to live this life of contradictions? How long shall we continue to deny equality in our social and economic life? If we continue to deny it for long, we will do so only by putting our political democracy in peril. We must remove this contradiction at the earliest possible moment or else those who suffer from inequality will blow up the structure of political democracy which is Assembly has to laboriously built up.

The second thing we are wanting in is recognition of the principle of fraternity. what does fraternity mean? Fraternity means a sense of common brotherhood of all Indians-if Indians being one people. It is the principle which gives unity and solidarity to social life. It is a difficult thing to achieve. How difficult it is, can be realized from the story related by James Bryce in his volume on American Commonwealth about the United States of America.

The story is I propose to recount it in the words of Bryce himself-that—

"Some years ago the American Protestant Episcopal Church was occupied at its triennial Convention in revising its liturgy. It was thought desirable to introduce among the short sentence prayers a prayer for the whole people, and an eminent New England divine proposed the words 'O Lord, bless our nation'. Accepted one afternoon, on the spur of the moment, the sentence was brought up next day for reconsideration, when so many objections were raised by the laity to the word nation' as importing too definite a recognition of national unity, that it was dropped, and instead there were adopted the words O Lord, bless these United States."

There was so little solidarity in the U.S.A. at the time when this incident occurred that the people of America did not think that they were a nation. If the people of the United States could not feel that they were a nation, how difficult it is for Indians to think that they are a nation. I remember the days when politically-minded Indians, resented the expression "the people of India". They preferred the expression "the Indian nation." I am of opinion that in believing that we are a nation, we are cherishing a great delusion. How can people divided into several thousands of castes be a nation? The sooner we realize that we are not as yet a nation in the social and psychological sense of the world, the better for us. For then only we shall realize the necessity of becoming a nation and seriously think of ways and means of realizing the goal. The realization of this goal is going to be very difficult–far more difficult than it has been in the United States. The United States has no caste problem. In India there are castes. The castes are anti-national. In the first place because they bring about separation in social life. They are anti-national also because they generate jealousy and antipathy between caste and caste. But we must overcome all these difficulties if we wish to become a nation in reality. For fraternity can be a fact only when there is a nation. Without fraternity equality and liberty will be no deeper than coats of paint.

These are my reflections about the tasks that lie ahead of us. They may not be very pleasant to some. But there can be no gainsaying that political power in this country has too long been the monopoly of a few and the many are only beasts of burden, but also beasts of prey. This monopoly has not merely deprived them of their chance of betterment, it has sapped them of what may be called the significance of life. These down-trodden classes are tired of being governed. They are impatient to govern themselves. This urge for self-realization in the down-trodden classes must no be allowed to devolve into a class struggle or class war. It would lead to a division of the House. That would indeed be a day of disaster. For, as has been well said by Abraham Lincoln, a House divided against itself cannot stand very long. Therefore the sooner room is made for the realization of their aspiration, the better for the few, the better for the country, the better for the maintenance for its independence and the better for the continuance of its democratic structure. This can only be done by the establishment of equality and fraternity in all spheres of life. That is why I have laid so much stresses on them.

I do not wish to weary the House any further. Independence is no doubt a matter of joy. But let us not forget that this independence has thrown on us great responsibilities. By independence, we have lost the excuse of blaming the British for anything going wrong. If hereafter things go wrong, we will have nobody to blame except ourselves. There is great danger of things going wrong. Times are fast changing. People including our own are being moved by new ideologies. They are getting tired of Government by the people. They are prepared to have Governments for the people and are indifferent whether it is Government of the people and by the people. If we wish to preserve the Constitution in which we have sought to enshrine the principle of Government of the people, for the people and by the people, let us resolve not to be tardy in the recognition of the evils that lie across our path and which induce people to prefer Government for the people to Government by the people, nor to be weak in our initiative to remove them. That is the only way to serve the country. I know of no better.

[Ambedkar resigned from the cabinet in 1951 following the stalling in parliament of his draft of the Hindu Code Bill, which sought to expound gender equality in the laws of inheritance and marriage. Ambedkar independently contested an election in 1952 to the lower house of parliament, the Lok Sabha, but was defeated in the Bombay (North Central) constituency by a little-known Narayan Sadoba Kajrolkar, who polled 138137 votes compared to Ambedkar's 123576 votes. He was appointed to the upper house, of parliament, the Rajya Sabha in March 1952 and would remain as member till death.]

□

Integral Humanism Lectures*

—Deendayal Upadhyaya

[Pandit Deendayal Upadhyaya was an Indian philosopher, economist, sociologist, historian, journalist, and political scientist. A revered icon of Integral Humanism, he was an ideologue, a guiding force for an alternative model of governance and politics, and one of the most important leaders of the Bharatiya Jana Sangh, the forerunner of the present day Bharatiya Janata Party.

He was born in 1916 in the village Chandrabhan, now called Deendayal Dham, near the Farah town in Mathura District, 26 km away from Mathura. His father, Bhagwati Prasad, was a well known astrologer and his mother Shrimati Rampyari was a religious-minded lady. Both his parents died when he was young and he was brought up by his maternal uncle. He excelled academically under the guardianship of his maternal uncle and aunt. He went to high school in Sikar, where he matriculated. He stood first in the board exam, obtainaing a Gold Medal from Maharaja Kalyan Singh of Sikar, along with a monthly scholarship of 10 rupees and an additional 250 rupees towards his books. He did Intermediate at the Birla College in Pilani, the predecessor of the present Birla Institute of Technology and Science. He did B.A. at the

---

* *Bombay, 22nd To 25th April, 1965*

Sanatan Dharma College, Kanpur in 1939 and graduated in first division. He joined St. John's College, Agra to pursue a Master's degree in English literature but was unable to appear for the final year exam on account of a cousin's illness. His maternal uncle persuaded him to sit for the Provincial Services Exam, where he got selected but declined to join the Services on account of his interest in working with the common man. He obtained a B.T. degree at Prayag and entered public service.

While he was a student at Sanatan College, Kanpur in 1937, he came into contact with the Rashtriya Swayamsevak Sangh (RSS) through his classmate Baluji Mahashabde. He met the founder of the RSS, K. B. Hedgewar, who engaged with him in an intellectual discussion at one of the shakhas. Sunder Singh Bhandari was also one of his classmates at Kanpur. This gave a fillip to his public life. He dedicated himself to full-time work in the RSS from 1942. He had attended the 40-day summer vacation RSS camp at Nagpur where he underwent training in Sangh Education. After completing second-year training in the RSS Education Wing, Upadhyaya became a lifelong pracharak of the RSS. He worked as the pracharak for the Lakhimpur district and, from 1955, as the joint prant pracharak (regional organiser) for Uttar Pradesh.

Deendayal Upadhyaya was a man of soaring idealism and had a tremendous capacity for organisation and reflected different aspects of a social thinker, economist, educationalist, politician, writer, journalist, speaker, organiser etc. He was regarded as an ideal swayamsevak of the RSS essentially because 'his discourse reflected the pure thought-current of the Sangh'. He started a monthly Rashtra Dharma from Lucknow in the 1940s. The publication was meant for spreading the ideology of nationalism. Though he did not have his name printed as editor in any of the issues of this publication but there was hardly any issue which did not have his long lasting impression due to his thought provoking writings. Later he started a weekly Panchjanya and a daily Swadesh.

In 1951, when Syama Prasad Mookerjee founded the Bharatiya Jana Sangh, Deendayal was seconded to the party by the RSS, tasked with moulding it into a genuine member of the Sangh Parivar. He was appointed as General Secretary of its Uttar Pradesh branch, and later the all-India General Secretary. The acumen and meticulousness shown by Deendayal deeply impressed Syama Prasad Mookerjee and elicited his famous remark: "If I had two Deendayals, I could transform the political face of India."

After Mookerjee's death in 1953, the entire burden of nurturing the orphaned organisation and building it up as a nation-wide movement fell on the young shoulders of Deendayal. For 15 years, he remained the outfit's general secretary and built it up, brick by brick. He raised a band of dedicated workers imbued them with idealism and provided the entire ideological framework of the outfit. He also contested for Lok Sabha from Uttar Pradesh, but did not get elected.

Upadhyaya conceived the political philosophy Integral Humanism–the guiding philosophy of Bharatiya Jana Sangh, the forerunner of the present day Bharatiya Janata Party. The philosophy of Integral Humanism advocates the simultaneous and integrated program of the body, mind and intellect and soul of each human being. His philosophy of Integral Humanism, which is a synthesis of the material and the spiritual, the individual and the collective, bears eloquent testimony to this. In the field of politics and economics, he was pragmatic and down to earth. He visualised for India a decentralised polity and self-reliant economy with the village as the base.

Deendayal Upadhyaya was convinced that India as an independent nation cannot rely upon Western concepts like individualism, democracy, socialism, communism, capitalism etc. and he was of the view that the Indian polity after independence has been raised upon these superficial Western foundations and not rooted in the timeless traditions of India's ancient culture. He was of the view that the Indian intellect was getting suffocated by Western theories and ideologies and consequently there was a big roadblock on the growth and expansion of original Bharatiya thought. He said that there was an urgent public need for a fresh breeze.

He welcomed modern technology but wanted it to be adapted to suit Indian requirements. Deendayal believed in a constructive approach. He exhorted his followers to co-operate with the government when it was right and fearlessly oppose when it erred. He believed in Swaraj (self governance) which was campaigned by Bharatheeya Janatha Party till end of last century. He placed nation's interest above everything else.

Pandit Deendayal Upadhyaya first presented his philosophy of Integral Humanism in a series of lecture in Bombay from 22nd to 25th April, 1965, form the basis of a system of governance that is suited to the Indian nation and its people, regardless of caste, religion or region, as an alternative for all round human development.

LECTURE-1 (22nd April, 1965)

I am asked to present my thoughts on the subject of "Integral Humanism" in a series of talks beginning this evening. Last January at Vijayavada, Bharatiya Jana Sangh adopted the statement of "Principles & Policies" in which 'Integral Humanism' has also been accepted. There have been scattered discussions here and there on the subject. It is necessary that we consider Integral Humanism in all its aspects. So long as the country was under the yoke of the British rule, all the movements and policies in the country had one principal 'aim to drive out the foreign rulers and to achieve independence'. But what would be the face of the new Bharat after independence? In which direction were we to advance? These questions were precisely thought out. It would not be correct to say that no thought was devoted to these aspects. There were people who even at that time had considered these questions. Gandhiji himself had set out his idea of the independent Bharat in his book "Hind Swaraj". Prior to this Lokmanya Tilak discussed the philosophical basis of the rejuvenation of Bharat in his book 'Gita Rahasya'. He gave a comparative discussion of various schools of thought current all over the world at that time.

Apart from these, the Congress and other political parties adopted various resolutions from time to time which contain references to this subject. However the subject requires much more serious study than was devoted to it at that time. It did not attract serious attention at that time because every one believed it was more important to think of ways to drive out the British and the other things could be discussed later on. It did not seem right to waste time in internal discussions while the foreign rule continued. Hence even if there might have been difference in views, they were shelved for the time being.

As a result, even those who held the view that socialism should be the basis of the future Bharat, worked inside the Congress as a socialist group. They did attempt to form as a separate party as such. The revolutionaries too, were working independence in their own way. All were agreed, however, that the foremost task was to gain independence. Having attained Independence, the question naturally ought to have occurred to us, "Now that we independent, what shall be the direction of our progress?" But is amazing that serious thought has not been to this question and today even after seventeen years independence we cannot say that a definite direction been decided upon.

Whither Bharat: From time to time, Congressmen or others have declared Welfare State, Socialism, Liberalism etc. as their aims. Slogans have been raised. But these ideology slogans attached little significance to the philosophies, apart from the slogans. I am saying this on the basis of personal discussions. A leading gentleman once suggested during a conversation that a joint front should be for against Congress, whereby a good fight can be given. Now-a-days political parties adopt this strategy. So, it was surprising to put forward this suggestion. However, naturally, I asked, "What programme shall we adopt? If such a joint front is formed some idea of the programme is essential. What will be out economic policy? What will our foreign policy? These questions should also be broadly tackled."

"Do not worry about it. Whatever you like you can adopt. We are ready to support, anything from extreme Marxist to downright capitalist program." The reply came as if this was natural. He had no difficulty in adopting any programme. The only object was somehow Congress should be defeated. Even now some declare that Congress must be defeated even with the cooperation of communists and all the rest.

Recently elections were held in Kerala. During the elections, Communists, Muslim League, Swatantra Party, S.S.P. Rebel Congress known as Kerala Congress, Revolutionary Socialist Party etc. entered into a variety of bilateral of multiple alliances. As. a result, it was difficult to imagine that any of these parties had a definite ideology, principles and aims. This is the situation as far as principles are concerned. Congress too, is in a similar state. Even though the Congress has proclaimed democratic socialism as its goal, the behaviour of various Congress leaders shows one thing clearly that there are no definite, principles, no single direction in Congress. There are staunch communists in Congress fold. There are also those who have faith in, Capitalism and oppose communism to the teeth. All brands of people are arrayed on Congress platform. If there can be a magic box which contains a cobra and a mongoose living together, it is Congress. We must ponder whether we can progress under such conditions. If we stop to analyze the reasons for the problems facing the country we will find that the confusion about our goal and the direction is mainly responsible for the chaos. I realize that all the. 450 million people of Bharat cannot agree on all or even on a single question. That is not possible in any country. Yet there is generally, what is called a more or less common desire of the people of any nation. If this popular longing is made the basis of our aims, the common man feels that the nation is moving in a proper direction, and that his own aspiration is reflected in the efforts of the nation. This also generates the greatest possible feeling of unity. The truth of the statement is borne out by the response of the people during the Chinese Invasion of October/November 1962. A wave of enthusiasm swept across the country. Action and sacrifice both obtained in abundance. There was no barrier between the government and the public or between various political parties. How did this happen? The external threat made us recognize ourselves. The government adopted that policy which reflected the widespread feeling in the people and which enhanced their sense of self-respect with a call for sacrifice. The result was we stood united.

The root of our problems—neglect of self: It is essential that we think about our national identity. Without this identity there is no meaning. Of neither independence, nor can independence become the instrument of progress and happiness. As long as we are unaware of our national identity, we cannot recognize develop all our potentialities. Under alien rule this identity is suppressed. That is why nations wish to remain independent so that they can progress according to their natural bent and can experience happiness in their endeavour. Nature is powerful. An attempt to go against nature or to disregard her leads to troubles. The natural instincts cannot be disregarded but it is possible to elevate this nature to the level of culture. Psychology informs us how by suppression of various natural instincts different mental disorders ensue. Such a person remains restless and dejected. His abilities slowly deteriorate and become perverted. The Nation too like the individual becomes a prey to numerous ills when its natural instincts are disregarded. The basic cause of the problems facing Bharat is the neglect of its national identity.

Opportunism has shaken the confidence of people in politics: A majority of those who lead the nation today as well as those who take active interest in the affairs of the country are not sufficiently aware of this root cause. Consequently opportunists with no principles reign in politics of our country. Parties and politicians have neither principles nor aims nor a standard code of conduct. A person feels nothing wrong in leaving one party and joining another. Even alliances and mergers of parties or their bifurcations are dictated not by agreement or by differences in principles by purely by gains in elections or in positions of power. In 1939 Shri Hafiz Mohammed Ibrahim was elected Muslim League ticket. Later when he joined Congress, in accordance with healthy principles of public conduct he resigned and sought re-election on Congress ticket and was once again elected. In 1948 when socialists left Congress and founded Socialist Party, all those who were members of legislature resigned and fought elections on socialist tickets. But thereafter this healthy tradition was forgotten. Now there is complete license in politics. As result, in public mind there is distrust for everyone. There is hardly any reason whose Integrity is beyond doubt in the public mind. This situation must be changed. Otherwise, unity and discipline cannot.

What should be our direction: The nation is at crossroads. Some people suggest that we must start from where we have left off one thousand years ago, when foreign invaders disrupted our life. But nation is not an inanimate object like a cloth so that weaving can be taken up after a gap in time. Besides it would not be rational to say that the thousand year old alien rule has interrupted the current of our national life so completely that from that time to this day we remained stationary and inactive. The nation has certainly put her genius to work, in the changing circumstances to meet the challenges thrown at her. We have struggled to continue our life forward and to wrest independence from the aliens. The current of our national life was not interrupted but has gone on ceaselessly. The task of turning the waters of Ganga back to some previous point would not be wise Ganga at Banaras may not be crystal clear as at Haridwar. But still it is the same holy Ganga. It has absorbed numerous rivulets with all their refuse. However, these have no separate existence but have become Ganga. The current Ganga must inevitably glow onwards. If this was all that happened, it would still not be a big problem. But there are other nations in the world. They have made phenomenal progress in the past one thousand years. Our entire attention was engaged in fighting for independence or staving off new hordes of invaders. We have not been able to contribute to the world progress. Now when we are free, is it not paramount that we fill this deficiency at the earliest and stand shoulder to shoulder with other advanced nations of the world?

Up to this point there is no room for difference of opinion. The difficulty arises when we fail to discern the reasons of the spectacular advance of the West, its effects, real and, apparent.

This is further complicated by the fact that Britishers a representative of the West, ruled this country for a century and, during this period adopted such measures whereby in the minds of our people a contempt for things Bharatiya and respect for everything Western were subtly created. Along with the scientific advance, their way of life, manners and food habits etc. came to this country. Not only material sciences but also their social, economic and political doctrines became our standards. Today the educated in this country clearly display this effect. We shall have to decide whether this effect is good or bad for us. We had taken pride in resisting things British while they ruled us, but strangely enough, now that the Britishers have left, westernisation has become synonymous with progress. It is true that a narrow sense of nationalism should not be allowed to obstruct the progress of the nation. However western science and the western way of life are two different things. Whereas western science is universal and must be absorbed by us if we wish to go forward, the same is not true about the western way of life and values. In fact thoughtless imitation of the West must be scrupulously discarded. There are those who consider economic and political doctrines of the West as epitome of progress and desire to transplant the same in our country. Therefore when we are trying to decide where wish to take our country and how, we must also take into consideration the basis of various economic and political doctrines of the west and their present position.

The rise of European nations: Among various Isms that affected the West, the principal ones are Nationalism, Democracy and Socialism. At the same time there have been some who cherish world unity and world peace and have made some efforts in that direction.

Among these, nationalism is the oldest and the strongest. After the fall of the Roman Empire and decline in the influence of the Catholic Church, Europe witnessed rise of several nations. History of Europe in the past on thousand years is the history of the rise of and conflict among various nations. These nations extended their expires beyond the European continent and subjugate other independent countries. Nationalism brought nation and state together resulting in nation states. At the same time the decline in the influence of the Roman Catholic Church gave rise either to national churches or to complete disappearance of religious influence on politics. Anyway the concept of secular state arose out of this situation.

Birth of democracy in Europe: A revolutionary concept which made a deep impact on the political life of Europe is Democracy. In the beginning, every nation had a king as its head but there was gradual awakening in the minds of people against the autocracy of the royalty. The industrial revolution and the international trade resulted in the rise of a business community in all nations. Naturally there ensued a conflict between these new centres of power and the established kings and feudal lords. This conflict, adopted 'democracy' as its philosophical basis. The origin of democracy was sought in the Greek city republics. The common man was attracted by the lofty ideals of equality, fraternity and liberty of every citizen. France witnessed a bloody revolution. In England too, there were periodic movements. The idea of democracy gained foothold in the mind of common man. The royalty was either liquidated or their powers were drastically' curbed and constitutional governments were established. Today democracy has been already accepted in Europe. Even those who have suppressed democracy do not denounce it. The dictators like Hitler, Mussolini and Stalin too paid lip service to democracy.

Individual was exploited: Every individual got a vote in the democratic setup. But real power stayed with those who had led the revolution. Industrial revolution had generated faith in the new methods of production. Instead of working in the freedom of home, workers had started working in the factories taking orders from the factory owners, the worker migrated from his home town to dwell in crowded cities. There was no provision of proper housing. There were hardly any rules in the factory to protect the worker. He was economically weak and not yet organized. He became a victim of exploitation, injustice and harassment. Those in whom political power was vested were members of the same group who exploited the workers. Hence there was no hope of redress from the state.

A number of persons led movements in protest against this injustice with the desire to improve the lot of workers. They called themselves socialists. Karl Marx was one of them. In an effort to lead the movement against injustice, he studied the entire history and structure presented his analysis of the situation. He claimed to have given a scientific basis to his theories. All the subsequent socialists might not have agreed with Marx but they all considerably influenced by his ideas.

Dictatorship of the proletariat: According to Marx analysis-dialectic materialism the root cause of exploitation lies in the private owners of the means of production. If these means are made the property of the society (for the Marxist, the Society synonymous with the State) then there will be no further exploitation. But before this, the state should be redeemed from the hands of the exploiters and ensured against their influence in future. Towards this end, dictatorship of proletariat must be established. In order that people tolerate this dictatorship, it was held as an ideal that when the exploiter class has been finally liquidated, and possibility of its resurgence exists, the states will replaced by a classless, stateless society. Marx also attempted to show that capitalism contains seeds of own destruction and that socialism is inevitable.

In some countries of Europe there was social revolution. Even where, socialism was not accepted, politicians had to accept the rights of workers. "Welfare State" was accepted as an ideal. Nationalism, democracy, socialism or equality (equality is there at the root of socialism; equality is different from equability), these three doctrines have dominated European social political thinking. Every now and then, apart from these ideals of world peace and world unity also cropped up. All these are good ideas. They reflect the higher aspirations mankind. But by itself each of these doctrines is incomplete. Not only that, each stands opposed to the rest in practice. Nationalism poses a threat to world peace. Democracy and capitalism join hands to give free reign exploitation. Socialism replaced capitalism and brought with it and to democracy and individual freedom. Hence the West is present faced with the task of reconciling these good ideals.

They have not succeeded to this day, in this task. They have tried combinations and permutations, by emphasis on one or the other ideal. England emphasized nationalism and democracy and developed her politico-social institutions along those lines, whereas France could not adopt the same. There, democracy resulted in political instability. The British Labour party wanted to reconcile socialism with democracy but people have raised doubts whether democracy will survive if socialism gains strength. Hence the labour party no longer supports socialism as strongly as the Marxist doctrines advocate. If socialism has been diluted considerably, Hitler and Mussolini adopted nationalist cum socialism and buried democracy. In the end socialism also became a tool for their nationalism which posed a great threat to world peace and unity. We may indeed seek some guidance from the western world but the fact is, it has no concrete suggestions to offer. It is itself at crossroads unable to decide what is good. Under such circumstances we cannot expect guidance from the West. On the contrary we must consider whether in this present state of the world, we can contribute something to resolve its dilemma. Having taken note of the progress of the world, can we add to the common store of Knowledge? As a member of the world community, we must discharge our responsibilities. If we possess something that may prove helpful to world progress we should not hesitate in imparting it to the world. In this era of adulteration, instead of adulterating ideas we must on the contrary scrutinize and improve upon them wherever possible before accepting them. Rather than being a burden on the world, we must attempt to resolve if possible the problems facing the world.

We must also consider what contribution our tradition and civilization make to the world culture. We shall consider this tomorrow evening.

LECTURE-2 (23rd April, 1965)

Yesterday we had seen that even after 17 years of independence, we have still to decide what direction we should adopt to realize our cherished dream of all round development in the lives of our countrymen. Normally people are not prepared to seriously consider this question. They think only of the problems which they face from time to time. Sometimes economic problems are viewed with concern and an attempt is made to resolve them, and at other times social or political problems come to the forefront claiming attention. Not knowing fundamentally the direction in which we to go al these efforts are not accompanied by sufficient enthusiasm not do they give a feeling of satisfaction to the people engaged in these efforts. These efforts produce only a fraction of the results which they ought to have produced.

Modern versus ancient: Those who advocate some define direction, include two distinct groups of people. There are some who suggest that we must go back to the position when we lost our independence and proceed from there. On the other hand there are people who would like to discard all that has originated here in Bharat and are not ready to think about it. They seem to think that western life and thoughts are the last word in progress and all of it should be imported here if we are to develop. Both these lines of thought are incorrect, thought they do represent partials truths and it will not be proper to discard them altogether.

Those who advocate starting from where we left off a thousand years ago, forget that whether it may or may not be desirable. It is definitely impossible. The flow of time cannot be reversed.

The past cannot be disowned: In the past one thousand years whatever we assimilated whether it was forced on us or we took with willingness cannot be discarded now. Besides, we too have created originality not a little. In the life of our society, we did not remain always mere passive witness to whatever new challenging situations arose; nor did we merely react to every alien action. We too have attempted to reshape our life as required to face the new situations. Therefore, it will not do, simply to close our eyes to all that has happened in the past one thousand years.

Foreign ideologies are not universal: Similarly those who would like to make western ideologies the basis of our progress forget that these ideologies have arisen in certain special situations and time. These are not necessarily universal. They cannot be free from the limitations of the particular people and their culture, which gave birth to these Isms. Besides, many of these ideas are already out of date. The principles of Marx have changed both with the changing times as well as with varying conditions to the extent that parrot like repetition of Marxism for problems facing our country would amount to a reactionary attitude rather than a scientific and pragmatic one. It is indeed surprising that those who claim to reform the society by removing dead traditions, themselves fall prey to some outdated foreign traditions.

Our country, our problems: Every country has its own peculiar historical. Social and economic situations and its leaders decide the remedies to the ills that beset the country from time to time taking into consideration its background. It is illogical to believe that remedies which the leaders of one country decided to try for their problems are likely to be applicable as such to all other peoples. A simple illustration will suffice. Even though the basic organic activity is the same in all human beings the drugs which may be helpful in England may not prove equally helpful in India. Diseases depend also upon climate, water, dietary habits and heredity. Even though the external symptoms may be apparently similar the same drug does not necessarily cure all persons. Those who apply a single panacea to all diseases must be considered quacks rather than doctors. Therefore Ayurveda states i.e. for the disease in each place remedy suitable to that place must be found. Therefore, it is neither possible nor wise to adopt foreign Isms in our country in the original from in toto. It will not be helpful in achieving happiness and prosperity.

Human knowledge is common property: On the other hand it needs, to be realized that not all the thoughts and principles that have sprung up elsewhere are necessarily local in space and time. The response of human beings in a particular place time and social atmosphere may, and does, in many cases have relation and use to other human beings elsewhere and at other times. Therefore to ignore altogether the developments in other societies, past or present is certainly unwise. Whatever truths these developments contain must be taken not of and accepted. The rest must be scrupulously avoided. While absorbing the wisdom of other societies it is only proper that we avoid their mistakes or perversities. Even their wisdom should be adapted to our particular circumstances. In brief, we must absorb the knowledge and gains of the entire humanity so far as eternal principles and truths are concerned. Of these the ones that originated in our midst have to be clarified and adapted to changed times and those that we take from other societies have to be adapted to our conditions.

The conflicting ideas: The western political thought has accepted Nationalism, Democracy and Socialism or equality as ideals. Besides now and then, there have been attempts directed at world unity which took the shape of the 'League of Nations' and after the Second World War, the 'United Nation Organizations'. For a variety of reasons those have not succeeded. However, those definitely were attempts in that direction.

All these ideals have in practice proved to be incomplete and mutually opposing. Nationalism led to conflict between nations and in turn to global conflict, whereas if status-quo is regarded as synonymous with world peace the aspirations of many small nations to be independent would have never been fulfilled. World unity and Nationalism conflict with each other. Some advocate suppression of Nationalism for world unity whereas other regard world unity as an utopian ideal and emphasize national interest to the utmost.

Similar difficulty arises in reconciling Socialism and Democracy. Democracy grants individual liberty but the same is used by capitalist system for exploitation and monopoly. Socialism was brought in to end exploitation but it eliminated the freedom and dignity of the individual. Mankind stands confused unable to decide what is the correct path for future progress. The West is not in a position to say with confidence that "this alone and no other" is the right path. It is itself groping. Therefore simply to follow the West would be an instance of a blind being led by another blind.

In this situation our attention is claimed by the Bharatiya culture. Is possible that our culture can point the direction to the world?

From the national stand point we shall have to consider our culture because that is our very nature. Independence is intimately related to one's own culture. If culture does not form the basis of independence then the political movement for independence would reduce simply to a scramble by selfish and power seeking persons independence can be meaningful only if it becomes instrument for the expression of our culture. Such expression will not only contribute to our progress but the effort required will also give us the experience of joy. Therefore, both from the national as well as human standpoint it has become essential that we think of the principles of the Bharatiya culture. If with its help we can reconcile the various ideals of the western political though then it will be an added advantages for us. These western principles are a product of revolution in human thought, and social conflict. They represent one or the other aspiration of mankind. It is not proper to ignore them.

Bharatiya culture is integrated: The first characteristic of Bharatiya culture is that it looks upon life as an integrated whole. It has an integrated view point. To think of parts may be proper for a specialist but it is not useful from the practical standpoint. The confusion in the West arises primarily from its tendency to think of life in sections and then to attempt to put them together by patch work. We do admit that there is diversity and plurality in life but we have always attempted to discover the unity behind them. This attempt is thoroughly scientific. The scientists always attempt to discover order in the apparent disorder in the universe, to find out the principles governing the universe and frame practical rules on the basis of these principles. Chemists discovered that a few elements comprise the entire physical world. Physicists went one step further and showed that even these elements consist only of energy. Today we know that the entire universe is only a form of energy.

Philosophers are also basically scientists. The western philosophers reached tip to the principle of duality; Hegel put forward the principle of thesis, anti-thesis and synthesis; Karl Marx used this principle as a basis and presented his analysis of history and economics. Darwin considered the principle of survival of the fittest as the sole basis of life. But we in this country saw the basic unity of all life. Even the dualists have believed the nature and spirit to be complementary to each other than conflicting. The diversity in life is merely an expression of the internal unity. There is complementary underlying the diversity. The unit of seed finds expression in various form - - the roots, the trunk, the branches the leaves, the flowers and the fruits of the tree. All these have different forms and colors and even to some extent different properties. Still we recognize their relation of unity with each other through seed.

Mutual conflict, the sign of cultural regression: Unity in diversity and the expression of unity in various forms has remained the central thought of Bharatiya culture. If this truth is wholeheartedly accepted then there will not exist any cause for conflict among various powers. Conflict is not a sign of culture of nature: rather it is a symptom of their degradation. The law of the jungle, "Survival of the Fittest" which the West discovered in recent years was known to our philosophers.

We have recognized desire, anger etc. among the six lower tendencies of human nature, but we did not use them as the foundation or the basis of civilized life or culture. There are thieves and robbers in the society. It is essential to save ourselves and the society from these elements. We cannot consider them as our ideals or standards for human behaviour. Survival of the fittest is the law of the jungle. The civilizations have developed not on the basis of this law but by consideration of how the operation of this law will be the least in human life. If we wish to progress, we have to keep this history of civilization before our minds.

Mutual co-operation: Co-operation also obtains in abundance just as conflict and competition in this world. Vegetation and animal life keep each other alive. We get our oxygen supply with the help of vegetation whereas we provide carbon dioxide so essential for the growth of vegetable life. This mutual co-operation sustains life on this earth.

The recognition of this element of mutual sustenance among different forms of life and taking that as the basis of an effort to make human life mutually sustaining is the prime characteristic of civilization. To mold the nature to achieve the social goals is culture but when this nature leads to social conflict it is perversion. Culture does not disregard or deny nature. Rather it enhances those elements in nature which are helpful in sustaining life in this universe and making it fuller richer, and curbs others which obstruct or destroy life. Let us take a simple illustration. The relationship such as brother, sister, mother and son, father and son are natural. These are same both in man as well as among animals. Just as two brothers are sons of one mother so also, two calves have a single mother cow. Where lies the difference? In animals by lack of memory the relation is short-lived. They cannot build up an edifice of civilization on these relations. But men use this natural relation as a basis to construct a more harmonious order in life, to establish other relationships flowing from these basic relationships so as to knit the whole society in single unit of co-operation. Thus various values and traditions are built. Standards of good and bad are constructed accordingly. In society we find instances of both affection as well as enmity between brothers. But we consider affection good and aim at enchanting affectionate brotherly relations. The opposite tendency is disapproved. If conflict and enmity is made the basis of human relationships and if on this basis history is analyzed, then it would be futile to dream of world peace to result out of such a course of action.

A mother brings up her children. Mother's love is held up as the highest love. On such a basis alone we can devise the rules regulating the life of mankind. Sometimes there are examples of selfishness and cruelty of a mother toward her child. Among some species of animal's mother devise her progeny to satisfy the hunger. On the other hand among monkeys mother carries her child long after its death. Both types of behaviour are found among living things. Which of these two principles of nature can be made the basis of civilized life? We cannot but conclude that alone which helps to sustain life can be chosen, the contrary cannot lead to civilized life. Human nature has tendencies, anger, and greed on the one hand and love, sacrifice on the other. All these are present in our nature. Anger etc. are natural to man and beasts. For the reason if we make anger a standard in our life and arrange our efforts accordingly then the result will be a lack of harmony in our life. Therefore the exhortation, "do not yield to anger". Even when the anger arises in one's mind one can exercise control over it and one should do so. Thus control becomes a standard of our life and not anger.

Such laws are known as the principles of ethics. These principles are not framed by anyone. They are discovered. A suitable analogy is that of the law of gravitation, that if we throw a stone it falls on the ground. This law of gravitation is not framed by Newton. He discovered it. When he saw an apple falling to the ground from the branch, he realized there must exists such a law. Thus he discovered this law, he did not frame it. Similarly there are certain principles of human relations such as, if one feels anger it is on the whole beneficial to mankind that one must control anger. These principles of ethics are then discovered.

"Do not tell lies to one another say what you know to be true." This is a principle. Its usefulness becomes apparent at every step in life. We appreciates truthful person. If we speak lie, we ourselves feels unhappy; life cannot go on; there will be great confusion.

Modern versus ancient–These principles constitute our Dharma: A child does not speak lie by nature. Often Parents, teach their child to speak untruths. When the child desires something, if parents do not wish that child should have it, they conceal the object and tell the child that the desired object has disappeared. The child may be fooled a couple of times but soon knows the real situation and learns to speak untruth. This fact that by nature a person is truthful is a law that is discovered. Many other principles of ethics are similarly discovered. They are not arbitrarily framed by someone. In Bharat these principles are termed "Dharma", laws of life. All those principles which bring about harmony, peace and progress in the life of mankind are included in this "Dharma". On the sound basis of 'Dharma' then, we must proceed with the analysis of life as an integral whole.

When Nature is channelled according to the principles of Dharma, we have culture and civilization. It is indeed this culture which will enable us to sustain and sublimate the life of mankind. 'Dharma' is translated here as law. The English word 'religion' is not the correct word for 'Dharma'. As pointed out earlier an integrated life is the foundation and the principle underlying this culture as well as its aims and ideals.

We have thought of life as Integrated not only in the case of collective or social life but also in the individual life. Normally an individual is thought of in the physical bodily forms. Physical comfort and luxury is considered happiness. But we know that mental worry destroys bodily happiness. Everyone desires physical comfort. But if a person is imprisoned and there he is given finest of food etc., will he be happy? A person does not experience joy on getting nice food if it is also accompanied by a few abuses. There is a well-known incident in Mahabharata. When Lord Krishna went to Hastinapur as an emissary of Pandavas, Duryodhan invited him to enjoy his hospitality. Lord Krishna declined his Invitation and went instead to Vidura's home. Overjoyed by the visit of this much revered guest, Vidura's wife served the banana skins while throwing away the pulp. But Lord Krishna enjoyed even the meal of banana skin. That is why it is said, "Even a modest meal served with dignity and affection tastes better than the best delicacies served with disrespect". It is necessary therefore to take not of the mental happiness.

Similarly there is an intellectual happiness which too must be considered. Even after a person gets comforts for the body, and importance, affection etc. Which please the mind? If he is involved in some intellectual confusion he is reduced to a state almost similar to madness. And what is madness itself? A lunatic may have all physical comforts, he may be perfectly healthy and properly cared for by his relatives; but he does not possess intellectual happiness. Intellectual peace is also essential and important. We will have to take all these things into consideration.

Modern versus ancient–the political aspirations of Man: Body, mind, intelligence and the soul.-these four make up an individual. But these are integrated. We cannot think of each part separately. The confusion that has arisen in the West is due to the fact that they have treated each of the above aspects of human being separately and without any relation to the rest. When there was movement for democratic structure, they proclaimed "man is a political animal" and therefore his political aspirations must be attended to. Why only one person should be the king and others his subjects'? Let everyone rule! In Order to satisfy this political man they gave him the right to vote. Now he did get the right to a vote, but at the same time other rights diminished. Then the questions arose. "The voting right is nice but what about food? What if there is nothing to eat?"

They wondered, "Now that you have voting right, you are the king. Why need you worry?" But man replied, "What shall I do with the state if I do not get any food? I have no use of this voting right. I want bread first." Then came Karl Marx and said, "Yes, bread is the most important thing. The state belongs to the 'haves'. So let us fight for bread. He saw man as primarily made up of body, wanting bread." But those who followed the path shown by Karl Marx came to realize that they had neither the bread nor voting-right.

At the opposite end there is USA. There is both bread as well as voting right. Even so there is lack of peace and happiness. USA has highest list in number of suicides, number of mental patients and number of persons using tranquilizers to get sleep. People are puzzled as to the cause of this new situation. Man obtained bread, he got his voting right, and still there is no peace, no happiness. Now they want back their peaceful sleep. Sound and undisturbed sleep is a scarce commodity in the present day America. Those who think realize that there is a basic mistake somewhere, whereby even after acquiring all good things of life, they are not happy.

The reason is that they have not thought of the integrated human being. In our country we have thoroughly considered this matter. That is why we have stated that progress of man means progress of the body, mind, intellect and soul of man, all together. Often it has been propagated that Bharatiya culture thinks only salvation of the soul. It does not bother about the rest. This is wrong. We do not think of the soul but it is not true that we do not consider body, mind and intellect of much importance. Other gave importance of body alone. Therefore our attention to the soul is unique. With time this created and impression that we are concerned only with the soul and not with other aspects of human being. A young unmarried boy cares for his mother, but after marriage he cares both for his wife as well as his mother, and discharges his responsibilities towards both of them. Now if anyone says that this man has no loves for his mother, it would be untrue. A wife also loves only her husband at first, but after the birth of child, she loves both her husband and child. Sometimes an unthoughtful husband feels that his wife neglects him, after the birth of their child. But this is generally not correct. If that is true then the wife has certainly slipped in her duty.

Similarly, while we recognize the need to pay attention to the soul, we do not neglect the body. Upanishads declare in unambiguous words i.e. weakling cannot realize the self. Again Body is truly the primary instrument to discharge the responsibilities that dharma in joins. The fundamental difference between our position and that of the west is that. Whereas they have regarded body and satisfaction of its desires as the aim, we regard the body as an instrument for achieving our aims. We have recognized the importance of the body only in this light. The satisfaction of our bodily needs is necessary, but we don't consider this to be the sole aim of all our efforts. Here in Bharat, we have placed before ourselves the ideal of the four fold responsibilities, of catering for the needs of body, mind, intellect and soul with a view of achieve the integrated progress of man. Dharma, Artha, Kama and Moksha are the four kinds of human effort. Purushartha means efforts which befit a man. The longings for Dharma, Artha, Kama and Moksha are inborn in man, and satisfaction. Of these four efforts too, we have thought in an integrated way. Even though Moksha has been considered the highest of these purusharthas, efforts for Moksha alone are not considered to give benefit to the soul. On the other hand, a person who engages in action, while remaining unattached to its fruits, is said to achieve Moksha inevitably and earlier.

Artha includes what is known as political and economic policies. According to the ancients, it used to include the justice and punishment also. Kama relates to the satisfaction of various natural desires. 'Dharma' defines a set of rules to regulate the social activity. So Artha and Kama progress in an integral and harmonious way, and attain not only Kama and Artha but also Moksha eventually.

Thus even though Dharma regulates Artha and Kama, all the three are interrelated and mutually complementary. Dharma helps achieve Artha. Even in business, one requires honesty, restraint, truthfulness etc. which are the attributes of Dharma. Without these qualities one cannot earn money. It must be admitted that Dharma is instrumental in attaining Artha and Kama. Americans proclaimed, "Honesty is the best business policy." In Europe they said, "Honesty is the best policy." We go one step forward and assert "Honesty is not a policy but a principle" i.e. we believe in dharma not just because it is instrumental in acquiring Artha but because it is a fundamental principle of civilized life.

Kama too can be attained only through Dharma. Having produced the material things such as nice food, when, where, how and in what measure it will be used can be determined only by Dharma. If a sick person eats food meant for a healthy one and vice-versa, both of them will be at a disadvantage. Dharma helps in restraining the natural tendencies of man, whereby he is able to determine what is beneficial to him apart from what is pleasurable. Hence Dharma is given the foremost place in our culture.

Dharma is of primary importance, but we should not forget that it is not possible to practice Dharma in the absence of Artha. There is a saying "What sin will not be committed by one who is starving? Those who have lost everything become ruthless." Even a rishi like Vishwamitra driven by hunger broke into the home of a hunter and ate the flesh of a dog. Therefore we are enjoined to see that there is enough wealth created continuously, since wealth also strengthens Dharma. Similarly the government has to maintain law and order and prevent chaos, which definitely destroys Dharma. At the time of Chaos, law of the jungle prevails where the strong feed upon the weak. Therefore stability in the state is also essential for the prevalence of Dharma.

In order to do these, educations, character building, spread of idealism, and suitable economic structures are all necessary. Governments also fall inside the realm of Artha. Excessive power of state is also harmful of Dharma. It was said that a king should be neither too harsh nor too soft with his people. Heavy reliance on harsh measures produces a feeling of revolt in people. When state usurps the rightful position of Dharma, then there is this evil of preponderance of power of the state. Dharma suffers thereby. This is the reason of the decline of Dharma in ruthless states.

When the state-acquires all powers, both political and economic, the result is a decline of Dharma. In this way if the state has unlimited powers, the whole society looks towards the state, for everything. Officers of the government neglect their duties and acquire vested interests. These are all signs of the preponderance of the powers of state.

Dharma staffers a setback, hence Artha should not be allowed to acquire hold in either of these two ways. Karma too has been considered on the same lines. I the physical needs are neglected, and desires entirely suppressed, Dharma does not grow. Dharma cannot be observed if one has no food to eat. If the fine arts which satisfy the mind are altogether stopped, then the civilizing influence on people will not be present. Mind will become perverse and Dharma neglected. On the other hand, if greediness of the gluttons of Rome or sensuousness of Yayati prevails, then the duties will be forgotten. Hence Kama too must be pursued consistent with Dharma. We have thus considered the life of an individual in a through and integrated manner. We have set the aim of developing body, mind intellect as well as soul in a balance way. We have tried to satisfy the manifold aspirations man taking care that efforts to satisfy two different aspirations are not mutually conflicting. This is the integrated picture of all the fourfold aspirations of and individual. This concept of a complete human being, integrate individual, is both our goal as well as our path. What should be the relation of this integrated human being with the society and how the interests of the society should be enhanced will be discussed tomorrow.

Lecture–3 (24th April, 1965)

Yesterday we considered man as an individual. There are different aspects of an individual personality, different levels of needs of an individual. In order to develop complete personality, to satisfy the needs progressively but simultaneously at all levels, certain specific kinds of efforts are needed. These, too, were considered. But man does not exist merely as an individual. The individual comprising of body, mind, intellect and soul as not limited to singular 'I' but is also inseparably related to the plural 'We'. Therefore we must also think of the group or the society. It is a simple truth treat society is a group of men. But how did society come into being? Many views have been put forward by philosophers. Those propounded in the West and on which the western socio-political structure is based can be broadly summarized as "society is a group of individuals brought into being by the individuals by an agreement among themselves." This view is known as "Social Contract Theory". Individual is given greater importance in this view. If there are any differences in different western views, these pertain only to the questions, namely, "If the individual produced a society then in whom the residual power remains vested, in the society or in the individual? Does the individual have the right to change the society? Can the society impose a variety or regulations on the individual and claim a right to the allegiance of the individual to itself? Or the individual is free as regards these questions?"

Individual versus society: There is a controversy in the West on this question. Some have opted for the society as supreme and from this a conflict has arisen. The truth is that the view that individuals have brought society into being, is fundamentally incorrect. It is true that the society is composed of a number of individuals. Yet it is not made by people, nor does it come into being by mere coming together of a number of individuals.

In our view society is self-born. Like an individual, society comes into existence in an organic way. People do not produce society. It is not a sort of club, or some joint stock company, or a registered co-operative society. In reality, society is an entity with its own 'Self', its own life; it is a sovereign being like an individual; it is an organic entity. We have not accepted the view that society is some arbitrary association. It has its own life. Society too has its body, mind, intellect and soul. Some western psychologists are beginning to accept this truth. McDougal has produced a new branch of psychology called group mind. He has accepted that the group has its own mind, its own psychology, its own methods of thinking and action.

Group has its feelings too. These are not exactly similar to the individual's feelings. Group feelings cannot be considered a mere arithmetic addition of individual feelings. Group strength too is not a mere sum of individual's strength. The intellect, emotions and energies, strength of a group, are fundamentally different from those of an individual. Therefore, at times it is experienced that even weakling, despite his individual weak physique turns out to be a heroic member of the society. Sometimes an individual may be ready to put up with an affront to his person, but is unwilling to tolerate an insult to his society. A person may be ready to forgive and forget a personal abuse to him, but the same man loses his temper if you abuse his society. It is possible that a person who is of a high character in his personal life, is unscrupulous as a member of the society. Similarly an individual can be good in society but not so in his individual life. This is a very important point.

Let me give you an illustration. Once during a conversation between Shri Vinobaji and the Sar Sanghachalak of Rashtriya Swayamsevak Sangh, Shri Guruji, a question arose as to where the modes of thinking of Hindus and Muslims differ. Guruji said to Vinobaji that there are good and bad people in every society. There can be found honest and good people in Hindus as well as in Muslims. Similarly rascals can be seen in both the societies. No particular society has a monopoly of goodness. However, it is observed that Hindus even if they are rascals individual life, when they come together in a group, they always think of good things. On the other hand when two Muslims come together, they propose and approve of things which they themselves in their individual capacity would not even think of. They start thinking in an altogether different way. This is an everyday experience. Vinobaji admitted that there was truth in this observation but had no reasons to explain it.

If we analyze this situation, we shall discover that the modes of thinking of an individual and of a society are always different. These two do not bear an arithmetic relation. If a thousand good men gather together it cannot be said for certain that they will think similarly of good things.

An average Indian student at present is a mild and meek young man. Compared to an average student of twenty years ago, he is weaker and milder in every way. But when a score of such students get together, the situation becomes difficult. Then they indulge in all sorts of irresponsible actions. Thus a single student appears disciplined but a group of students become undisciplined. We shall have to consider why this change comes about. This is known as mob-mentality as distinct from individual mentality. This mob-mentality is a small aspect of mind. When a group of persons collect for a short time, the collective mentality obtained in that group is known as mob-mentality. But society and social mentality evolves over a much longer period. There is a thesis is that when a group of people live together for a long time, by historical tradition and association, by continued intercourse, they begin to think similarly and have similar customs. It is true that some uniformity is brought about by staying together. Friendship arises between two persons of similar inclination. However a nation or a society does not spring up from mere co-habitation.

Why mighty nations of antiquity perished: It is known that some ancient nations disappeared. The ancient Greek nation came to end. Egyptian civilization similarly disappeared. Babylonian and Syrian civilizations are a matter of history. Cynthia's perished. Was there ever a time when the citizens of those nations stopped living together? It was only the fact that there were wide differences among people that led to the downfall of these nations. The Greece in the past produced Alexander and Heredotes, Ulysis and Aristotle, Socrates and Plato and the present day Greece is inhabited by people of the same hereditary stock. There was no interruption in their heredity, because there never was a time when the whole of Greece was devoid of human population and when a new race inhabited that country. Such a thing never happened. Father and son tradition of old Greece was never interrupted. It is possible to trace the ancestry of present day Greeks to the old Greeks, some 250 to 500 generation back. Despite all the old Greek Nation is non-existent. So also the old Egyptian Nation Is no longer there. New nations have arisen in those places. How did this happen? This simple fact is indisputable, that nations do not come into existence by a mere co habitation. There was never a time in the lives of the citizens of these decadent nations, when they stopped living in a group. On the other hand Israeli Jews lived for centuries with other peoples scattered far and wide, yet they did not get annihilated in the societies in which they lived because of cohabitation. It is clear therefore that the source of national feeling is not in staying on a particular piece of land, but is in something etc.

What is a nation: That source is in the goal which is put before the people. When a group of persons lives with a goal, ideal and mission and looks upon a particular place of land as motherland, this group constitutes a nation. If either of the two-an ideal and a motherland-is not there, then there is no nation. There is a 'Self' in the body, the essence of the individual; upon the severance of its relation with the body, a person is said to die. Similarly there is this idea, ideal, or fundamental principle of a nation, its soul. Although it is believed that man take birth again and again, yet the re-born person is a different individual. They are treated as two separate beings. The same soul leaves one body and enters another, but the previous and the latter are two different individuals. The end of a person is nothing but the departure of his soul from his body. The other components of the body also undergo change. From childhood to old age, there is a drastic change! The biologists tell us that in course of a few years, every cell of our body is replaced by a new one. A variety of changes takes place. Because the soul resides in the body without interruption, the body continues its existence; such a relation is known as "the law of identity" in logic. It is due to this identity that we admit the continued existence of any entity. In this connection a nice illustration of a barber's razor is sometimes advanced.

Once while shaving a customer, a barber, prided in his razor being 60 years old. His father too had worked with the same razor. The customer was surprised especially because the handle was quite shiny and new In appearance. "Why the handle is quite shiny? How have your preserved the brightness for sixty years?" He asked. Barber too was amused with this. "Is it possible to preserve the handle in a brand new appearance for sixty years? It has been replaced only six months ago", he replied naturally. The customer was curious and asked and how old is the steel? Three years was the reply. In brief, the handle was replaced, the steel was also replaced, but the razor remained old! Its identity was intact. Similarly a nation too has a soul. There is a technique name for it. In the 'Principles arid Policies' adopted by the Jana Sangh, this name is mentioned. The word is 'Chiti'. According to McDougal, it is the innate nature of a group. Every group of persons has an innate nature. Similarly every society has an innate nature, which is inborn and is not the result of historical circumstances.

A human being is born with a soul. Human personality, Soul and character are all distinct from one another.. Personality results from a cumulative effect of all the actions, thoughts and impressions of an individual. But Soul is unaffected by this history. Similarly national culture is continuously modified and enlarged by the historic reasons and circumstances. Culture does include all those things which by the association, endeavours and the history of the society, have come to be held up as good and commendable. But these are not added on to Chiti. Chiti is fundamental and is central to the nation from its very beginning. Chiti determines the direction in which the nation is to advance culturally. Whatever is in accordance with Chiti, is included in culture.

Chiti, Culture, and Dharma: By way of an illustration consider the story of Mahabharata. Kauravas were defeated, and Pandavas won. Why did we hold up the conduct of Pandavas as Dharma? Or why this battle was not considered just a battle for a kingdom? The praise for Yudhistir and the dishonour heaped on Duryodhana are not a result of political causes Krishna killed his uncle Kansa, the established king of the times. Instead of branding this as a revolt, we consider Krishna as an Avatar of God, and Kansa as an Asura.

Rama was assisted in his invasion of Lanka by Vibhishana, brother of Ravana. Such conduct of Vibhishana instead of being branded as treason is considered good and exemplary. He betrayed his brother and his king even as Jaichand had one later on. He might be branded as a 'quisling'. But Vibhishana is not called "quisling' by any one. On the contrary he is highly praised for his conduct, and Ravana actions are disapproved. Why so? The reason behind this is not political.

If there is any standard for determining the merits and demerits of particular action, it is this Chiti; from nature whatever is in accordance with 'Chiti', is approved and added on to culture. These things are to be cultivated. Whatever is against 'Chiti,' is discarded as perversion, undesirable, is to be avoided. 'Chiti' is the touchstone on which each action, each attitude is tested, and determined to be acceptable or otherwise. 'Chitti' is the soul of the nation. On the strength of this 'Chiti', a nation arises, strong and virile if it is this 'Chiti' that is demonstrated in the actions of every great man of a nation.

An individual is also in instrument in bringing forth the soul of the nation 'Chiti'. Thus apart from his own self, an individual also represents his nation. Not only that, but he also mans the various institutions that are created for the fulfillment of the national goal. Therefore he represents these too. The groups larger than nation such as 'mankind' are also represented by him. In short, an individual has a multitude of aspect, but they are not conflicting; there is co-operation, unity and harmony in them. A system based on the recognition of this mutuality complementary nature of the different ideals of mankind, their essential harmony, a system which devises laws, which removes the disharmony and enhances this mutual usefulness and co-operation, alone can bring peace and happiness to mankind; can ensure steady development.

Institution–a means to fulfill national needs: According to Darwin's theory, living beings develop various organs as per the requirements dedicated by the circumstances. In our 'shastras', it was stated slightly differently, that the soul constructs, using the strength of 'Prana', various organs as the need is felt, for the purpose of continuing life. Just as the soul produced these different organs in the body, so also in the nation many different organs are produced as instruments to achieve national goals. Like various departments in a factory, building, machinery, sales, production, maintenance etc. nations also produce different departments, which are called institutions. These institutions are created to fulfil the needs of a nation. Family, castes, guilds, (which are now known as trade unions) etc., are such institutions. Property, marriage are also institution. Formerly there were no marriages. Later on some Rishi established this practice of marriage. He produced the institution of marriage. Similarly Gurukul and Rishkul were institutions. In the same way, the state is also an institution. The Nation creates it. A lot of trouble in the West is due to the fact that they confused the state with the nation, they considered the state synonymous with the nation. Truly speaking, nation and state are not the same. In our country, the state was produced as per social contract theory. Formerly there was no king. Mahabharata describes that in Krityuga, there was no state or king. Society was sustained and protected mutually by practicing Dharma.

Later on interruption and disorganization came into existence. Greed and anger dominated. Dharma was on the decline and the rule "might is right" prevailed. The Rishis were perturbed over the developments. They all went to Brahma to seek counsel, Brahma gave them a treatise on "Law and the Functions of the State", which he had himself writer. At the same time, he asked Manu to become the first King. Manu declined saying that a king will have to punish other persons, put them in jail and so on; he was not prepared to commit all these sins. There upon Brahma said, your actions in the capacity of king will not constitute sin, a long as they are aimed at securing conditions under which the society can live peacefully and according to Dharma. This will be your duty, your Dharma. Not only that but you will also have a share of the Karma of your subjects, whereby you will gain Dharma considerably if your subjects maintain conduct according to Dharma. Although it is not explicitly stated here, but I believe that if the society under any king committed sin, a part of that too must automatically go to the account of the king. It is not proper if only good things are shared by the king and not the bad ones; both must be shared in the same proportion. Thus state came into existence as a contract. This contract theory can be applied to the state but not to the nation. In the West, it was exactly opposite. Society as a nation, according to them, was a contract, but the king claimed a divine right and proclaimed himself the sole representative of God. This is wrong. In our Country, the king may have been first recognized in antiquity but the society as a nation is considered self-born. State is only an institution.

Similarly other institutions, like the state, are created from time to time as the need is felt. Every individual is a limb of one or more of these institutions. A person is a member of his family, as well as his community; he may also be a member of some association of his fellow professionals, if he pursues a profession. Above all he is a member of the nation and society. If we consider even larger sphere he is a member of the whole mankind, and then the entire universe, truly speaking an individual is not merely a single entity but a plural entity. He is a part of not just one, but a member of many institutions. He lives a variety of lives. The most important aspect is that despite this multiple personality, he can and should behave in a way which does not bring different aspects of his life into mutual conflict but which is mutually sustaining, complementary and unifying. This quality is inherent in man.

A person, who uses this quality properly, becomes happy and on the other hand one, who does not do so, reaps unhappiness. Such a person will not have balanced development in the life. As an illustration, a man is son of another, husband of his wife, brother of his sister and father of his son. A single individual is a father and is also a son, he is brother and also husband. He has to maintain all these relation with intelligence, understanding and tact. Where a person fails to do so, there is conflict. If he sides with one party the other feels wronged. The conflicts between his wife and his sisters, his wife and mother result from his inability to behave properly. There upon some of his relations are strained. He is pained because his duties towards his mother and towards his wife clash. When he can resolve this conflict, and fulfil all his obligations properly, it can be said that his development will be integrated.

Society and individual not conflicting: We do not accept the view that there is any permanent inevitable conflict among the multifarious personality of an individual, and different institutions of the society. If a conflict does exist, it is a sign of decadence perversion and not of nature or culture. The error in western thinking lies in that some people there believe that human progress is a result of this fundamental conflict. Therefore they consider the conflict between the individual and the state as a natural occurrence, on the same basis they also theorized on the class conflict.

Classes do exist in a society. Here too, there were castes, but we had never accepted, conflict between one caste and another as fundamental concept behind it. In our concept of four castes, they are thought of as analogous to the different limbs of Virat-purusha. It was suggested that from the head of the Virat-Purusha Bhrahmins were created, Kshatriyas from hands, Vaishyas from his abdomen and Shudras from legs. If we analyze this concept we are faced with the question whether there can arise any conflict among the head, arms, stomach and legs of the same Virat Purusha. If conflict is fundamental, the body cannot be maintained. There cannot be any conflict in the different parts of the same body. On the contrary 'one man' prevails. These limbs are not only complementary to one another, but even further, there is individual unity. There is a complete identity of interest identity of belonging. The origin of the caste system was on the above basis. If this idea is not kept alive; the castes, instead of being complementary, can produce conflict. But then this is distortion. It is not a systematic arrangement, rather it is absence of any plan, any arrangement. This is indeed the present condition of our society.

This process of deterioration can set in the various institutions of a society due to a variety of reasons. If the soul of the society weakens, then all the different limbs of the society will grow feeble and ineffective. Any particular institution may be tendered useless or even harmful. Besides, the need and the usefulness of any particular institution may change with time, place and circumstances. While examining the present state of an institution we ought at the same time, to think of what it should be like; mutual complementary and a sense of unity, alone can be the standards of proper conduct. Family, Community, Trade Union, Gram Panchayat, Janapada, State and such other institutions are various limbs of the nation and even of mankind. They are interdependent, initially complementary. There should be a sense of unity through all of them. For this very reason, there should be a tendency toward mutual accommodation in them instead of conflict or opposition.

State is one of the several institutions, an important one, but it is not above all other. One of the major reasons for the problems of the present day world is that almost everyone thinks of the state to be synonymous with the society. At least in practice, they consider the state as the sole representative of the society. Other institutions leave declined in their effectiveness while the state has become dominant to such an extent that all the powers are gradually being centralized in the state.

We had not considered the state to be the sole representative of the nation. Our national life continued uninterruptedly even after the state went in the hands of foreigners. The Persian nation came to an end with their loss of independence. In our country, there were foreign rules now and then in various parts of the country. At the sometime the Pathans seized the throne of Delhi, and then the Turks; the Mughals and the British too established their rules. Despite all this, our national life went on, because the state was not its centre. If we had considered state as the centre, we would have been finished as a nation long time ago. In some tale for children, it is described that an evil spirit resided in some parrot and to kill the evil spirit one had to kill that parrot. Those nations, whose life centered in the state, were finished with the end of the state. On the other hand, where state was not believed central to its life, the nation survived the transfer of political power.

This had its effects also. Late Dr. Ambedkar had said that our Gram Panchayats were so strong that we neglected the throne of Delhi. We did not remain alert as regards the state as much as we ought to have done, thinking that nation's life did not depend on the state. We forgot that, though it may not be central. The state is definitely an important institution serving some needs of the nation, just as a limb of the body. It is possible to pluck a hair without much harm but along with the hair, if some skin is also removed, and a little further, if the head too is cut off, then there will be great loss for the body. Therefore the body must be protected. Although the various limbs of the body are not absolutely indispensable yet each of them serves an important purpose. From the same standpoint, state, too, should have been deemed important in the life of a nation. There were persons who attended to this aspect. It was for this reason that the great teacher of Shivaji, Samarth Ramdas Swami, directed him to establish his kingdom. Dharma wields its own power. Dharma is important in life. Shri Ramdas would as well have preached to Shivaji to become a mendicant and spread Dharma following his own example. But on the contrary, he inspired Shivaji to extend his rule, because state too, is an important institution of the society. However, to consider something important is different from saying that it is supreme. The state is not supreme. The question arises, then, that if the state is not of fundamental importance, what is that is absolutely important. Let us consider this question.

Dharma sustains the society: We shall have to examine the reasons why the state was established. No one will dispute that the state must have some specific aim, some ideal. Then this aim or ideal must be considering of highest importance rather than the state which is created to fulfil this ideal. A watchman is not deemed greater than the treasure he supposed to protect, nor is a treasure. The state is brought into existence to protect the nation: produce and maintain conditions in which the ideals of the nation can be translated into reality. The ideals of the nation constitute 'Chiti', which is analogous to the soul of an individual. It requires some effort to comprehend 'Chiti'. The laws that help manifest and maintain 'Chiti' of a Nation are termed Dharma of that nation. Hence it is this 'Dharma' that is supreme. Dharma is the repository of the nation's soul. If Dharma is destroyed the Nation perishes. Anyone who abandons Dharma betrays the nation.

Dharma is not confined to temples or mosques. Worship of God is only a part of Dharma. Dharma is much wider. In the past, temples have served as effective medium to educate people in their Dharma. However just as schools themselves do not constitute knowledge, so also temples do not constitute Dharma. A child may attend school regularly and yet may remain uneducated. So also, it is possible that a person may visit temple or mosque without break and yet he may not know his Dharma. To attend temple or mosque constitutes a part of religion, sect. creed, but not necessarily 'Dharma'. Many misconceptions that originated from faulty English translations include this most harmful confusion of Dharma with religion.

Dharma and religion are different: On the one hand we used the word religion as synonymous with 'Dharma' and on the other hand increasing ignorance, neglect of our society and Dharma, and greater acceptance of European life, became the outstanding features of our education. As a result all the characteristics of a narrow religion, especially as practiced in the West were attributed automatically to the concept of Dharma also. Since in the West, injustice atrocities, were perpetrated, bitter conflicts and battles were fought in the name of religion, all these were unblock listed on the debit side of 'Dharma' also. We felt that in the name of Dharma also battles were fought. However 'battles of Religion' and 'battles for Dharma' are two different things. Religion means a creed or a sect; it does not mean Dharma. Dharma is very wide concept. It is concerned with all aspects of life. It sustains the society. Even further, it sustains the whole world. That which sustains is 'Dharma'.

The fundamental principles of Dharma are eternal and universal. Yet, their implementation may differ according to time, place and circumstances. It is a fact that a human being requires food for maintaining his body. However, what a particular person should eat in, how much quantity, at what intervals is all decided according to circumstances. It is possible at times that even fasting is advisable. If a typhoid patient is given normal food, the consequences may be disastrous. For such a person, keeping away from food is necessary; similarly the principles of Dharma have to be adapted to changing times and pace.

Some rules are temporary and others are valid for longer periods. There are some rules regulating our conduct at this meeting. One of the rules is that I speak and you listen with attention. If a contravention of this rule, you start conversing with one another or addressing the gathering at the same time, than there will be disorder; our work will not progress: the meeting will not be sustained. It can be said that you have not observed your Dharma. Thus it is our Dharma that we observed your Dharma. Thus it is our Dharma that we observed the rules by winch the meeting proceeds smoothly. But this rule is applicable only as long as this meeting lasts. If after the meeting is over, even when you reach home, you continue to observe this rule and do not speak, a different problem will arise. Your family might have to call in a doctor. At home, the rules suitable there will have to be observed. The complete treatise on the rules in general and their philosophical basis is the meaning of Dharma. These rules cannot be arbitrary. They should be such as to sustain and further existence and progress of the entity which they serve. At the same time they should be in agreement with and supplementary to the larger framework of Dharma of which they form a part. For instance, when we form a registered society, we have the right to frame the rules and regulations, but these cannot be contradictory to the constitution of the society. The constitution itself cannot violate the Societies Registration Act. The act has to be within the provision of the constitution of the country. In other words, the constitution of the country is a fundamental document which governs the formulation of all acts in the country. In Germany the constitution is known as the 'Basic Law'.

Is the constitution too, not subject to some principles of more fundamental nature? Or is it a product of any arbitrary decisions of the constituent assembly? On serious consideration, it will be clear that even the constitution has to follow certain basic principles of Nature. Constitution is for sustaining the nation. If instead it is instrumental in its deterioration, then it must be pronounced improper. It must be amended. The amendment is also not solely dependent on majority opinion. Now-a-days the majority is much talked of. Is the majority capable of doing anything and everything? Is the action of the majority always just and proper? No. In the West, the king used to be the sovereign. Thereafter when royalty was deprived of its so-called divine rights, sovereignty was proclaimed to be with the people. Here in Our country neither the kings, nor the people, nor the parliament have had absolute sovereignty. Parliament cannot legislate arbitrarily.

It is said about the British parliament that it is sovereign and can do anything. They say that "British Parliament can do everything except making a woman a man and vice versa." But is it possible for the parliament to legislate that every Englishman must walk on his head? It is not possible. Can they pass an act that everyone in England must present himself before the local authority once every day? They cannot. England has no written constitution. They regard tradition highly. But their traditions too have undergone change. What is the basis for making changes in their traditions? Whichever tradition proved an obstacle in the progress of England, was discarded. Those which were helpful in the progress were consolidated.

The traditions are respected everywhere, just as in England. We have written constitution, but even these written constitutions cannot go contrary to the traditions of this country. In as much as it does go contrary to our traditions, it is not fulfilling Dharma. That constitution which sustains the nation is in tune with Dharma. Dharma sustains the nation. Hence we have always given primary importance to Dharma, which is considered sovereign. All other entities, institutions or authorities derive their power from Dharma and are subordinate to it.

If we examine our constitution from the point of view of the growth of the nation, we find that our constitution needs amendment. We are one nation, one society. That is why we did not entertain any special rights on the basis of language, province, caste, religion, etc. but gave everyone equal citizenship. There are separate states. There is no separate citizenship of state and of Union. We are all citizens of Bharat. By the same token, we have denied the right to secede to individual state. Not only that the power to demarcate the boundaries of state and to choose their names, is vested in the parliament, and not in assemblies. This is as it should be; in tune with the nationalism and tradition of Bharat. However, despite all this, we made our constitution federal, whereby what we have adopted in practice, we have rejected in principle. In a federation constituent units have their own sovereignty. These voluntarily relinquish their sovereignty to the federation, by an agreement. It may be that they surrender all their rights and thereby the centre requires sovereignty. But these powers are given to the Union. It has no power of its own. Thus the federal constitution considers the individual states as fundamental power, and the centre as merely a federation of states. This is contrary to the truth. It runs counter to the unity and indivisibility of Bharat. There is no recognition of the idea of Bharatmata, Our sacred motherland, as enshrined in the hearts of our people.

According to the first para of the Constitution, "India that is Bharat will be a federation of States", i.e. Bihar Mata, Banga Mata, Punjab Mata, Kannada Mata, Tamil Mata, all put together make Bharat Mata. This is ridiculous. We have thought of the provinces as limbs of Bharat Mata and not as individual mother. Therefore our constitution should be unitary instead of federal.

A unitary State does not mean concentration of all powers in the Centre; just as the head of the family does not have all the powers with him even though all the transactions are carried out in his name. Others also share the executive power. In our body also, does the soul possess all powers? Thus a unitary State does not mean a highly autocratic centre nor does it entail the elimination of provinces. The provinces will have various executive powers. Even the various entities below the provincial level, such as the Jana Padas, will also have suitable powers. The Panchayats too should have powers. Traditional, the Panchayats had a very important position. Nobody could dissolve Panchayats. Today, however, our constitution does not have any place for these Panchayats. There are no powers to these Panchayats in their own right. They exist at the mercy of the state only as delegated authorities. It is necessary that their powers be considered fundamental. In this way, the decentralization of power will be accomplished. The authority will be distributed to the lowest level, and will be fully decentralized. At the same time, all these entities of power will be centered on the unitary State. This arrangement will embody Dharma.

If we carry this concept of Dharma even further, not only the State and the nation but the nature of the entire mankind will have to be considered. In other words, the constitution of a nation cannot be contrary to the natural law. There are a number of norms of behaviour which are not found in any statute book, yet they do exist. At times they are even stronger and more binding than any statutory law. The precept that one should respect one's parents is not written in any law. The present day governments which are turning out variety of laws, day in and day out have not passed a law to this effect. Still, people respect their parents. Those who do not are criticized. If tomorrow there arises a discussion, even in a court. it will be generally accepted that as long as a person does not attain majority, he should accept his parent's decisions and should respect them.

Thus the fundamental law of human nature us the standard for deciding the propriety of behaviour in various situations. We have termed this very law as' Dharma'. The nearest equivalent English term for Dharma can be 'Innate law', which, however, does not express the full meaning of Dharma. Since 'Dharma' is supreme, our ideal of the state has been 'Dharma Rajya'. The king is supposed to protect Dharma. In olden times at the coronation ceremony the king used to recite three times. "There is no authority which can punish me." (Similar claim was made by kings in the western countries. i.e., it was said, "King can do no wrong", and hence there too, nobody could punish the king). Upon this, the Purohit used to strike the king on his back with a staff saying, "No, you are subject to the rule of Dharma. You are not sovereign." The king used to run around the sacred fire and the Purohit would follow him striking him with the Staff. Thus after completing three rounds, the ceremony would came to an end thereby the king was unambiguously told that he was not an un-punishable sovereign. Dharma was above him, that even he was subject to Dharma. Can the people do whatever they please? It may be contended that democracy means just that. The people can do what they please. But in our country, even in people wish, they are not free to act contrary to Dharma. Once a priest was asked, "If the God is omnipotent, can he act contrary to Dharma. If he does, then he is not omnipotent." This was a dilemma. Can God practice Adharma or is lie not omnipotent? Actually God cannot act contrary to Dharma. If he does, then he is not omnipotent.

Adharma is a characteristic of weakness, not of strength. If fire instead of emitting heat dies out it is no longer strong. Strength lies not in unrestrained behaviour, but in well regulated action. Therefore God who is omnipotent is also self- regulated and consequently fully in tune with Dharma. God descends in human body to destroy Adharma and re-establish Dharma, not to act on passing whims and fancies. Hence even God can do everything but cannot act contrary to Dharma. But for the risk of being misunderstood, one can say that Dharma is even greater than God. The universe is sustained because he acts according to Dharma. The king was supposed to be a symbol of Vishnu, in as much as he was the chief protector of Dharma Rajya.

Dharma Rajya does not mean a theocratic state. Let us be very clear on this point, where a particular sect and its prophet or Guru, rule supreme, that is a theocratic state. All the rights are enjoyed by the followers of this particular sect. Others either cannot live in that country or at best enjoy a slave-like, secondary citizen's status. Holy Roman Empire had this basis. The same concept was existed behind 'Khilafat'. The Muslim kings world over used to rule in the name of Khalifa. After the First World War, this came to an end. Now efforts are afoot to revive it. Pakistan is the most recent theocratic state. They call themselves an Islamic State. There, apart from Muslims all the rest are second class citizens. Apart from this difference there is no other sign of Islam in Pakistan's administration. Quran, Masjid, Roja, Eid, Namaz etc. are same both in Bharat as well as in Pakistan. There is no need to the state and religion. By such a tie-up, there is no increase in an individual's capacity to worship God. The only result is that the state slips in its duty. This does not happen in a Dharma Rajya. Rather there is freedom to worship according to one's religion. In a theocratic state one religion has all the rights and advantages, and there are direct or indirect restrictions on all other religions. Dharma Rajya accepts the importance of religion in the peace, happiness and progress of an individual. Therefore the state has the responsibility to maintain an atmosphere in which every individual can follow the religion of his choice and live in peace. The freedom has its inherent limits. I have the freedom to swing my hand, but as soon as there is conflict between my hand and someone else's nose, my freedom has to be restricted. I have no freedom to swing my hand so as to hit another person's nose. Where other person's freedom is likely to be encroached upon my freedom ends. The freedom of both parties has to be ensured. Similarly every religion has the freedom to exist. But this freedom extends only as far as it does riot encroach upon the religion of others. If such encroachment is carries on, it will have to be condemned as misuse of freedom and will have to be ended. Such limitations will be required in all aspects of life. Dharma Rajya ensures religious freedom and is not theocratic state.

Now-a-days the word 'secular state' is being uses as opposed to theocratic state. The adoption of this work is mere imitation of the western thought pattern. We had no need to import it. We called it a secular state to contrast it with Pakistan. There is some misunderstanding arising out of this. Religion was equated with Dharma and then secular state was meant to be a state without Dharma. Some said ours is a state (without Dharma), whereas others trying to find a better sounding word, called it Dharmanirpeksha (indifferent to Dharma state). But all these words are fundamentally erroneous. For a state can neither be without Dharma nor can it be indifferent dharma just as fire cannot be without hear. If fire loses heat, it does not remain fire any longer. State which exists fundamentally to maintain Dharma to maintain law and order can neither be Needharma nor Dharmanirpeksha. If it is Needharma– it will be lawless state, and where there is lawlessness, where is the question of the existence of any state? In other words Dharma and State are self-contradictory. State can only be Dharma Rajya (rule of Dharma) nothing else. Any other definition will conflict with the reason of its very existence.

In a Dharma Rajya, the state is not absolutely powerful. It is subject Dharma. We have always vested sovereignty in Dharma. Presently there has arisen a controversy. Parliament is sovereign or the Supreme Court? Legislature is higher or judiciary? This quarrel is like a quarrel whether left hand is more important or right hand? Both are limbs of the state, the Legislature is well as Judiciary. Both have distinct functions to perform in their individual sphere each is supreme. To consider either one above the other would be mistake. Yet the legislators say, "we are higher", On the other hand members of the Judiciary assert that they have a higher authority, since they interpret the laws which the legislature makes. The Legislature claims to have given powers to the Judiciary. If necessary, legislature can change the constitution. Hence it claims sovereignty. Now since powers are bestowed by constitution, they are talking of amendment to the constitution. But I believe that even if by a majority the constitution is amended, it will be against Dharma. In 'reality' both the Legislature and the Judiciary are on an equal plane. Neither the Legislature is higher nor the Judiciary. Dharma is higher than both. The Legislature will have to act according to Dharma and the Judiciary will have to act according to Dharma. Dharma will specify limits of both. The Legislature, the Judiciary or the people none of these is supreme. Some will say, "Why! People are sovereign. They elect." But even the people are not sovereign because people too have no right to act against Dharma. If an elected government allows people to go against Dharma and does not punish. Then that government is in reality a government of thieves. Even the general will cannot go against Dharma. Imagine the situation if by some manoeuvring, thieves gain a majority in the government and send one of their ranks as an executive! What will be the duty of the minority if the majority is of thieves and elects a thief to rule? The duty clearly will be to remove the representative elected by the majority.

During the Second World War then Hitler attacked France, the French army could not stall the onward march of Nazi troops. The then Prime Minister of France Marshall Petain decided to surrender. The French public supported the decision, but De Gaulle escaped to London where he declared that he did not accept the surrender. France is independent and will remain so. From London, he formed a Government of France in Exile and eventually liberated France. Now if the majority rule is to be considered supreme, then De Gaulle's action will have to be condemned. He had no right to fight in the name of independence. De Gaulle derived his right from the fact that the French nation was above the majority public opinion. The national Dharma is above all. Independence is Dharma of every nation. To preserve independence and to strive for regaining it when lost is the duty of every citizen.

Even in our country a majority had not risen against the Britishers; only a few had. Some revolutionaries arose; some brave people arose and fought. Lokmanya declared, "Freedom is my Birth right." He did not declare this birthright with the support of a majority or by a referendum from the public. Now a day's people advocate that the merger of Goa should be decided by referendum, that there should be plebiscite in Kashmir etc., etc. This is wrong. National unity is our Dharma. Decision concerning this cannot be made by plebiscite. This type of a decision has already been taken by the nature. Elections and majority can decide as to who will form the government. The truth cannot be decided by the majority. What the government will do will be decided by Dharma.

You all know that in the USA where they swear by democracy, at one time Lincoln did not accept wrong public opinion. On the question of the abolition of slavery when the southern states declared their intention to secede Lincoln stood firm and told them, "You have no right to secede even in a democracy." He fought against this and did not allow them to secede. Nor did he tolerate slavery. He did not show readiness for a compromise whereby there may continue partial slavery to accommodate southern states. He did not accept the principle of meeting halfway. He categorically declared that the system of slavery was against tradition, the Dharma, the principle which was at the basis of American nation. Therefore the system of slavery had to be abolished. When the Southerners decided to secede he told them "You cannot secede." On this point there was a civil war and Lincoln did not compromise with Adharma.

Here in our country the situation in this regard is very much like old Hindu marriages where a married couple could not divorce even if both the parties wished. The principle was that their behaviour should be regulated not by their sweet will but by Dharma. The same is case with the nation. If the four million people of Kashmir say that they want to secede, if the people of

Goa say they want to secede, some say they want the Portuguese to return, all this is against Dharma. Of the 45 million people of India, even if 449,999,999 opt for something which is against Dharma, even then this does not become truth. On the other hand, even if a person stands for something which is according to Dharma, that constitutes truth because truth resides with Dharma. It is the duty of this one person that he treads the path of truth and change people. It is from this basis that persons drive the right to proceed according to Dharma.

Let us understand very clearly that Dharma is not necessarily with the majority of with the people. Dharma is eternal. Therefore in the definition of democracy to say that it is a government of the people. It is not enough; it has to be for the good of the people. What constitutes the good of the people? Dharma alone can decide. Therefore, a democratic Government 'Jana Rajya' must also be rooted in Dharma i.e. a 'Dharma Rajya'. In the definition of 'Democracy' viz. "government of the people, by the people and for the people", of stands for independence, 'by' stands for democracy and 'for' Indicates Dharma. Therefore, the true democracy is only where there is freedom as well as Dharma encompasses all these concepts.

Lecture–4 (25th April, 1965)

Yesterday we had discussed the functions of State in a Nation. According to the Bharatiya traditions, a nation is an organic living entity which has come into existence on its own and has not been made up or created by any group of persons. A nation brings forth a variety of institutions to fulfil its needs, as well as to give concrete shape to its inner fundamental nature. The State is one of these institutions which though being an important institution, is not supreme. In our literature where the duties of a king are referred to, his importance is definitely recognized. This is so, perhaps, to make him realize his immense responsibility. He exercised tremendous influence on the lives and character of the people. Hence he had to give due attention to his own behaviour. Bhishma has said the same thing, in Mahabharat when he was asked whether circumstances make a king or a king makes the circumstances. He categorically stated that the king shapes the circumstances. Now some persons interpret this to mean that the considered the king above all. But this is not true. He did not suggest that the king was above Dharma. It is true that the king wielded a great deal of influence. and that he was the protector of Dharma in society, but the king could not decide what constitutes Dharma. He only saw to it that people led their lives according to Dharma. In a way he was equivalent to present day executive.

In the present State, the executive has the responsibility to execute the laws properly, but does not enact laws. When the executive does not function with honesty and efficiency, the laws are entirely disregarded, as we see very well around us. We can well say today "Executive is responsible for the present evils to a great extent." After all why has prohibition failed? Who is responsible for the failure? When those very persons who have been entrusted with the task of implementing prohibition. Start taking monthly allowances from the bootleggers, how is the prohibition policy to succeed? The executive is, therefore, responsible for the proper enforcement of law. This is the meaning of Bhishma's statement. It would be a mistake to interpret it as acceptance of approved supremacy of a monthly allowances from the bootleggers, how is the prohibition policy to succeed? The executive is therefore, responsible for the proper enforcement of law. This is the meaning of Bhisma statement. It would be a mistake to interpret it as acceptance of approved supremacy of a king. If this were so, how was it that the tyrant king Venu was removed by the Rishis and Prithu was enthroned? This action by the Rishis was never condemned by any one in history. On the contrary it was hailed by everyone. When the supremacy of Dharma is accepted as a principle, then, though the authority of Dharma, the Rishis derive a right to remove a king who defaults in his duty. Otherwise, it would have been absolutely illegal to remove a king from his throne. Thus if a King does not act according to Dharma, it becomes the duty of everyone to remove him.

In Western countries, either a King was removed by some other king or people rejected the sovereignty of king altogether. There king was a representative of God and could under no circumstances be removed at least in principle.

In our socio-political set-up, the king and the State were never considered supreme. Not only that, there were other important institutions, (besides the State, which was only one of them) to regulate and to help carry on the social life. Those institutions had been organized both on horizontal and vertical level, i.e. on original and occupation basis. We have evolved Panchayats and Janapada Sabhas. The mightiest of the king did not ever disturb the Panchayats. Similarly there were associations on the basis of trade. These two were never disturbed by the State; on the contrary their autonomy was recognized. They devised their own rules and regulations in their fields. The Panchayats of different communities, shrines, nigams, Village Panchayats, Janapada Sabhas and such other Organization used to set-up regulations. The function of the state was mostly to see that these rules are observed by the persons concerned. The State never interfered with the affairs of these associations. Thus the State was concerned only with some aspects of life of the Society.

Similarly, in the economic field many institutions are created. We have to think what should be the nature of our economic structure. We must have such an economic system which helps in the developments of our human qualities, or civilization and enables us to attain a still higher level of all round perfection. We should have a system which does not overwhelm our humane quality; which does not make us slaves of its own grinding wheels. According to our concept, man attains God like perfection as a result of development. What structure. what regulation should be specified in our economic system if we wish to achieve this goal? Let us, consider this point.

Economic system must achieve the production of all the basic things essential for the maintenance and development of people as well as the protection and development of the Nation. Having satisfied the basic minimum requirements, the question naturally arises, whether there should be more production for greater property and happiness. The Western societies consider it most essential and even desirable to go on continuously and systematically increasing the desires and needs of man. There is no upper limit in the context. Normally desire precedes the efforts at producing the things desired. But now the position is reverse. People are induced to desire and use the things that have been and are being produced. Instead of producing to meet the demand, the search is on the markets for the goods already produced; if the demand does not exist, systematic efforts are made to create demand. This has become the chief characteristic of the western economic movement. Earlier, production followed the demand, now demand allows the production. Consider the use of tea for example. Tea was produced because people desired and wanted it. But Tea was produced and we were induced to develop taste for tea. Now tea is a common man's drink. It has become a part of our life. Similar is the case of vegetable ghee. Did anyone ever want to use it? It was first produced and then we were taught to use it. If whatever is manufactured is not consumed, there will be depression. Some of us many remember the great depression of 1930-32. There was abundance of goods at that time but there was no demand. Therefore factories had to be closed down. Bankruptcy and unemployment were widespread. Thus now-a-days it is most important that what is being produced must be consumed.

The Editor of 'Organiser', an English Weekly, had gone to USA for a visit sometime ago. Upon his return, he related an interested instance. There is a factory producing 'Potato-peelers', a device for peeling potatoes. The production of this factory outstripped the demand for the device. The management of the firm faced the problem of finding some way by which people may be induced to buy more potato peelers. They called a meeting of all the salesmen of the firm. Among the suggestions put forward, one was to make the color of the handle similar to that of potato peel. So that along with the peel. the peeler may also be dumped in the garbage, often by mistake. Thus there may be greater demand. Also, the product was offered in a more attractive packing. Now this economic structure is not merely consumption oriented but is clearly leading to destruction. Throw away the old one and buy a new one! Rather than satisfying the need and demand from people to create fresh demand has become the aim of modern economics. Supposing that we need not worry about the limited supply of natural resources, there is yet the question of balance in Nature. There is a relationship in different parts of Nature. If from the three sticks standing with mutual support, one is removed, the other two will automatically fall. The present economic system and system of production are fast disturbing this equilibrium of nature. As a result on the one hand new products are manufactured for satisfying ever increasing desires, on the other hand new problem arise every day, threatening the very existence of the entire humanity and civilization.

It is essential, therefore, to use up that portion of the available natural resources which the nature will be able to recoup easily. When the fruits are taken, the fruit tree is not injured: it may even be helpful to the tree. However, in the effort to take a greater harvest from the land chemical fertilizers are used which in a few years time render the land altogether infertile. Lakhs of acres of land lie barren in America due to this factor. How long this dance of destruction can go on?

The destruction provides for depreciation fund to replace the machines when worn out. Then how can we neglect the depreciation fund for nature. From this point of view, it must be realized that the object of our economic system should be, not extravagant use of available resources, but a well regulated use. The physical objects necessary for a purposeful, happy and progressive life must be obtained. The Almighty has provided as much. It will not be wise, however, to engage into a blind rat-race of consumption and production as if man is created for the sole purpose of consumption. Engine needs coal for its proper working, but it has not been produced merely to consume coal. On the contrary it is only proper always to see that with the minimum coal-consumption, maximum energy is produced. This is the economic view point. Keeping in view the aim of human life, we must endeavour to see how with the minimum of fuel, man proceeds to his goal with the maximum speed. Such a system alone can be called civilization. This system will not think of merely a single aspect of human life but of all its aspects including the ultimate aim. This system will not thrive on the exploitation of nature but will sustain nature and will in turn itself be nourished. Milking rather than exploitation should be our aim. The system should be such that overflow from nature is used to sustain our lives.

If such human angle inspires the economic system than our thinking on the economic question will undergo through transformation. In the Western economics, whether it is capitalist or socialist, value has the most important and central position. All economic theories centre on value. It may be that the analysis of value is very important from the point of view of the economist but, those social philosophers which are based entirely on value are for incomplete, inhuman and to some extent unethical take. For example, the slogan commonly heard now-a-days "one must earn his bread". Normally communists use this slogan but even the capitalists are not fundamentally in disagreement with it. If there is any difference between them, it is only as regards who earns and how much. The capitalists consider capital and enterprise as important components of production and hence if they take a major share of profits. They think it is their due. On the other hand, communists believe only labour to be the main factor in production. Therefore they concede major share of production to the labourers. Neither of these ideas is correct. Really speaking, our slogan should be that the one who earns will feed and every person will have enough to eat. The right to food is a birthright. The ability to earn is a result of education and training. In a society even those who do not earn must have food. The children and the old, the diseased and the invalids, all must be eared for by the society. Even society generally fulfils this responsibility. The social and cultural progress of mankind ties in the readiness to fulfil this responsibility. The economic system must provide for this task. Economics as a science does not account for this responsibility. A man works not merely for bread alone, but also to shoulder this responsibility. Otherwise those who have had their meals would no longer work.

Any economic system must provide for the minimum basic necessities of human life to everyone. Food, clothing and shelter constitute, broadly speaking these basic necessities. Similarly, the society must enable the individual to carry out his obligations to the society by properly educating him. Lastly, in the event of an individual falling a prey to any disease. Society must arrange for his treatment and maintenance. If a government provides these minimum requirements, then only it is a rule of Dharma. Otherwise, it is a rule of Adharma.

Describing the King Dilip, Kalidas has said in Raghuvansha "Being responsible for the maintenance. Protection and education of his subjects, he was their true farther. Others were merely instrumental in giving them their birth". The description of king Bharat after whom our country has been named Bharat, also runs similarly, i.e. "by maintaining and protecting his subjects he was called Bharat." This is his country, Bharat, if in this country maintenance and protection are not guaranteed, and then the name Bharat is meaningless.

Education–A Social Responsibility: To educate a child is in the interest of the Society itself. By birth a child is an animal. He becomes a responsible member of the society only by education and culture. To charge fees for something which is in the interest of the society itself a rather odd. If due to the inability to pay the fees, children are left without education, will the society endure the situation for long? We do not charge fee from trees for sowing the seed and caring for the supplying. On the contrary we invest our money and efforts. We know that when the tree grows, we shall reap fruits.

Education is a similar investment. An educated individual will indeed serve the society. On the other hand it will not be surprising if people grow indifferent to the society which leaves them to fend for themselves. Before 1947, in all the princely states in India, no fees were charged for education. The highest education was free. In the Gurukulas, even food and lodging were arranged without any charge. The student used to go to the society for 'Bhiksha'. No householder would refuse the Bhiksha to the student. In other words, society used to bear the burden of education.

Similarly, it is rather surprising that medical treatment must be paid for. In fact, medical treatment also should be free as it was in this country in the past. Now-a-days one has to pay even to gain entrance to a temple. In Tirupathi, to enter the Balaji temple, there is a charge of 0.25 paise. However, at noon for one hour, there is Dharma Darshan, which means, during that time, no ticket is needed, as if at other times there is Adharma Darshan. The society should guarantee to all members minimum requirements for maintenance and progress of every individual. Now the question arises that if everyone is to be guaranteed the minimum necessities, where will the resources for all this come from?

Guarantee of Work: It is clear that the resources must be produced by our own efforts. Therefore, where a right to a guaranteed minimum is recognized, any individual who does not share in the efforts to produce is a burden to the society. Similarly any system which obstructs the production activity of the people is self destructive. Such a system will not enable the individuals to fulfil their responsibility. Not only that, but even if the requirements of an individual are met, while he does not share in the efforts, his personality will not develop fully, his progress as a human being will be distorted and lop-sided. Man has stomach as well is hands. If he has no work for his hands, he will not get happiness even if he gets food to satisfy his hunger. His progress will be obstructed. Just as a barren woman experiences emptiness in life and consequent dissatisfaction, so does a man without work.

The guarantee of work to every able bodied member of the society, should be the aim of our economic system. Today we witness a very strange situation. On the one hand, a ten-year-old child and seventy-year-old man are toiling and on the other hand youth of twenty five is driven to suicide for want of work. We shall have to remove this mismanagement. God has given hands to every man but by themselves hands have a limited capacity to produce. They need assistance of capital in the form of machines. Labour and capital bear the same relation to each other as that between man and nature. The world is a creation of these two. Neither of them can be neglected.

Capital Formation: For capital formation it is essential that a part of production be saved from immediate consumption and be used for further production, in future. Thus capital can be formed only by restraint on consumption. This is the basis of capital formation to which Karl Marx refers to as "surplus value" in his treatise. In the capitalist system the industrialist creates capital with the help of this surplus value. In a socialist system, the state undertakes this task. In both the systems, the entire production is not distributed among the workers. If production is carried on through centralized large-scale industries, the sacrifice on the part of the worker in creating the capital is not given due recognition. The advantage in decentralization is in the fact that the workers have a sense of direct participation in the management of this surplus value or capital. Machine is the most common form of capital. Machine was created in order to reduce the content of physical labour in production and to increase the productivity of the worker. Machine, therefore, is an assistant of the worker and not his competitor. However, where the human labour came to be considered as a commodity to be purchased with money, the machine became the competitor of the human being. The principal drawback of the capitalist view point in the fact that by making the machine a competitor of human labour and thereby displacing and competitor of human labour and thereby displacing and subjecting human being to privations the very purpose of creating machine has been defied. Machine cannot be blamed for this. It is the fault of the economic and social system which cannot distinguish between the object and the instrument. We shall have to take into account the limitations on usefulness of machines and decide on its field of application. From this point of view to import the machinery from Western countries, where shortage of manpower was the guiding factor in the design of machines would be a serious mistake. The merits of machine are, not independent of time and place. Machines are a product of the modern science but not its representatives. Scientific knowledge is not a monopoly of any particular country. But its application has to take into account the particular condition of each country and its requirements. Our machines must not only, by tailored for our specific economic means, but also must, at least, avoid conflict with our socio-political and cultural objectives, if not support them.

Professor Vishvesaraya has said in one of his books, that while considering the system of production one must take into account the seven 'M's. These are man, material, money, management, motive power, market and machine. The skill and ability of the workers or those who should be provided with work must be considered. Easy availability of the required raw material and the quality and properties of the raw materials available cannot be ignored. We must also think of how much money is available as capital. How this capital can be increased and at what rate? How best it can be utilized for maximum production? How much of it should be put in the fixed assets and how much should be kept in the liquid form? We must also pay attention to the form of power available in the country in addition to the human and animal labour. Wind, water, steam oil, gas, electricity and atomic power can supply the motive power. Of these, which form of power can be obtained in what quantity and without being uneconomic must be thought of while deciding upon our methods of production. In the same way managerial skills are also important and deserve the attention. If the ability to co-ordinate the efforts of a dozen workers are wanting, all of them will remain unemployed. It is also necessary to think of the usefulness of the goods produced to the society. This means that production of any particular commodity cannot be justified economically without the consideration of the market it commands. Taking into consideration all these factors we should design suitable machines. Instead, we find now-a-days that we install the machines first and try to coordinate all other factors afterwards. Other countries of the world did not progress in this fashion. Otherwise new machines would not have been invested. We are importing the machines and hence, we have little knowledge. We shall have to develop a Bharatiya technology.

None of the seven factors is unchangeable. In fact each one keeps constantly changing. Those who are entrusted with the task of planning must think of how the change is directed towards progress, how physical hardship is reduced, and waste of energy is minimized. As an illustration let us take the low productivity of our worker. It can be increased by using machines, and it is necessary to do so. But if the machine is such that requires only a few men to run it, then the rest of the people will be thrown out of employment. If the machine has to be imported from other countries at such a heavy cost that the additional production it causes will be insufficient to make it economic, then such a machine is not suitable to our requirements. Just as to let a part of the installed capacity of a factory remain unutilised is a losing proposition, so also to let the people of this country remain unemployed is a losing proposition. May, this is even worse. Whereas a machine ties up only the capital invested in it in past, the unemployed people have to be fed, which is continuous and unending drain on resources, consumed at double the speed. Therefore instead of the usual exhortation "Every worker must get food", we must think of "Everyone who eats must get work", as the basis of our economy. No doubt charakha has to be replaced by machines but not necessarily automatic machines everywhere. Full employment must be a primary consideration and then the rest of the six factors suit this.

Man's place in the economy: The use of manpower and the employment question will have to be thought of in the context of the human being as a whole, as an integral being. The economic theories of the past few centuries and the structure of society based on these theories, have resulted in a thorough devaluation of the human being. His personality is altogether irrelevant to the economic set up. Capitalist economy recognizes only an 'economic man', whose all decisions are based entirely on calculations of gain and loss, in terms of material wealth. For this economic man, five rupees are always more than four rupees. He works solely to gain more wealth, and execs to get the maximum gain. For him, just like other commodities, human labour is a commodity to be bought and sold In the market. This is free enterprise. It holds all other restriction and regulations unjust, save the brake of competition. In the race no one is prepared to stop and give a helping land to the weak, which is left behind; elimination of the weak is considered just and natural. He is uneconomic, marginal unit, not fit to exist. This is what it advocates. By the elimination of such marginal units, the economic power accumulates in the hands of a few. This is considered normal and natural is capitalist system. But when monopoly is a established, even the check of competition ceases to operates. In such a. situation the incentive resulting from competition is no longer available. Prices are arbitrarily fixed and quality of products deteriorates.

Even as regards the consumer's needs, the capitalist is guided not by the necessities and desires of the consumer, but by his purchasing power. The needs of the wealthy and the well fed are attended to rather than those of the poor and the hungry. As a result where countless varieties of goods are produced for he needs of the wealthy, even the basic necessities of life for the poor become scarce. The centralization and monopolization of reduction totally undermine the influence of the consumer. The markets are so organized that the consumer has to go by standard products. This standardization is on the increase at such a pace that individual preference of the consumer is ignored. Like the books in the library, even human beings are allotted numbers as consumers. The system which boasts of giving highest importance to the individual has ironically destroyed all individuality. Clearly, the capitalist system is incapable of helping the development of an integral human being.

Socialist system is a reaction: Socialism arose as a reason to capitalism. But even socialism failed to establish the importance of the human being. Socialists contented themselves by merely transferring the ownership of capital in the hands of the State. But the State is even more of an impersonal institution. All the business of the State is conducted by rigid rules and regulations. Generally, there is no place for individual discretion and even where such discretion is allowed, the slightest laxity in the sense of duty and social responsibility on the part of the administrator's results in corruption and favouritism. The capitalistic system thought merely of the economic man, but left him free in other fields where they could exercise his individuality. The socialist system went much further thinking only of the abstract man. After that, there was no scope for the development of the individual personality based on diverse tastes and abilities. The needs and preferences of individuals have as much importance in the socialist system as in a prison manual. There is no such thing as individual freedom in the socialist system.

State's claims on individual: There is no private property in a socialist society. This removes the problems attendants to the institution of private property. However the incentive for production and conservation of resources and economy in utilization accompany the institution of private property. There has been no alternative arrangement to preserve these. The State is made supreme and sole authority in all matters. Individual citizen is reduced to mere cog in this giant wheel. There is no provision to inspire the individual to fulfil his role. As Djilas states, the class of old fashioned exploiters has been eliminated, but a new class of bureaucratic exploiter has come into existence. Karl Marx put forward, in his analysis of history, that capitalism contains the seeds of its own destruction and that communism is a natural and inevitable successor to capitalism.

This concept may be helpful in fostering faith in the communist about their ultimate victory but certainly such a determinist view destroys the urge for reforms and dynamism in man. He is no longer the creator of a new order; he is merely incidental to a predetermined historic process. His task is only to accelerate the process. Therefore, even as he tries to organize workers, he cares little for their welfare, but uses them as mere tools for the revolution. The dialectic materialism of Marx, too, operates only so long as state is note established as supreme after destroying the capitalists. Thereafter, the state puts a stop to the operation of the principle of dialectic materialism. In the name of crushing and counter revolutionaries, the state becomes more and more totalitarian. The day when the state is to wither away yielding place to a stateless society remains a mere dream. In fact according to the Marxist view, to obstruct the process of this antithesis, is itself reactionary. Marx is thus falsified by his own standards.

These systems, capitalist as well as communist, have failed to take account of the Integral Man, his true and complete personality and his aspirations. One considers him a mere selfish being lingering after money, having only one law, the law of fierce competition, in essence the law of the jungle; whereas the other has viewed him as a feeble lifeless cog in the whole scheme of things, regulated by rigid rules, and incapable of any good unless directed. The centralization of power, economic and political, is implied in both. Both, therefore, result in dehumanization of man.

Man, the highest creation of God is losing his own identity. We must re-establish him in his rightful position, being him the realization of his greatness, reawaken his abilities and encourage him to exert for attaining divine heights of his latest personality. This is possible only through a decentralized economy.

We want neither capitalism nor socialism. We aim at the progress and happiness of 'Man', the Integral Man.

The protagonists of the two systems fight with 'Man' on the state. Both of them do not understand man, nor do they care for his interests.

Our economic system: The Objectives of our Economy should be

1. An assurance of minimum standard of living to every individual and preparedness for the defense of the nation.
2. Further increase above this minimum standard of living whereby the individual and the nation acquires the means to contribute to the world progress on the basis of its own 'Chiti'.
3. To provide meanings employment to every able bodies citizens by which the above two objectives can be realized and to avoid waste and extravagance in utilizing natural resources.
4. To develop suitable machines for Bharatiya conditions (Bharatiya Technology) taking note of the availability and nature of the various factors of production (Seven 'M's).
5. This system must help and not disregard the human being, the individual. It must protect the cultural and other values of life. This is requirement which cannot be violated except at a risk of great peril.
6. The ownership, state, private or any other form of various industries must be decided on a pragmatic and practical basis.

These are a few general directions which we must bear in mind while developing our economy. 'Swadeshi' and 'Decentralization' are the two words which can briefly summarize the economic policy suitable for the present circumstances. Centralization and monopolization have been the order of the day for all these years, knowingly or unknowingly. The planners have become prisoners of a belief that only large-scale centralized industry is economic and hence without worrying about its ill-effects, or knowingly but helplessly, they have continued in that direction. The same has been the fate of 'Swadeshi'.

The concept of 'Swadeshi' is ridiculed as old fashioned and reactionary. We proudly use foreign articles. We have grown over independent upon foreign aid in everything from thinking, management, capital, methods of production, technology, etc. to even the standards and forms of consumption. This is not the road to progress and development. We shall forget our individuality and become virtual slaves once again. The positive content of 'Swadeshi' should be used as the cornerstone of reconstruction of our economy.

For want of time, I have not touched the natural aspects of economic structure. But one thing is clear that many old institutions will yield place to new ones. This will adversely affect those who have vested interests in the old institutions. Some others who are by nature averse to change will also suffer by efforts of reconstruction. But disease must be treated with medicine. Strength can be gained only from exercise and hard work. Therefore, we still have to discard the status-quo mentality and usher in a new era. Indeed our efforts at reconstruction need not be clouded by prejudice or disregard for all that is inherited from our past. On the other hand, there is no need to cling to past institutions and traditions which have outlived their utility. We have considered what the direction of change should be.

We have in the last four days thought over the integrated from of Humanism. On the basis we shall be able to reconcile nationalism, democracy, socialism and world peace with the traditional values of Bharatiya Culture and think of all these ideals in an integrated form. The mutual conflict among these ideals can be removed and they can supplement mutually. Thereby the "Man can gain his lost status and attain the aims of his life".

We have here discussed the philosophy. But the members of the Bharatiya Jana Sangh are not mere philosophers or academicians. We have set out with the determination to make this nation strong, happy and prosperous through the medium of the Bharatiya Jana Sangh. Therefore, we must carry on practical programs for the nationalist reconstruction on this foundation. We have taken due note of our ancient culture. But we are no archaeologists. We have to intention of becoming the custodians of a vast archaeological museum. Our goal is not merely to protect the culture but to revitalize it so as to make it dynamic and in tune with the times. We must ensure that our nation stands firm on this foundation and our society is enabled to live a healthy, progressive and purposeful life. We shall have to end a number of traditions and set in reforms which are helpful in the development of values and of national unity in our society. We shall remove those traditions which obstruct this process. Whereas one need not mourn the limitations of the human body, one must undergo the required social operation if any part of the body has cancerous growth. There is no need to amputee healthy limbs. If today, the society is gripped with evils like untouchability which lead men to treat other human beings as lower than themselves and thereby threaten the national unity, we shall have to end such evils.

We shall be required to produce such institutions as will kindle the spirit of action in us, which will replace the self-centeredness and selfishness by a desire to serve the nation, which will produce not only sympathy towards our brethren, but a sense of affection and oneness with them. Such institutions can truly reflect our 'Chiti'.

'Chiti' is a nation's soul. The strength and energy activating the nation is called 'Virat' and channelled by 'Chiti'. The place of 'Virat' in the life of nation is similar to that of Prana in the body. Just as 'Prana' infuses strength in various organs of the body, refreshed the intellect and keeps body and soul together; so also in a nation, with a strong 'Virat' alone can democracy succeed and the government be effective. Then the diversity of our nation does not prove an obstacle to our national unity. The difference of languages, occupations, etc. are present everywhere. However, when the 'Virat' is awake, diversity does not lead to conflicts and people co-operates with each other like the various limbs of the human body or like the members of a family.

We have to undertake the task of awakening our nation's 'Virat'. Let us go forward in this task with a sense of pride for our heritage, with a realistic assessment of the present and a great ambition for the future. We wish neither to make this country a shadow of some distant past nor an imitation of Russia or America.

With the support of Universal knowledge and our heritage, we shall create a Bharat which will excel all its past glories, and will enable every citizen in its fold to steadily progress in the development of his manifold latent possibilities and to achieve through a sense of unity with the entire creation, a state even higher than that of a complete human being; to become Narayan from 'Nar'. This is the external divine from of our culture. This is our message to humanity to cross roads. May God give us strength to succeed in this task!

BHARAT MATA KI JAI!

□

The Last Speech*

—Indira Gandhi

[Her speech had its meaning. What a philosophical speech delivered by the great lady. She had predicted her death and delivered the speech knowingly or unknowingly. Mrs. Indira Gandhi delivered her speech at Parade Ground in Bhubaneswar on 30th October, 1984 and she was gunned down by her own security guards at her home lawn in New Delhi on 31st October, 1984]

India, in our long history, has never attacked by country. There have been many invasions against us. People from outside came here and many of them settled here. They proved to be good Indians. Later, they participated with us in the fight for freedom; all of them expressed their solidarity with the people of India. They stood like a solid wall and faced the challenges. The prime need of the hour is to revive once again the same spirit of solidarity in the hearts and minds of the people. It is not a case of strengthening the hands of Indira Gandhi alone. It means that the hands of millions of people, who live in India, should be strengthened.

The hands of men and women, old and young, scheduled castes and scheduled tribes, people belonging to backward classes indeed, of everybody who is living in India, should be

* *Parade Ground, Bhubneshwar (Orissa), 30th October, 1984*

strengthened. They should have the courage and they should have the strength which will take this country along the road of development. All of us should work hard. It is not only a question of manual labour, it also concerns the mind. Let new ideas be brought in from different sources, so that in this scientific age India could progress.

Whenever I happen to meet scientists I have only one massage for them, "Do something which of use to the whole country." But if along with this a scientific temper is not cultivated, if we remain prisoners of superstitions, if we continue to quarrel among ourselves, if we tolerate communalism and do not fight against it, if we let casteism or regionalism develop or grow or if we start quarrelling in the name of language, how will we be able to preserve the unity of India? If unity is not preserved, how will we protect our independence? Do not think that if we have won freedom once, we will be able to preserve it for all time to come. Eternal vigilance is the price of freedom. We have to think about it and do something about it every day. We have to preserve that freedom for our poorer masses, particularly for the people who are backward and living in backward areas. We should make freedom a reality for them.

Actually, the real work started from that point and the Congress took upon itself two things. First, democracy should be nurtured because until each and everybody's voice is not heard, freedom would not be complete. Secondly, the Congress adopted the path of socialism. Without economic equality, and without equal opportunities for all, freedom could not be considered complete. If there are acute inequalities in the society, the gap between the rich and the poor will widen, resulting in increased tension and class struggle.

If there is no peace in the society, freedom cannot be secure and development projects cannot be executed, progress cannot be made. Therefore, from the very beginning we made strides towards self-reliance. If you travel, you will see how the picture of our country is changing in the post-independence India. As we go forward, we face new problems. There are chronic problems, like poverty and economic backwardness. But there are also problems which are the result of progress and development.

Several countries are rich. Even then, they have failed to root out unemployment, or control rising prices. As a matter of fact, both the problems have aggravated there in the recent years. Even then, we have to find out a way, so that we are able to avoid these problems. These are not new challenges. These are old problems and we are making efforts to solve them. How will unemployment be removed, and how do we get over price rise? When we increase our production, people will get employment opportunities. We have to see that when production is increased and we achieve success, the fruits of these reach all the people.

We have to take to the masses our programs regarding education and healthcare, particularly to those areas where people have been victims of social and economic injustice for centuries. This must be remedied. This is our object and we are moving towards the direction. We were doing it before, we are doing it now and we will continue to pursue out path as before whether we are in the office or out of office.

So, everything is interrelated. We have to co-ordinate everything and move forward. We have to strike a balance in our social structure. We can do this only when there is peace in the society. If agitation coupled with violence are launched and people hate each other and the opposition parties encourage such agitations without considering the long-term effects on the social fabric of our country, then we will not be successful. All of us must think how much pain, agony and hardship it will cause to our countrymen.

Some agitations have been launched which have harmed the country's unity. The slogans which are raised by these agitators were not originated in the country. These have been coined in foreign countries by those who live outside India. Many anti-social and treacherous elements found their way into these agitations. In the shadow of these agitations, they indulge in evil work. What happened in Punjab is known all of you.

What happening in Jammu and Kashmir is also known to you. It was not a question of an individual at any place. Neither was it a question of a particular caste or creed or religion or party. The real question was that the things which were happening were not beneficial to the country and were creating difficulties for India. They were likely to create hazards and crises in the country in future. But no government can support any deed or any action which would weaken the country, whatever the price.

The citizens of India must think of India first. We may belong to any religion or caste or creed, but nationalism is supreme, the love for our country must get priority over everything. But today some people think that they should support or back any agitation which may help in getting votes to them during the elections. But people in Orissa and the people living in different states and indeed the people of the whole country, must realize that such agitations will pose a greater danger to our country.

Our policy is to have friendly relations with all countries. But we shall not give up our self-respect or overlook the interest of India. Many times India has faced invasions and there were five attacks in recent years. We should always be prepared to face such a contingency. We have already assured our people and people of the world that we will never attack anybody. We shall continue to pursue our policy of friendship with all people. The same is our policy at home.

Our progress has been acknowledged by other nations. Be it big universities or big international economic organizations, everybody acknowledges that India has pursued the path of progress, despite difficulties, without incurring big debts or without being trapped into any crisis. Since, 1980, every year, we have done something or the other which is remarkable and every time it has helped to enhance the reputation of the country in the comity of nations. The young generation of India and the intellectuals of this country have new opportunities to achieve name and fame and expand their scope of knowledge. That is why we have to see that Indian continues to move forward on this path.

India does not raise her voice only for her own sake. If we raise our voice it is not on behalf of the Congress. We are speaking here on behalf of the people of India, on behalf of the weaker sections of India, on behalf of women of India, on behalf of the younger generation of India, for the future belongs to them. If they move forward on the right path and if they engage themselves in constructive activities and do not indulge in sabotage then a bright future awaits them.

They can also build their states and the country. So this is our view of India. This applies to all the under-developed nation of the world. What we say here is also criticized. Our aid is discontinued. But whatever injustice is perpetrated, India always is the first to raise its voice against it because we know if there is injustice at one place and the people are suppressed, then it will affect the whole world.

My father used to say that freedom cannot be divided. In the same manner, progress is also indivisible, development is also indivisible. Many countries of the world have become prosperous through scientific development and they are also collecting wealth very rapidly and using it for raising their standard. They are very powerful and even then, they want to influence other nations.

It is not like the older type of slavery. In that system, imperialist powers used to dispatch their forces and occupy territories. But in the new system, they try to influence people by their ideology. They try to break the morale of the people. Even if the weaker nations do some good works, the powers try to show that the under-developed countries have done nothing.

I had to resort to emergency for a very brief period. But even today I am being criticized. I am being described as authoritarian and dictatorial. But the same people are fully helping the other authoritarian regimes with money, resources and arms. For them, that dictatorship is not dictatorship. Therefore we have to learn from all this and know after all what they want, why they want India should not go forward. No outsider will take care of our interest or think about us. We have to look after ourselves. This is not exclusively my responsibility.

I am here today; I may not be here tomorrow, but the responsibility to look after national interest in on the shoulder of every citizen of India. I have often mentioned this earlier. Nobody knows how many attempts have been made to shoot me; lathies have been used to beat me. In Bhubaneswar itself, a brickbat hit me. They have attacked me in every possible manner. I do not care whether I live or die. I had lived a long life and I am proud that I spend the whole of my life in the service of my people. I am only proud of this and nothing else. I shall continue to serve until my last breath and when I die, I can say that every drop of my blood will invigorate India and strengthen it.

I hope that youth, women and others, all will think together. They should shoulder the responsibilities and it cannot be done by accepting others as leaders. Leaders come and go.

When the struggle for the freedom was on, many time we were in jail. But because of our absence, the struggle never ceased. In every state, province and district, new leaders came up. It is our wish that every section of the people living in Orissa, whether they are from scheduled tribes or happen to belong to other caste, will think, "This is my country. This is our country." We must make our nation strong. We must reinforce its integration and it our responsibility, it is every citizen's responsibility. We cannot make Indira Gandhi or the Congress or any other leader responsible for this work. We want that spirit should develop and envelop the country.

When we talk about self-reliance, it means we want self-reliance in the material sense. But we also want psychological self-reliance. The people must feel confident that they have the strength to do the job and I know that this strength is in the masses. I fully believe that the masses of India will never take a wrong path. The people of world know about it. Many cultures and civilizations have disappeared into oblivion. But as the poet Iqbal once said, "We have survived, whereas all those ancient civilizations have perished. Our civilization is still there."

It means that there is some inherent strength in us; that is why we are surviving. That strength is there inside everybody. But you have to let it develop. If you do not allow it to develop, if you are frustrated, then inner strength will not take its shape and it will negatively. There are weakness and courage, if we do not have the necessary morale, then we shall not be able to get over those shortcomings and weaknesses. Without doing this, good work cannot be done. So, it is in your hands, in the hands of the people of Orissa and in the hands of the people of this country what they want to do.

We can only formulate policies and programs. We are there to help. But development work must go on. You must see that Orissa progress. It is your responsibility. Everybody should search his heart and ask himself why he would do this job. I fully believe that this beautiful state, where art and other things have developed so much, will also develop economically. You should not do anything to strike at the roots of your art or traditions. These should also develop along with economic progress.

You have heard me very patiently. I shall repeat that you must give top priority to the unity and integrity of the country. Everything else is secondary. We have to face today's challenges in such a manner that we emerge stronger and our strength continues to grow. If we gain something for the short term and it weakens us tomorrow or day after, then it is not a thing worth pursuing.

Jai Hind

□

The Presidential System*

—J.R.D. Tata

Jamsetji Ratanji Dadabhoy (JRD) Tata entered the his family business as an unpaid apprentice in December 1925. His mentor in business was John Peterson, a Scotsman who had joined the group after serving in the Indian Civil Service. At 22, soon after his father passed away, JRD was on the board of Tata Sons, the group's flagship company. In 1929, aged 25, he surrendered his French citizenship to embrace the country that would become the central motif of his life.

The first of JRD's big adventures in business was born of his childhood fascination for flying. He had grown up in France watching the famous aviator Louis Bleriot's early flights, and had taken a joyride in an airplane as a 15-year-old. In 1929, JRD became one of the first Indians to be granted a commercial pilot's licence. A year later, a proposal landed at the Tata headquarters to start an airmail service that would connect Bombay, Ahmedabad and Karachi. JRD needed no prompting, but it would take Peterson to convince Dorabji Tata, then Chairman of the Tatas, to let the young ace have his way.

After three years of negotiations Tata Aviation Service won a contract to carry the mail in April 1932 and in July 1932

---

* *Indian Merchant's Chamber's Annual General Meeting, Bombay, 20th February, 1968*

the Aviation Department of Tata Sons was formed. On 15th October, 1932, J.R.D. Tata flew a single-engined De Havilland Puss Moth carrying air mail (postal mail of Imperial Airways) from Karachi's Drigh Road Aerodrome to Bombay's Juhu Airstrip via Ahmedabad.

That pre-1940 period had four main Indian airlines: apart from Tata there was Indian Trans-Continental Airways, Indian National Airways (both linked to Imperial Airways) and Air Services of India. After 1940 several shortlived services came up –Deccan, Himalaya, Ambica, Mistri. As these flew into problems, the government got involved in trying to keep them going, and slowly got closer into the aviation business. JRD watched this with foreboding, regularly pointing out the folly of its involvement in a business that required both quick decisions and a service focus. "On both these counts, State enterprise, with its rigid and slow moving administration and its inevitable red tape and conservatism, cannot possibly compare with private enterprise," he said to the Times in 1946.

Yet JRD knew it was best not to resist the trend too much. His personal closeness to Jawaharlal Nehru, despite differences over economic policy, made him realise the need to work with the government, and his plans to take Tata Airlines international seemed the ideal meeting point. First he took it public in 1946, renaming it Air India. Then the next year he submitted a plan to the government to set up an international airline for India, with the government holding 49%, Tatas holding 25% and the balance 26% with the public. And acknowledging that the government would probably want majority control soon, it was given the option of taking over 2% from the Tatas. The government agreed and Air India was incorporated in 1948 and launched its Bombay-London service three months later. This seemed an ideal balance. The government was involved, but the service was run by Tata, and JRD threw himself into making it one of the best in the world.

Foreign experts were flown in to train the new staff,

with special emphasis on the air-hostesses providing the best service. Bobby Kooka, the legendary marketing head of Air India was brought on board and given absolute freedom to develop strategy for the airline, which resulted in the maharaja mascot. India was a fresh, exotic and glamorous new country at that time, and Air India based its strategy around this image. Yet, if one was superstitious, there was a bad portent early on. The plane that launched Air India's international operations was a Lockheed Constellation named Malabar Princess which left Bombay for London on 8th June, 1948. Barely two years later, on 3rd November, 1950 had this same plane crashed into Mount Blanc with the loss of 48 lives (16 years later, the Air India plane Kanchenjunga would crash in almost the same place).

JRD's hopes for a proper public-private partnership with Air India would crash three years later when on 25th August 1953 the Government of India exercised its option to purchase a majority stake in the carrier and Air India International Limited was born as one of the fruits of the Air Corporations Act that nationalised the air transportation industry. At the same time all domestic services were transferred to Indian Airlines (now a part of Air India). As a grace note, Nehru asked JRD to stay on as chairman.The Air India saga certainly hurt JRD, but he wasn't the kind to bear a grudge. Nehru insisted that he continue to head the national carrier and that's what JRD did, right up to 1977, when another act of government forced him out. Indira Gandhi, when she came back to power, reinstated JRD to the chairmanship, but by then he no longer had the appetite for the responsibility.

Actually, Jawaharlal Nehru didn't have a very high opinion of businessmen. He disliked wealthy men in general and intrusive businessmen in particular. Nehru had first met Birla in 1924. Mahatma Gandhi, just out of jail, was recuperating in the industrialist's beach-facing house in Mumbai. That's when the two met. A year later, Nehru told Mahatma Gandhi that he was a little tight for money. Gandhi said that he could find him work somewhere. Gandhi mentioned Nehru's plight to Birla. Almost overnight, Birla turned up at Nehru's home at Allahabad and offered to help him out of the situation. Nehru was incensed but managed to conceal his anger from his visitor. Their differences became serious in the days to come. Nehru thought Birla supported the Hindu lobby within the Congress. Agnostic to the core, Nehru found no place for religion in public life. Birla, on the other hand, found Nehru's sympathies for the Soviet Union and his socialist bent of mind a bit too much to handle. Independence didn't help matters. Birla had to junk his plans to set up a steel plant at Durgapur in West Bengal because Nehru had decided that it was the job of the public sector to make steel.

When he was short of money, Nehru had toyed with the idea of working with the House of Tata. He had even used a Tata aircraft during his campaign in 1937. The Tatas were Parsis and did not wear their religion on their sleeves. They had built assets like the steel mill in Jamshedpur and the Taj Mahal hotel in Mumbai, which had done all Indians proud. Under J.R.D. Tata, they had earned a name as an ethical business house which did things the right way. In fact, the Tatas were one of the few groups that came out unscathed from the probe into super-normal profits during the Second World War.

But fractures in the relationship began to emerge soon after Independence. Tata did not approve of Nehru's economic policies. Nehru once told Tata that he hated the word profit. "Jawaharlal, I am talking about the need of the public sector making a profit," Tata shot back. "Never talk to me about the word profit; it is a dirty word," Nehru retorted. Tata, unsure of the prime minister's socialist bent of mind, turned down his invitation to join a delegation to the United Nations on the ground that there was so much to do inside the country. Giving the same argument, he declined Nehru's invitation to head Indian Rare Earths, one of the first public sector units floated after Independence. In turn, Tata's Air India, Air India International and insurance outfit were nationalised by the government.

Indira Gandhi, being the only child of Jawaharlal Nehru, served as the Chief of Staff of her father's highly centralised administration between 1947 and 1964 and came to wield considerable unofficial influence in government. She was elected Congress President in 1959. Upon her father's death in 1964, Gandhi refused to enter Congress party leadership contest and instead chose to become a cabinet minister in the government led by Lal Bahadur Shastri. In Congress' party parliamentary leadership election held in early 1966 upon the death of Shastri, she defeated her rival, Morarji Desai, to become leader and thus succeed Shastri as the prime minister of India.

Indira was more prejudiced against big-business than her father. So, particularly be between 1964 and 1969 Congress Government appointed four powerful panels to curb big businesses: the Mahalanobish Committee (1964), the Monopolies Inquiry commission (1965); the R.K. Hazari Committee (1966) and the Industrial Licensing Policy Committee (1969). The Monopolistic and Restrictive Trade Practice (MRTP) Act promulgated. JRD Tata decried the mud-slinging against big-businesses and demanded better deal for private sector at every Tata annual general meeting. He begged politicians and bureaucrats to work with and not against business; and to shed their preconceptions that 'the profit motive is dishonourable, that profit is synonymous with profiteering, that about 3 percent net is a fair return of risk capital, that the population solved itself, that mechanization means unemployment, that it is more important to impoverish to rich than to enrich the poor, that a welfare state can be built without first creating the means to pay for it, that nationalization creates additional wealth.'

JRD's frustration with anti-capitalist propaganda often spilled over. One occasion was the annual general meeting of the Indian Merchant' Chamber on 20th February, 1968 in Bombay. In his keynote speech to fellow business elite of Bombay, J.R.D. could not be able to contain his personal and in general his fellow business brethren's frustration against

Indira led India Government. At that point he had lost faith in the Wetminiter parliamentary model imposed on India, and advocated for why the presidential system was more relevant for India. Even after so many decades, his great vision and words still have relevance.

While I have always advocated, and still do, that businessmen should not mix business with politics, this does not mean that in their capacity of educated and responsible citizens, they should not take interest in political matters and form rational views on them. In fact, in our tightly planned, regulated and controlled economy, no intelligent analysis of economic issues is possible without taking into account the dominating influences of politics.

In the last fifteen years and more, our Five-Year Plans have been formulated by the government and passed by Parliament, our economic activity controlled by a spate of legislation and executive decisions. All economic power has been centered in ministers and members of central and state legislatures and in the bureaucracy. Today also, more than ever before, every problem is considered and every decision made on the basis of political consideration.

Unless the political system in force functions effectively, unless there is political stability and the rule of law prevails, all efforts to improve the economic climate must be frustrated. On the basis of this criterion and in the light of the recent outrageous events in Bengal and our other legislative assemblies, the proliferation of parties and groups within parties, the scramble for power or for the retention of power, the disintegration of law and order in many parts of the country, the increasing weakness of the Central Government, is there no justification for the view I hold that the political system of government we have adopted is in the process of failing?

On that assumption, the thesis I put before you today is that the British parliamentary system of government, which have enshrined in our Constitution is unsuited to the conditions in our country, to the temperament of our people and to our historical background. Take a look at the broad geographical sweep south of /Europe, from the Atlantic in the West to the Pacific in the East, from Morocco up to Japan and you will find no country except India, Ceylon and Malaysia where this system successfully prevails. It is worth noting also that only in countries of considerably greater political maturity and with a much smaller population than outs, has the system worked, or still working, usually in a modified form.

It may be argued that other countries like France, for instance, have in the past been politically unstable for decades and yet survived and progressed, that the present political instability in our country is a passing phase—the growing pains of an infant democracy—that India will survive intact as it has survived thousands of years of even more severe political instability. I fear this is dangerous wishful thinking, which ignores the tremendous changes—political, economic and technological—those are taking place here and in the rest of the world, quiet apart from the tremendous impact of our population explosion.

I venture to suggest that India is one of the twentieth century's major political anachronisms. The parliamentary system, which was evolved over a thousand years of trial and error for the government of a small, occidental island, and is predicted on the existence and smooth working of a sophisticated two-party system through a single Parliament is sought to be adapted to administering an Asian subcontinent through the machinery of what is developing into multi-multi-party system clashing in Parliament and in a number of state legislatures.

The British system has been worked by generations of trained professional and highly skilled politicians and administrators. In contrast, most of India's politicians are untrained and inexpert in the complex management of a modern society, while the main responsibility for administering the country is borne by an overworked cadre of senior civil servants whose number is grossly inadequate to cater effectively to the needs of over half a billion people.

In addition, the machine has been burdened with the most ambitious economic planning and development programme ever attempted outside Soviet Russia and with immensely difficult problems of defense, external affairs and finance. Up to the 1960s, the strain on the machine was hidden by the dominating personality of the great leader, while a benevolent one-party autocracy maintained a facade of political stability and democracy in action. With Nehru gone, the facade has begun to crack and the machine is showing increasing signs of breaking down.

The process is being accelerated by the disillusionment of the Indian people, who after twenty years of planning and controls and the expenditure of enormous amounts of money, find themselves little better off than when they started on their great adventure. The search of new leadership and new political ideas is further fragmenting a multiplicity of parties, most of which seem to be so bankrupt in ideas that they continue to use slogans and clichés of nineteenth century socialism. Frustration and loss of faith are rapidly eroding our nationhood and encouraging a tendency for India to withdraw again into mutually antagonistic regional divisions.

To come back to our thesis that the parliamentary form of government we have adopted is in the process of failing, the next question is whether this is due to inherent defects in the system itself or to the failings of the politicians charged with operating it? I think it is due to both.

If the majority of professional politicians of India, elected to the central and state legislatures, were as mature, as civic minded, as well-informed and as responsible as their counterparts in more politically advanced countries, we would at least have a measure of political stability, a better informed and intellectually higher level of debate and a greater respect of law and order. We would still suffer, however, from what I suggest is the major failure of the system under our conditions, namely, the constitutional requirement that cabinets at the Centre and in the states can be formed only from Members of Parliament and the respective legislatures and are made directly responsible to them in their day to day conduct of the country's or states' affairs.

The Problem to be tackled by the Executive and the Legislative branches of the government are nowhere in the world as numerous, varied and complex as in India. The great majority of them are certainly not political problems. Is it not obvious, therefore, that they should be tackled mainly by experts, technicians, scientists, economists, industrial managers and other professionally trained men and women? Can we blame our politicians, untrained and uninformed in any of the specialized disciplines involved in the management of a vast country such as ours, if they fail to understand, let alone to solve, the problem they face and to adapt themselves to the rapidly changing conditions of today? If, except for a few outstandingly able and dedicated men and women to whom we must extend our profound respect and gratitude, they have in this new game of parliamentary politics been mainly concerned with maintaining their own political position and status? Can we blame them for succumbing to the lust for power and for the many privileges attached to political power?

Between now and the next General Election in 1972, so overwhelming may be the disillusion of our voters that they may turn their faces totally away from the procedures and practices of parliamentary democracy. Even if this does not happen, it is not likely that the trend which emerged in the last elections (1967) may be even more pronounced in 1972? If so, we may be faced, both in the Centre and in most of the states, with a dangerously fluid situation in which a host of parties will constantly man oeuvre for power in series of ever changing coalitions, defections and floor-crossings, where the authority of the government and Parliament will be debased that the nation many sink into anarchy, be captured and ruled by a dictatorship, or cease to exist as a united India.

Can we afford such a risk and what will be the fate of our hundreds of millions of hungry, and by then angry people, if we do and gamble fails?

What then is alternative? Might it not be a Presidential System of Federal Government in which a Chief Executive at the Centre and the elected Governors in the states are elected for a term of years, during which they are irremovable and free to govern through cabinets of experts appointed by them and who may, but need not, include professional politicians?

There can be many variations of such a system, many way of electing a President and governors, but its main characteristics, however, are stability on the one hand and expert management of affair on the other. The executives of such a government will not, as in the British system, be directly responsible to Parliament in their day to day management of a country's affairs and constantly vulnerable to political skullduggery, but would be subject to constant and vigilant scrutiny by Parliament, which, of course, must remain the only body entrusted with law making.

I am well aware that this alternative was considered by the Constituent Assembly before our Constitution was enacted and that the British system was preferred to it, but since then, we have had a full twenty years of experience in its working and the conditions visualized in 1947 are certainly not those which we find in existence today. We have, in these twenty years, already amended the Constitution almost a many times, and four of the amendments have been major ones. Need we be afraid of a further amendment intended to provide the country with a more stable and more expert government than we have today?

What, in practice, should we do? I suggest that the first step should be the appointment by Parliament of a high powered commission to undertake a comprehensive study of the problem and to recommend such revision of our Constitution as would ensure the attainment of the desired objective. The commission should consist of outstanding experts in the fields of politics, law, education and other profession.

This will, I know, require an act of great courage but on it will depend the future of on-seventh of the human race as well as of the whole experiment of welding our people together permanently into a single united nation.

Meanwhile, we cannot even afford to wait till courage comes. We have to find the intermediate ways and means of restoring a degree of stability to our politics and more than a degree of safety to our citizens. Whatever be the politics of the parties or coalitions of parties in individual states, communication links must be kept going and at least selected strategic industries must be kept free from intimidation and sabotage.

Although such action obviously lies in the realm of the government, we businessmen, particularly those of us whose activities spread beyond a single state, can do much by our example and by word and action to help to break through the parochial barriers of creed and language, which we see being put up throughout the country.

In addition to the many tasks and duties of a purely economic trading and managerial nature to which we must dedicate ourselves in the coming years, let us also play our part in maintaining the integrity our country and the survival of our democratic way of life.

□

A Tryst with Destiny*

—Jawaharlal Nehru

Jawaharlal Nehru was India's royal figure, its matinee idol, its most gifted prime minister. He combined a unique array of talents: compelling oratory, a brilliant mind, good looks, a keen political sense, but he also suffered from brooding isolation. He left an indelible mark on both the country he led to independence, and the world in which he lived. Yet even though Nehru wrote more about himself than did any other modern Indian, 'Panditji's' true face has always remained veiled. "Tryst with Destiny" was a speech made by Jawaharlal Nehru, the first Prime Minister of independent India, to the Indian Constituent Assembly in the Parliament, on the eve of India's Independence, towards midnight on 14th August, 1947. It focusses on the aspects that transcend India's history. It is considered to be one of the greatest speeches of all time and to be a landmark oration that captures the essence of the triumphant culmination of the largely non-violent Indian independence struggle against the British Empire in India.

Long years ago, we made a tryst with destiny, and now the time comes when we shall redeem our pledge, not wholly or in full measure, but very substantially.

At the stroke of the midnight hour, when the world sleeps, India will awake to life and freedom. A moment comes, which

* *Parliament House, New Delhi on 14th August, 1947*

comes but rarely in history, when we step out from the old to the new, when an age ends, and when the soul of a nation, long suppressed, finds utterance.

It is fitting that, at this solemn moment, we take the pledge of dedication to the service of India and her people and to the still larger cause of humanity.

At the dawn of history, India started on her unending quest, and trackless centuries are filled with her striving and the grandeur of her success and her failures. Through good and ill fortune alike, she has never lost sight of that quest or forgotten the ideals which gave her strength. We end today a period of ill fortune and India discovers herself again.

The achievement we celebrate today is but a step, an opening of opportunity, to the greater triumphs and achievements that await us. Are we brave enough and wise enough to grasp this opportunity and accept the challenge of the future?

Freedom and power bring responsibility. The responsibility rests upon this assembly, a sovereign body representing the sovereign people of India. Before the birth of freedom, we have endured all the pains of labour and our hearts are heavy with the memory of this sorrow. Some of those pains continue even now. Nevertheless, the past is over and it is the future that beckons to us now.

That future is not one of ease or resting but of incessant striving so that we may fulfil the pledges we have so often taken and the one we shall take today. The service of India means the service of the millions who suffer. It means the ending of poverty and ignorance and disease and inequality of opportunity.

The ambition of the greatest man of our generation has been to wipe every tear from every eye. That may be beyond us, but as long as there are tears and suffering, our work will not be over.

And so we have to labour and to work, and work hard, to give reality to our dreams. Those dreams are for India, but they are also for the world, for all the nations and peoples are too closely knit together today for anyone of them to imagine that it can live apart.

Peace has been said to be indivisible; so is freedom, so is

prosperity now, and so also is disaster in this one world that can no longer be split into isolated fragments.

To the people of India, whose representatives we are, we make an appeal to join us with faith and confidence in this great adventure. This is no time for petty and destructive criticism, no time for ill will or blaming others. We have to build the noble mansion of free India where all her children may dwell.

The appointed day has come – the day appointed by destiny– and India stands forth again, after long slumber and struggle, awake, vital, free and independent. The past clings on to us still in some measure and we have to do much before we redeem the pledges we have so often taken. Yet the turning point is past, and history begins anew for us, the history which we shall live and act and others will write about.

It is a fateful moment for us in India, for all Asia and for the world. A new star rises, the star of freedom in the east, a new hope comes into being, a vision long cherished materialises. May the star never set and that hope never be betrayed!

We rejoice in that freedom, even though clouds surround us, and many of our people are sorrow-stricken and difficult problems encompass us. But freedom brings responsibilities and burdens and we have to face them in the spirit of a free and disciplined people.

On this day, our first thoughts go to the architect of this freedom, the father of our nation, who, embodying the old spirit of India, held aloft the torch of freedom and lighted up the darkness that surrounded us.

We have often been unworthy followers of his and have strayed from his message, but not only we but succeeding generations will remember this message and bear the imprint in their hearts of this great son of India, magnificent in his faith and strength and courage and humility. We shall never allow that torch of freedom to be blown out, however high the wind or stormy the tempest.

Our next thoughts must be of the unknown volunteers and soldiers of freedom who, without praise or reward, have served India even unto death.

We think also of our brothers and sisters who have been cut off from us by political boundaries and who unhappily cannot share at present in the freedom that has come. They are of us and will remain of us whatever may happen, and we shall be sharers in their good and ill fortune alike.

The future beckons to us. Whither do we go and what shall be our endeavour? To bring freedom and opportunity to the common man, to the peasants and workers of India; to fight and end poverty and ignorance and disease; to build up a prosperous, democratic and progressive nation, and to create social, economic and political institutions which will ensure justice and fullness of life to every man and woman.

We have hard work ahead. There is no resting for any one of us till we redeem our pledge in full, till we make all the people of India what destiny intended them to be.

We are citizens of a great country, on the verge of bold advance, and we have to live up to that high standard. All of us, to whatever religion we may belong, are equally the children of India with equal rights, privileges and obligations. We cannot encourage communalism or narrow-mindedness, for no nation can be great whose people are narrow in thought or in action.

To the nations and peoples of the world, we send greetings and pledge ourselves to cooperate with them in furthering peace, freedom and democracy.

And to India, our much-loved motherland, the ancient, the eternal and the ever-new, we pay our reverent homage and we bind ourselves afresh to her service. Jai Hind [Victory to India].

□

Speech on Visionary Leadership

—Kiran Bedi

Now I'm going to give you a story. It's an Indian story about an Indian woman and her journey. Let me begin with my parents. I'm a product of this visionary mother and father. Many years ago, when I was born in the '50s—'50s and '60s didn't belong to girls in India. They belonged to the boys. They belonged to boys who would join business and inherit business from parents, and girls would be dolled up to get married. My family, in my city, and almost in the country, was unique. We were four of us, not one, and, fortunately, no boys. We were four girls and no boys. And my parents were part of a landed property family. My father defied his own grandfather, almost to the point of disinheritance, because he decided to educate all four of us. He sent us to one of the best schools in the city and gave us the best education. As I've said, when we're born, we don't choose our parents, and when we go to school, we don't choose our school. Children don't choose a school. They just get the school which parents choose for them. So, this is the foundation time which I got. I grew up like this, and so did my other three sisters. And my father used to say at that time, "I'm going to spread all my four daughters in four corners of the world." I don't know if he really meant [that], but it happened. I'm the only one who's left in India. One is a British, another is an American, and the third is a Canadian. So, we are four of us in four corners of the world.

And since I said they're my role models, I followed two things which my father and mother gave me. One, they said, "Life is on an incline. You either go up, or you come down." And the second thing, which has stayed with me, which became my philosophy of life, which made all the difference, is: 100 things happen in your life, good or bad. Out of 100, 90 are your creation. They're good. They're your creation. Enjoy it. If they're bad, they're your creation. Learn from it. Ten are nature-sent over which you can't do a thing. It's like a death of a relative, or a cyclone, or a hurricane, or an earthquake. You can't do a thing about it. You've got to just respond to the situation. But that response comes out of those 90 points. Since I'm a product of this philosophy, of 90/10, and secondly, 'life on an incline', that's the way I grew up to be valuing what I got. I'm a product of opportunities, rare opportunities in the '50s and the '60s, which girls didn't get, and I was conscious of the fact that what my parents were giving me was something unique. Because all of my best school friends were getting dolled up to get married with a lot of dowry, and here I was with a tennis racket and going to school and doing all kinds of extracurricular activities. I thought I must tell you this. Why I said this, is the background.

This is what comes next. I joined the Indian Police Service as a tough woman, a woman with indefatigable stamina, because I used to run for my tennis titles, etc. But I joined the Indian Police Service, and then it was a new pattern of policing. For me the policing stood for power to correct, power to prevent and power to detect. This is something like a new definition ever given in policing in India — the power to prevent. Because normally it was always said, power to detect, and that's it, or power to punish. But I decided no, it's a power to prevent, because that's what I learned when I was growing up. How do I prevent the 10 and never make it more than 10? So, this was how it came into my service, and it was different from the men. I didn't want to make it different from the men, but it was different, because this was the way I was different. And I redefined policing concepts in India. I'm going to take you on two journeys, my policing journey and my prison journey. What you see, if you see the title called 'PM's car held"? This was the first time a prime minister of India was given a parking ticket. (Laughter) That's the first time in India, and I can tell you, that's the last time you're hearing about it. It'll never happen again in India because now it was once and forever. And the rule was, because I was sensitive, I was compassionate, I was very sensitive to injustice, and I was very pro-justice. That's the reason, as a woman, I joined the Indian Police Service. I had other options, but I didn't choose them.

So, I'm going to move on. This is about tough policing, equal policing. Now I was known as 'here's a woman that's not going to listen'. So, I was sent to all indiscriminate postings, postings which others would say 'no'. I now went to a prison assignment as a police officer. Normally, police officers don't want to do prison. They sent me to prison to lock me up, thinking, 'Now there will be no cars and no VIPs to be given tickets to. Let's lock her up.' Here I got a prison assignment. This was a prison assignment which was one big den of criminals. Obviously, it was. But, 10,000 men, of which only 400 were women—10,000—9,000 plus about 600 were men. Terrorists, rapists, burglars, gangsters—some of them I'd sent to jail as a police officer outside. And then how did I deal with them? The first day when I went in, I didn't know how to look at them. And I said, "Do you pray?" When I looked at the group, I said, "Do you pray?" They saw me as a young, short woman wearing a pathan suit. I said, "Do you pray?" And they didn't say anything. I said, "Do you pray? Do you want to pray?" They said, "Yes." I said, "All right, let's pray." I prayed for them, and things started to change. This is a visual of education inside the prison.

Friends, this has never happened, where everybody in the prison studies. I started this with community support. Government had no budget. It was one of the finest, largest volunteerisms in any prison in the world. This was initiated in Delhi prison. You see one sample of a prisoner teaching a class. These are hundreds of classes. Nine to eleven, every prisoner went into the education program—the same den in which they thought they would put me behind the bars and things would be forgotten. We converted this into an ashram—from a prison to an ashram—through education. I think that's a bigger change. It was the beginning of a change. Teachers were prisoners. Teachers were volunteers. Books came from donated schoolbooks. Stationery was donated. Everything was donated, because there was no budget of education for the prison. Now if I'd not done that, it would have been a hellhole.

That's the second landmark. I want to show you some moments of history in my journey, which probably you would never ever get to see anywhere in the world. One, the numbers you'll never get to see. Secondly, this concept. This was a meditation program inside the prison of over 1,000 prisoners. One thousand prisoners who sat in meditation. This was one of the most courageous steps I took as a prison governor. And this is what transformed. You want to know more about this, go and see this film, 'Doing Time, Doing Vipassana'. You will hear about it, and you will love it. And write to me on KiranBedi.com, and I'll respond to you. Let me show you the next slide. I took the same concept of mindfulness because why did I bring meditation into the Indian prison? Because crime is a product of a distorted mind. It was a distortion of mind which needed to be addressed to control. Not by preaching, not by telling, not by reading, but by addressing your mind. I took the same thing to the police because police, equally, were prisoners of their minds, and they felt as if it was 'we' and 'they', and that the people don't cooperate. This worked.

This is a feedback box called a petition box. This is a concept which I introduced to listen to complaints, listen to grievances. This was a magic box. This was a sensitive box. This is how a prisoner drew how they felt about the prison. If you see somebody in the blue—yeah, this guy—he was a prisoner, and he was a teacher. And you see, everybody's busy. There was no time to waste.

Let me wrap it up. I'm currently into movements, movements of education of the under-served children, which is thousands—India is all about thousands. Secondly is about the anti-corruption movement in India. That's a big way we, as a small group of activists, have drafted an ombudsman bill for the government of India. Friends, you will hear a lot about it. That's the movement at the moment I'm driving, and that's the movement and ambition of my life.

Thank you very much. (Applause) Thank you. Thank you very much. Thank you. Thank you. Thank you. Thank you.

□

Towards Freedom*

—Lala Lajpat Rai

[After studying law at the Government College in Lahore, Lajpat Rai practised at Hissar and Lahore, where he helped to establish the nationalistic Dayananda Anglo-Vedic School and became a follower of Dayananda Sarasvati, the founder of the reformist Hindu society Arya Samaj (Society of Noble People). After joining the Indian National Congress, and taking part in political agitation in the Punjab, Lajpat Rai was deported to Mandalay, Burma (Myanmar), without trial, in May 1907. In November, however, he was allowed to return when the viceroy, Lord Minto, decided that there was insufficient evidence to hold him for subversion. Lajpat Rai's supporters attempted to secure his election to the presidency of the party session at Surat in December 1907, but elements favouring co-operation with the British refused to accept him, and the party split over the issues.

Lala Lajpat Rai had left India in 1913 and gave the following reason for his departure: 'I began to suspect that I was being spied on by my own servant who lived with me in the same compound. Life became intolerable and I lost my sleep and appetite, so I decided to leave India.' He had gone to England via Japan and when World War I broke out in

---

* *Shandarama Chawl, Bombay, 20th February, 1920*

July 1914, he left for America where he lived for six years. In America he did a good deal of propaganda on India's behalf and founded the Indian Home Rule League in 1917.

After six years of self-imposed exile when Lala Lajpat Rai reached Bombay on 20th February, 1920, he was given a hero's welcome. The following extempore speech was delivered by him during the very first reception on his arrival at Shandarama Chawl.]

This is not the time for me nor the occasion for me to give you my opinion of the present political situation in this country. I shall beg leave of you to give me time before I express myself on the subject. However, there are some fundamental truths which I have learnt, to my pleasure, during my travels abroad which I am going to place before you as my message to 'Young India'. My friends, I must tell you that henceforth we should recognize it as a fundamental doctrine that the unity of the Hindus and Mohammedans will be a great asset to our political future. In this unity we shall not be guided by the temporary benefit of this community. We shall not adopt it as a measure of political expediency, but adopt it as a fundamental doctrine of our faith, which we have to stand by till our death and until we win our freedom. Not only till then, but thereafter too, we shall live in this country as brothers determined to work together, determined to resist together, and determined to win. That is one of the fundamental doctrines which we must adopt as a first article of our political faith.

Coming to the second article, I must tell you, that do not place any faith in anybody but yourself. You can rise only by your own efforts. Remember 'Nations are by themselves made.' We shall welcome cooperation. We shall welcome advice. We shall welcome guidance also, in certain matters. But we shall resent patronage and dictation. We are not little children. We have behind us the wisdom of six thousand years at least, not to say more.

I may add that I have travelled practically all over the world and I have seen three of the great self-ruling nations of the world at least, the Japanese, the Americans and the Englishmen. Take it from me, that except perhaps in areas of modern knowledge, we are inferior to none on this earth. What are we inferior in? We have been inferior in the capacity to unite, we have been inferior to a certain extent in adapting to modern times, we have been inferior in learning the lesson of modern diplomacy. Therein lies our inferiority. If we had learnt the art of telling lies on a broad scale, if we had swept away our past and had entered into the great arena of violence, if we had done all these things, which at the present moment represent power in the world, we might have been considered by the great nations of the world as worthy of self-government. We, however, lack these qualities. There is one of these qualities I want you to learn. We have been a righteous nation in all our history and we shall continue to be righteous and to win on the basis of righteousness. I want you to be true to your civilization. Seek truth, speak truth and act truth and I promise you shall win. The modern world is being managed, modern politics are being based upon the rights of the superior and the inferior. We recognise none as inferior or superior. We don't want for our country anything that we are not prepared to concede to other people on the globe. What we want is equality and nothing else.

There are some friends who are often tempted by the term imperialism. They want to be partners in the great imperial system. I do not want it. Ladies and gentlemen, there is no word coined by man more vicious, more sinful, and more criminal than imperialism. I for one do not want to be a partner in any imperial system. All that I want for my country is a position of equality first in the British Commonwealth and then in the nations of the world. With our connection with Great Britain, we want to cooperate with those British statesmen and politicians, thinkers and workers, who want to convert the British Empire into a British Commonwealth. I may add that world movements foreshadow coming events and unless the British Empire is soon converted into a British Commonwealth it will go to the dogs as other empires have gone. Its safety lies in converting to a British Commonwealth and we as Indians, as constitutional workers, as Indians believing in the destiny of the entire world, are prepared to cooperate constitutionally with our entire thinking force, to convert that Empire into a commonwealth of equal and free nations. My dear friends, there are some people who tell us that the opinion of others does not count for much. They tell us that the opinion of the British people who are the present rulers of this country naturally matters for our progress. I do not accept that dictum.

[He was elected President of the Congress party in the Calcutta Special Session of 1920. In 1921, He founded Servants of the People Society, a non-profit welfare organisation, in Lahore. In 1928, the British government set up the Commission, headed by Sir John Simon, to report on the political situation in India. The Indian political parties boycotted the Commission, because it did not include a single Indian in its membership, and it met with country-wide protests. When the Commission visited Lahore on 30th October, 1928, Lajpat Rai led silent march in protest against it. The superintendent of police, James A. Scott, ordered the police to lathi (baton) charge the protesters and personally assaulted Rai. Despite being injured, Rai subsequently addressed the crowd and said that "I declare that the blows struck at me today will be the last nails in the coffin of British rule in India". He did not fully recover from his injuries and died on 17th November, 1928 of a heart attack. Doctors thought that Scott's blows had hastened his death. However, when the matter was raised in the British Parliament, the British Government denied any role in Rai's death.]

□

The Quit India Speeches*

—Mahatma Gandhi

[Gandhi initially favoured offering "nonviolent moral support" to the British effort when World War II broke out in 1939, but the Congressional leaders were offended by the unilateral inclusion of India in the war without consultation of the people's representatives. Following this declaration by the then British Governor-General of India, Lord Linlithgow, the Congress Working Committee at its meeting on 10th October, 1939, passed a resolution condemning the aggressive activities of the Germans. At the same time the resolution also stated that India could not associate herself with war unless it was consulted first. Responding to this declaration, the Viceroy issued a statement on 17th October wherein he claimed that Britain is waging a war driven by the motif to strengthen peace in the world. He also stated that after the war, the government would initiate modifications in the Act of 1935, in accordance to the desires of the Indians.

Gandhi's reaction to this statement was; "the old policy of divide and rule is to continue. The Congress has asked for bread and it has got stone." According to the instructions issued by High Command, the Congress ministers were directed to resign immediately. Congress ministers from

* *All India Congress Committee (Aicc), Gowaliar Tank Maidan, Bombay On 8th August, 1942*

eight provinces resigned following the instructions. The resignation of the ministers was an occasion of great joy and rejoicing for leader of the Muslim League, Mohammad Ali Jinnah. He called the day of 22nd December, 1939 'The Day of Deliverance'. Gandhi urged Jinnah against the celebration of this day, however, it was futile. At the Muslim League Lahore Session held in March 1940, Jinnah declared in his presidential address that the Muslims of the country wanted a separate homeland, Pakistan.

In the meanwhile, crucial political events took place in England. Chamberlain was succeeded by Churchill as the Prime Minister and the Conservatives, who assumed power in England, did not have a sympathetic stance towards the claims made by the Congress. In order to pacify the Indians in the circumstance of worsening war situation, the Conservatives were forced to concede some of the demands made by the Indians. On 8th August, the Viceroy issued a statement that has come to be referred as the "August Offer". However, the Congress rejected the offer followed by the Muslim League.

In the context of widespread dissatisfaction that prevailed over the rejection of the demands made by the Congress, Gandhi at the meeting of the Congress Working Committee in Wardha revealed his plan to launch Individual Civil Disobedience. Once again, the weapon of satyagraha found popular acceptance as the best means to wage a crusade against the British. It was widely used as a mark of protest against the unwavering stance assumed by the British. Vinoba Bhave, a follower of Gandhi, was selected by him to initiate the movement. Anti war speeches ricocheted in all corners of the country, with the satyagrahis earnestly appealing to the people of the nation not to support the Government in its war endeavors. The consequence of this satyagrahi campaign was the arrest of almost fourteen thousand satyagrahis. On 3rd December, 1941, the Viceroy ordered the acquittal of all the satyagrahis. In Europe the war situation became more critical with the Japanese attack on Pearl Harbor and the Congress realized the necessity for appraising their program. Subsequently, the movement was withdrawn.

The Cripps' Mission and its failure also played an important role in Gandhi's call for The Quit India Movement. In order to end the deadlock, the British government on 22nd March, 1942, sent Sir Stafford Cripps to talk terms with the Indian political parties and secure their support in Britain's war efforts. A Draft Declaration of the British Government was presented, which included terms like establishment of Dominion, establishment of a Constituent Assembly and right of the Provinces to make separate constitutions. These would be, however, granted after the cessation of the Second World War. According to the Congress this Declaration only offered India a promise that was to be fulfilled in the future. Commenting on this Gandhi said; "It is a post dated cheque on a crashing bank." Other factors that contributed were the threat of Japanese invasion of India and realization of the national leaders of the incapacity of the British to defend India.

The Congress Working Committee meeting at Wardha (Gujrat) on 14th July, 1942 passed a resolution demanding complete independence from the British government. The draft proposed massive civil disobedience if the British did not accede to the demands. However, it proved to be controversial within the party. A prominent Congress national leader Chakravarti Rajgopalachari quit the Congress over this decision, and so did some local and regional level organizers. Jawaharlal Nehru and Maulana Azad were apprehensive and critical of the call, but backed it and stuck with Gandhi's leadership until the end. Sardar Vallabhbhai Patel, Dr. Rajendra Prasad and Dr Anugrah Narayan Sinha openly and enthusiastically supported such a disobedience movement, as did many veteran Gandhians and socialists like Asoka Mehta and Jayaprakash Narayan.

The Congress had little success in rallying other political forces under a single flag and program. Smaller parties like the Hindu Mahasabha opposed the call. The Communist

Party of India strongly opposed the Quit India movement and supported the war effort because of the need to assist the Soviet Union, despite support for Quit India by many industrial workers. In response the British lifted the ban on the party. The movement had less support in the princely states, as the princes were strongly opposed and funded the opposition. Muslim leaders opposed Quit India. Muhammad Ali Jinnah's opposition to the call led to large numbers of Muslims cooperating with the British, and enlisting in the army. The Muslim League gained large numbers of new members. Congress members resigned from provincial legislatures, enabling the League to take control in Sindh, Bengal and Northwest Frontier.

Anyhow, the Quit India Movement (Bharat Chhodo Andolan), or the India August Movement (August Kranti), a civil disobedience movement, was launched in India on 8th August 1942 by Mohandas Karamchand Gandhi. The All-India Congress Committee proclaimed a mass protest demanding what Gandhi called "an orderly British withdrawal" from India. It was for the determined, which appears in his call to Do or Die, issued on 8th August at the Gowaliar Tank Maidan, since renamed August Kranti Maidan (August Revolution Ground), in Bombay (Mumbai) in 1942.

The British were prepared to act. Almost the entire INC leadership, and not just at the national level, was imprisoned without trial within hours after Gandhi's speech. Most spent the rest of the war in prison and out of contact with the masses. The British had the support of the Viceroy's Council (which had a majority of Indians), of the Muslims, the Communist Party, the princely states, the Imperial and state police, the Indian Army, and the Indian Civil Service. Many Indian businessmen were profiting from heavy wartime spending and did not support Quit India. Many students paid more attention to Subhas Chandra Bose, who was in exile and supporting the Axis. The only outside support came from the Americans, as President Franklin D. Roosevelt pressured Prime Minister Winston Churchill to give in to Indian demands. The Quit India campaign was effectively crushed. The British refused to grant immediate independence, saying it could happen only after the war ended.

One of the achievements of the movement was to keep the Congress party united through all the trials and tribulations that followed. The British already alarmed by the advance of the Japanese army to the India-Burma border, responded by imprisoning Gandhi. All the members of the Party's Working Committee (national leadership) were imprisoned as well. Due to the arrest of major leaders, a young and till then relatively unknown Aruna Asaf Ali presided over the AICC session on 9th August and hoisted the flag; later the Congress party was banned. These actions only created sympathy for the cause among the population. Despite lack of direct leadership, large protests and demonstrations were held all over the country. Workers remained absent en masse and strikes were called. Not all demonstrations were peaceful, at some places bombs exploded, government buildings were set on fire, electricity was cut and transport and communication lines were severed.

The British swiftly responded with mass detentions. Over 100,000 arrests were made, mass fines were levied and demonstrators were subjected to public flogging. Hundreds of civilians were killed in violence many shot by the police army. Many national leaders went underground and continued their struggle by broadcasting messages over clandestine radio stations, distributing pamphlets and establishing parallel governments. The British sense of crisis was strong enough that a battleship was specifically set aside to take Gandhi and the Congress leaders out of India, possibly to South Africa or Yemen but ultimately did not take that step out of fear of intensifying the revolt.

The Congress leadership was cut off from the rest of the world for over three years. Gandhi's wife Kasturbai Gandhi and his personal secretary Mahadev Desai died in months and Gandhi's health was failing, despite this Gandhi went on a 21-day fast and maintained his resolve to continuous resistance. Although the British released Gandhi on account of his health in 1944, Gandhi kept up the resistance, demanding the release of the Congress leadership.

By early 1944, India was mostly peaceful again, while the Congress leadership was still incarcerated. A sense that the movement had failed depressed many nationalists, while Jinnah and the Muslim League, as well as Congress opponents like the Communists sought to gain political mileage, criticizing Gandhi and the Congress Party. Anyhow, Gandhi was successful to ignite the hearts and minds of the millions of Indians through his remarkable speech.]

Before you discuss the resolution, let me place before you one or two things. I want you to understand two things very clearly and to consider them from the same point of view from which I am placing them before you. I ask you to consider it from my point of view, because if you approve of it, you will be enjoined to carry out all I say. It will be a great responsibility. There are people who ask me whether I am the same man that I was in 1920, or whether there has been any change in me. You are right in asking that question.

Let me, however, hasten to assure that I am the same Gandhi as I was in 1920. I have not changed in any fundamental respect. I attach the same importance to non-violence that I did then. If at all, my emphasis on it has grown stronger. There is no real contradiction between the present resolution and my previous writings and utterances.

Occasions like the present do not occur in everybody's and but rarely in anybody's life. I want you to know and feel that there is nothing but purest Ahimsa in all that I am saying and doing today. The draft resolution of the Working Committee is based on Ahimsa, the contemplated struggle similarly has its roots in Ahimsa. If, therefore, there is any among you who has lost faith in Ahimsa or is wearied of it, let him not vote for this resolution.

Let me explain my position clearly. God has vouchsafed to me a priceless gift in the weapons of Ahimsa. I and my Ahimsa are on our trial today. If in the present crisis, when the earth is being scorched by the flames of Himsa and crying for deliverance, I failed to make use of the God given talent, God will not forgive me and I shall be judged unworthy of the great gift. I must act now. I may not hesitate and merely look on, when Russia and China are threatened.

Ours is not drive for power, but purely a non-violent fight for India's independence. In a violent struggle, a successful general has been often known to effect a military coup and to set up a dictatorship. But under the Congress scheme of things, essentially non-violent as it is, there can be no room for dictatorship. A non-violent soldier of freedom will covet nothing for himself, he fights only for the freedom of his country. The Congress is unconcerned as to who will rule, when freedom is attained. The power, when it will belong to the people of India, and it will be for them to decide to whom it should be entrusted. May be that the reins will be placed in the hands of the Parsis, for instance—as I would love to see happen—or they may be handed to some others whose names are not heard in the Congress today. It will not be for you then to object saying, "This community is microscopic. That party did not play its due part in the freedom's struggle; why should it have all the power?" Ever since its inception the Congress has kept itself meticulously free of the communal taint. It has thought always in terms of the whole nation and has acted accordingly....

I know how imperfect our Ahimsa is and how far away we are still from the ideal, but in Ahimsa there is no final failure or defeat. I have faith, therefore, that if, in spite of our shortcomings, the big thing does happen, it will be because God wanted to help us by crowning with success our silent, unremitting Sadhana for the last twenty-two years.

I believe that in the history of the world, there has not been a more genuinely democratic struggle for freedom than ours. I read Carlyle's French Revolution while I was in prison, and Pandit Jawaharlal has told me something about the Russian revolution. But it is my conviction that inasmuch as these struggles were fought with the weapon of violence they failed to realize the democratic ideal. In the democracy which I have envisaged, a democracy established by non-violence, there will be equal freedom for all. Everybody will be his own master. It is to join a struggle for such democracy that I invite you today. Once you realize this you will forget the differences between the Hindus and Muslims, and think of yourselves as Indians only, engaged in the common struggle for independence.

Then, there is the question of your attitude towards the British. I have noticed that there is hatred towards the British among the people. The people say they are disgusted with their behavior. The people make no distinction between British imperialism and the British people. To them, the two are one. This hatred would even make them welcome the Japanese. It is most dangerous. It means that they will exchange one slavery for another. We must get rid of this feeling. Our quarrel is not with the British people, we fight their imperialism. The proposal for the withdrawal of British power did not come out of anger. It came to enable India to play its due part at the present critical juncture. It is not a happy position for a big country like India to be merely helping with money and material obtained willy-nilly from her while the United Nations are conducting the war. We cannot evoke the true spirit of sacrifice and valour, so long as we do not feel that it is our war, so long as we are not free. I know the British Government will not be able to withhold freedom from us, when we have made enough self sacrifice. We must, therefore, purge ourselves of hatred. Speaking for myself, I can say that I have never felt any hatred. As a matter of fact, I feel myself to be a greater friend of the British now than ever before. One reason is that they are today in distress. My very friendship, therefore, demands that I should try to save them from their mistakes. As I view the situation, they are on the brink of an abyss. It, therefore, becomes my duty to warn them of their danger even though it may, for the time being, anger them to the point of cutting off the friendly hand that is stretched out to help them. People may laugh, nevertheless that is my claim. At a time when I may have to launch the biggest struggle of my life, I may not harbor hatred against anybody.

I congratulate you on the resolution that you have just passed. I also congratulate the three comrades on the courage they have shown in pressing their amendments to a division, even though they knew that there was an overwhelming majority in favour of the resolution, and I congratulate the thirteen friends who voted against the resolution. In doing so, they had nothing to be ashamed of. For the last twenty years we have tried to learn not to lose courage even when we are in a hopeless minority and are laughed at. We have learned to hold on to our beliefs in the confidence that we are in the right. It behooves us to cultivate this courage of conviction, for it ennobles man and raises his moral stature. I was; therefore, glad to see that these friends had imbibed the principle which I have tried to follow for the last fifty years and more.

Having congratulated them on their courage let me say that what they asked this Committee to accept through their amendments was not the correct representation of the situation. These friends ought to have pondered over the appeal made to them by the Maulana to withdraw their amendments; they should have carefully followed the explanations given by Jawaharlal. Had they done so, it would have been clear to them that the right which they now want the Congress to concede has already been conceded by the Congress.

Time was when every Musalman claimed the whole of India as his motherland. During the years that the Ali brothers were with me, the assumption underlying all their talks and discussions was that India belonged as much to the Musalmans as to the Hindus. I can testify to the fact that this was their innermost conviction and not a mask; I lived with them for years. I spent days and nights in their company. And I make bold to say that their utterances were the honest expression of their beliefs. I know there are some who say that I take things too readily at their face value, that I am gullible. I do not think I am such a simpleton, nor am I so gullible as these friends take me to be. But their criticism does not hurt me. I should prefer to be considered gullible rather than deceitful.

What these Communist friends proposed through their amendments is nothing new. It has been repeated from thousands of platforms. Thousands of Musalmans have told me, that if Hindu-Muslim question was to be solved satisfactorily, it must be done in my lifetime. I should feel flattered at this; but how can I agree to a proposal which does not appeal to my reason? Hindu-Muslim unity is not a new thing. Millions of Hindus and Musalmans have sought after it. I consciously strove for its achievement from my boyhood. While at school, I made it a point to cultivate the friendship of Muslim and Parsi co students. I believed even at that tender age that the Hindus in India, if they wished to live in peace and amity with the whole communities, should assiduously cultivate the virtue of neighbourliness. It did not matter, I felt, If I made no special effort to cultivate the friendship with Hindus, but I must make friends with at least a few Musalmans. It was as counsel for a Musalman merchant that I went to South Africa. I made friends with other Musalmans there, even with the opponents of my client, and gained a reputation for integrity and good faith. I had among my friends and co-workers Muslims as well as Parsis. I captured their hearts and when I left finally for India, I left them sad and shedding tears of grief at the separation.

In India too I continued my efforts and left no stone unturned to achieve that unity. It was my lifelong aspiration for it that made me offer my fullest cooperation to the Musalmans in the Khilafat movement. Muslims throughout the country accepted me as their true friend.

How then is it that I have now come to be regarded as so evil and detestable? Had I any axe to grind in supporting the Khilifat movement? True, I did in my heart of hearts cherish a hope that It might enable me to save the cow. I am a worshipper of the cow. I believe the cow and myself to be the creation of the same God, and I am prepared to sacrifice my life in order to save the cow. But, whatever my philosophy of life and my ultimate hopes, I joined the movement in no spirit of bargain. I co-operated in the struggle for the Khilafat solely in order to discharge my obligation to my neighbour who, I saw, was in distress. The Ali brothers, had they been alive today, would have testified to the truth of this assertion. And so would many others bear me out in that it was not a bargain on my part for saving the cow. The cow like the Khilafat, stood on her own merits. As an honest man, a true neighbour and a faithful friend, it was incumbent on me to stand by the Musalmans in the hour of their trial.

In those days, I shocked the Hindus by dining with the

musalmans, though with the passage of time they have now got used to it. Maulana Bari told me, however, that though he would not allow me to dine with him, lest some day he should be accused of a sinister motive. And so, whenever I had occasion to stay with him, he called a Brahmana cook and made special arrangements for separate cooking. Firangi Mahal, his residence, was an old-styled structure with limited accommodation; yet he cheerfully bore all hardships and carried out his resolve from which I could not dislodge him. It was the spirit of courtesy, dignity and nobility that inspired us in those days. The members of each community vied with one another in accommodating members of sister communities. They respected one another's religious feelings, and considered it a privilege to do so. Not a trace of suspicion lurked in anybody's heart. Where has all that dignity, that nobility of spirit, disappeared now? I should ask all Musalmans, including Quaid-i-Azam Jinnah, to recall those glorious days and to find out what has brought us to the present impasse. Quaid-i-Azam Jinnah himself was at one time a Congressman. If today the Congress has incurred his wrath, it is because the canker of suspicion has entered his heart. May God bless him with long life, but when I am gone, he will realize and admit that I had no designs on Musalmans and that I had never betrayed their interests. Where is the escape for me, if I injure their cause or betray their interests? My life is entirely at their disposal. They are free to put an end to it, whenever they wish to do so. Assaults have been made on my life in the past, but God has spared me till now, and the assailants have repented for their action. But if someone were to shoot me in the belief that he was getting rid of a rascal, he would kill not the real Gandhi, but the one that appeared to him a rascal.

To those who have been indulging in a campaign of abuse and vilification I would say, "Islam enjoins you not to revile even an enemy. The Prophet treated even enemies with kindness and tried to win them over by his fairness and generosity. Are you followers of that Islam or of any other? If you are followers of the true Islam, does it behove you to distrust the words of one who makes a public declaration of his faith? You may take it from me that one day you will regret the fact that you distrusted and killed one who was a true and devoted friend of yours." It cuts me to the quick to see that the more I appeal and the more the Maulana importunes, the more intense does the campaign of vilification grow. To me, these abuses are like bullets. They can kill me, even as a bullet can put an end to my life. You may kill me. That will not hurt me. But what of those who indulge in abusing? They bring discredit to Islam. For the fair name of Islam, I appeal to you to resist this unceasing campaign of abuse and vilification.

Maulana Saheb is being made a target for the filthiest abuse. Why? Because he refuses to exert on me the pressure of his friendship. He realizes that it is a misuse of friendship to seek to compel a friend to accept as truth what he knows is an untruth.

To the Quaid-i-Azam I would say: "Whatever is true and valid in the claim for Pakistan is already in your hands. What is wrong and untenable is in nobody's gift, so that it can be made over to you. Even if someone were to succeed in imposing an untruth on others, he would not be able to enjoy for long the fruits of such coercion. God dislikes pride and keeps away from it. God would not tolerate a forcible imposition of an untruth."

The Quaid-i-Azam says that he is compelled to say bitter things but that he cannot help giving expression to his thoughts and his feelings. Similarly I would say: "I consider myself a friend of Musalmans. Why should I then not give expression to the things nearest to my heart, even at the cost of displeasing them? How can I conceal my innermost thoughts from them? I should congratulate the Quaid-i-Azam on his frankness in giving expression to his thoughts and feelings, even if they sound bitter to his hearers. But even so why should the Musalmans sitting here be reviled, if they do not see eye to eye with him? If millions of Musalmans are with you can you not afford to ignore the handful of Musalmans who may appear to you to be misguided? Why should one with the following of several millions be afraid of a majority community, or of the minority being swamped by the majority? How did the Prophet work among the Arabs and the Musalmans? How did he propagate Islam? Did he say he would propagate Islam only when he commanded a majority? I appeal to you for the sake of Islam to ponder over what I say. There is neither fair play nor justice in saying that the congress must accept a thing, even if it does not believe in it and even if it goes counter to principles it holds dear.

Rajaji said: "I do not believe in Pakistan. But Musalmans ask for it, Mr. Jinnah asks for it, and it has become an obsession with them. Why not then say "yes" to them just now? The same Mr. Jinnah will later on realize the disadvantages of Pakistan and will forgo the demands." I said : "It is not fair to accept as true a thing which I hold to be untrue, and ask others to do so in the belief that the demand will not be pressed when the time comes for setting it finally. If I hold the demand to be just, I should concede it this very day. I should not agree to it merely in order to placate Jinnah Saheb. Many friends have come and asked me to agree to it merely for the time being to placate Mr. Jinnah, disarm his suspicions and to see how he reacts to it. But I cannot be party to a course of action with a false promise. At any rate, it is not my method."

The congress has no sanction but the moral one for enforcing its decisions. It believes that true democracy can only be the outcome of non-violence. The structure of a world federation can be raised only on a foundation of nonviolence, and violence will have to be totally abjured from world affairs. If this is true, the solution of Hindu-Muslim question, too, cannot be achieved by a resort to violence. If the Hindus tyrannize over the Musalmans, with what face will they talk of a world federation? It is for the same reason that I do not believe in the possibility of establishing world peace through violence as the English and American statesmen propose to do. The Congress has agreed to submitting all the differences to an impartial international tribunal and to abide by its decisions. If even this fairest of proposal is unacceptable, the only course that remains open is that of the sword, of violence. How can I persuade myself to agree to impossibility? To demand the vivisection of a living organism is to ask for its very life. It is a call to war. The Congress cannot be party to such a fratricidal war. Those Hindus who, like Dr. Moonje and Shri Savarkar, believe in the doctrine of the sword may seek to keep the Musalmans under Hindu domination. I do not represent that section. I represent the Congress. You want to kill the Congress which is the goose that lays golden eggs. If you distrust the Congress, you may rest assured that there is to be perpetual war between the Hindus and the Musalmans, and the country will be doomed to continue warfare and bloodshed. If such warfare is to be our lot, I shall not live to witness it.

It is for that reason that I say to Jinnah saheb, "You may take it from me that whatever in your demand for Pakistan accords with considerations of justice and equity is lying in your pocket; whatever in the demand is contrary to justice and equity you can take only by the sword and in no other manner."

There is much in my heart that I would like to pour out before this assembly. One thing which was uppermost in my heart I have already dealt with. You may take it from me that it is with me a matter of life and death. If we Hindus and Musalmans mean to achieve a heart unity, without the slightest mental reservation on the part of either, we must first unite in the effort to be free from the shackles of this empire. If Pakistan after all is to be a portion of India, what objection can there be for Musalmans against joining this struggle for India's freedom? The Hindus and Musalmans must, therefore, unite in the first instance on the issue of fighting for freedom. Jinnah saheb thinks the war will last long. I do not agree with him. If war goes on for six months more, how shall we be able to save China?

I, therefore, want freedom immediately, this very night, before dawn, if it can be had. Freedom cannot now wait for the realization of communal unity. If that unity is not achieved, sacrifices necessary for it will have to be much greater than would have otherwise sufficed. But the congress must win freedom or be wiped out in the effort. And forget not that the freedom which the congress is struggling to achieve will not be for the congressmen alone but for all the forty crores of the Indian people. Congressmen must for ever remain humble servants of the people.

The Quaid-i-azam has said that the Muslim League is prepared to take over the rule from the Britishers if they are prepared to hand it over the Muslim Leaue, for the British took over the empire from the hands of the Muslims. This, however, will be Muslim Raj. The offer made by Maulana Saheb and by me does not imply establishment of Muslim Raj or Muslim domination.

The Congress does not believe in the domination of any group or any community. It believes in democracy which includes in its orbit Muslims, Hindus, Christians, Parsis, Jews—every one of the communities inhabiting this vast country. If Muslim Raj is inevitable, then let it be; but how can we give it the stamp of our assent? How can we agree to the domination of one community over the others?

Millions of Musalmans in this country come from Hindu stock. How can their homeland be any other than India? My eldest son embraced Islam some years back. What would his home land be—Porbandar or the Punjab? I ask the Musalmans : "If India is not your homeland, what other country do you belong to? In what separate homeland would you put my son who embraced Islam?" His mother wrote him a letter after his conversion, asking him if he had on embracing Islam given up drinking which Islam forbids to its followers. To those who gloated over the conversion, she wrote to say: "I do not mind his becoming a Musalman so much as his drinking. Will you as pious Musalmans, tolerate his drinking even after his conversion? He has reduced himself to the state of a rake by drinking. If you are going to make a man of him again, his conversion will have been turned to good account. You will, therefore, please see that he as a Musalman abjures wine and woman. If that change does not come about, his conversion goes in vain and our non-co-operation with him will have to continue."

India is without doubt the homeland of all the Musalmans inhabiting this country. Every Musalmans should therefore co-operate in the fight for India's freedom. The Congress does not belong to any one class or community; it belongs to the whole nation. It is open to Musalmans to take possession of the Congress. They can, if they like, swamp the Congress by their numbers, and can steer it along the course which appeals to them. The Congress is fighting not on behalf of the Hindus but on behalf of the whole nation, including the minorities. It would hurt me to hear of a single instance of a Musalman being killed by a Congressman. In the coming revolution, Congressmen will sacrifice their lives in order to protect the Musalmans against a Hindu's attack and vice versa. It is a part of their creed, and is one of the essentials of non-violence. You will be expected on occasions like these not to lose your heads. Every Congressman, whether a Hindu or a Musalman owes this duty to the organization to which he belongs. The Musalman who will act in this manner will render a service to Islam. Mutual trust is essential for success in the final nation-wide struggle that is to come.

I have said that much greater sacrifice will have to be made this time in the wake of our struggle because of the opposition from the Muslim League and from Englishmen. You have seen the secret circular issued by Sir Frederick Puckle. It is a suicidal course that he has taken. It contains an open incitement to organizations which crop up like mushrooms to combine to fight the Congress. We have thus to deal with an empire whose ways are crooked. Ours is a straight path which we can tread even with our eyes closed. That is the beauty of Satyagraha.

In Satyagraha, there is no place for fraud or falsehood or any kind of untruth. Fraud and untruth today are stalking the world. I cannot be helpless witness to such a situation. I have travelled all over India as perhaps nobody in the present age has. The voiceless millions of the land saw in me their friend and representative, and I identified myself with them to an extent it was possible for a human being to do. I saw trust in their eyes, which I now want to turn to good account in fighting this empire upheld on untruth and violence. However gigantic the preparations that the empire has made, we must get out of its clutches. How can I remain silent at this supreme hour and hide my light under the bushel? Shall I ask the Japanese to tarry awhile? If today I sit quite and inactive, God will take me to task for not using up the treasure He had given me, in the midst of the conflagration that is enveloping the whole world. Had the condition been different, I should have asked you to wait yet awhile. But the situation now has become intolerable, and the Congress has no other course left for it.

Nevertheless the actual struggle does not commence this moment. You have only placed all your powers in my hands. I will now wait upon the Viceroy and plead with him for the acceptance of the Congress demand. That process is likely to take two or three weeks. What would you do in the meanwhile? What is the programme, for the interval, in which all can participate? As you know, the spinning wheel is the first thing that occurs to me. I made the same answer to the Maulana. He would have none of it, though he understood its import later. The fourteenfold constructive programme is, of course, there for you to carry out. What more should you do? I will tell you. Everyone of you should, from this moment onwards, consider yourself a free man or woman, and act as if you are free and are no longer under the heel of this imperialism.

It is not a make-believe that I am suggesting to you. It is the very essence of freedom. The bond of the slave is snapped the moment he considers himself to be a free being. He will plainly tell the master: "I was your bondslave till this moment, but I am a slave no longer. You may kill me if you like, but if you keep me alive, I wish to tell you that if you release me from the bondage, of your own accord, I will ask for nothing more from you. You used to feed and clothe me, though I could have provided food and clothing for myself by my labour. I hitherto depended on you instead of on God, for food and raiment. But God has now inspired me with an urge for freedom and I am today a free man, and will no longer depend on you."

You make take it from me that I am not going to strike a bargain with the Viceroy for ministries and the like. I am not going to be satisfied with anything short of complete freedom. May be, he will propose the abolition of salt tax, the drink evil, etc. But I will say, "Nothing less than freedom."

Here is a mantra,1 a short one, that I give you. You may imprint it on your hearts and let every breath of yours give expression to it. The mantra is : 'Do or Die'. We shall either free India or die in the attempt; we shall not live to see the perpetuation of our slavery. Every true Congressman or woman will join the struggle with an inflexible determination not to remain alive to see the country in bondage and slavery. Let that be your pledge. Keep jails out of your consideration. If the Government keep me free, I will spare you to the trouble of filling the jails. I will not put on the Government the strain of maintaining a large number of prisoners at a time, when it is in trouble. Let every man and woman live every moment of his or her life hereafter in the consciousness that he or she eats or lives for achieving freedom and will die, if need be, to attain that goal. Take a pledge, with God and your own conscience as witness, that you will no longer rest till freedom is achieved and will be prepared to lay down your lives in the attempt to achieve it. He who loses his life will gain it; he who will seek to save it shall lose it. Freedom is not for the coward or the fainthearted.

A word to the journalists; I congratulate you on the support you have hitherto given to the national demand. I know the restrictions and handicaps under which you have to labour. But I would now ask you to snap the chains that bind you. It should be the proud privilege of the newspapers to lead and set an example in laying down one's life for freedom. You have the pen which the Government can't suppress I know you have large properties in the form of printing presses, etc., and you would be afraid lest the Government should attach them. I do not ask you to invite an attachment of the printing press voluntarily. For myself, I would not suppress my pen, even if the press was to be attached. As you know my press was attached in the past and returned later on. But I do not ask from you that final sacrifice. I suggest a middle way. You should now wind up your standing committee, and you may declare that you will give up writing under the present restrictions and take up the pen only when India has won her freedom. You may tell Sir Frederick Puckle that he can't expect from you a command performance, that his press notes are full of untruth, and that you will refuse to publish them. You will openly declare that you are wholeheartedly with the Congress. If you do this, you will have changed the atmosphere before the fight actually begins.

From the Princes I ask with all respect due to them a very small thing. I am a well-wisher of the Princes. I was born in a State. My grandfather refused to salute with his right hand any Prince other than his own. But he did not say to the Prince, as I feel he ought to have said, that even his own master could not compel him, his minister, to act against his conscience. I have eaten the Prince's salt and I would not be false to it. As a faithful servant, it is my duty to warn the Princes that if they will act while I am still alive, the

Princes may come to occupy an honourable place in free India. In Jawaharlal's scheme of free India, no privileges or the privileged classes have a place. Jawaharlal considers all property to be State-owned. He wants planned economy. He wants to reconstruct India according to plan. He likes to fly; I do not. I have kept a place for the Princes and the Zamindars in India that I envisage. I would ask the Princes in all humility to enjoy through renunciation. The Princes may renounce ownership over their properties and become their trustees in the true sense of the term. I visualize God in the assemblage of people. The Princes may say to their people: "You are the owners and masters of the State and we are your servants." I would ask the Princes to become servants of the people and render to them an account of their own services. The empire too bestows power on the Princes, but they should prefer to derive power from their own people; and if they want to indulge in some innocent pleasures, they may seek do so as servants of the people. I do not want the Princes to live as paupers. But I would ask them: "Do you want to remain slaves for all time? Why should you, instead of paying homage to a foreign power, not accept this sovereignty of your own people?" You may write to the Political Department: "The people are now awake. How are we to withstand an avalanche before which even the large empires are crumbling? We, therefore, shall belong to the people from today onwards. We shall sink or swim with them." Believe me, there is nothing unconstitutional in the course I am suggesting. There are, so far as I know no treaties enabling the empire to coerce the Princes. The people of the States will also declare that though they are the Princes' subjects, they are part of the Indian nation and that they will accept the leadership of the Princes, if the latter cast their lot with the people but not otherwise. If this declaration enrages the Princes and they choose to kill the people, the latter will meet death bravely and unflinchingly, but will not go back on their word.

Nothing, however, should be done secretly. This is an open rebellion. In this struggle secrecy is a sin. A free man would not engage in a secret movement. It is likely that when you gain freedom you will have a C.I.D. of your own, in spite of my advice to the contrary. But in the present struggle, we have to work openly and to receive bullets on our chest, without taking to heels.

I have a word to say to Government servants also. They may not, if they like, resign their posts yet. The late Justice Ranade did not resign his post, but he openly declared that he belonged to the Congress. He said to the Government that though he was a judge, he was a Congressman and would openly attend the sessions of the Congress, but that at the same time he would not let his political views warp his impartiality on the bench. He held Social Reform Conference in the very Pandal3 of the Congress. I would ask all the Government servants to follow in the footsteps of Ranade and to declare their allegiance to the Congress as an answer to the secret circular issued by Sir Frederick Puckle.

This is all that I ask of you just now. I will now write to the Viceroy. You will be able to read the correspondence not just now but when I publish it with the Viceroy's consent. But you are free to aver that you support the demand to be put forth in my letter. A judge came to me and said: "We get secret circulars from high quarters. What are we to do?" I replied, "If I were in your place, I would ignore the circulars. You may openly say to the government: 'I have received your secret circular. I am, however, with the Congress. Though I serve the Government for my livelihood, I am not going to obey these secret circulars or to employ underhand methods."

Soldiers too are covered by the present programme. I do not ask them just now to resign their posts and to leave the army. The soldiers come to me, Jawaharlal and the Maulana and say: "We are wholly with you. We are tired of the Government tyranny." To these soldiers I would say: You may say to the Government, "Our hearts are with the Congress. We are not going to leave our posts. We will serve you so long as we receive your salaries. We will obey your just orders, but will refuse to fire on our own people."

To those who lack the courage to do this much I have nothing to say. They will go their own way. But if you can do this much, you may take it from me that the whole atmosphere will be electrified. Let the Government then shower bombs, if they like. But no power on the earth will then be able to keep you in bondage any longer.

If the students want to join the struggle only to go back to their studies after a while, I would not invite them to it. For the present, however, till the time that I frame a programme for the struggle, I would ask the students to say to their professors: "We belong to the Congress. Do you belong to congress, you need not vacate your posts. You will remain at your posts but teach us and lead us unto freedom." In all fights for freedom, the world over, the students have made very large contributions.

If in the interval that is left to us before the actual fight begins, you do even the little I have suggested to you, you will have changed the atmosphere and will have prepared the ground for the next step.

There is much I should yet like to say. But my heart is heavy. I have already taken up much of your time. I have yet to say a few words in English also. I thank you for the patience and attention with which you have listened to me even at this late hour. It is just what true soldiers would do. For the last twenty-two years, I have controlled my speech and pen and have stored up my energy. He is a true Brahmachari4 who does not fritter away his energy. He will, therefore, always control his speech. That has been my conscious effort all these years. But today the occasion has come when I had to unburden my heart before you. I have done so, even though it meant putting a strain on your patience; and I do not regret having done it. I have given you my message and through you I have delivered it to the whole of India.

[The following is the concluding portion of Gandhiji's speech before the A.I.C.C. at Bombay on 8-8-'42 which was delivered in English:]

I have taken such an inordinately long time over pouring out, what was agitating my soul, to those whom I had just now the privilege of serving. I have been called their leader or, in the military language, their commander. But I do not look at my position in that light. I have no weapon but love to wield my authority over any one. I do sport a stick which you can break into bits without the slightest exertion. It is simply my staff with the help of which I walk. Such a cripple is not elated, when he has been called upon to bear the greatest burden. You can share that burden only when I appear before you not as your commander but as a humble servant. And he who serves best is the chief among equals.

Therefore, I was bound to share with you such thoughts as were welling up in my breast and tell you, in as summary a manner as I can, what I expect you to do as the first step.

Let me tell you at the outset that the real struggle does not commence today. I have yet to go through much ceremonial as I always do. The burden, I confess, would be almost unbearable. I have to continue to reason in those circles with whom I have lost my credit and who have no trust left in me. I know that in the course of the last few weeks I have forfeited my credit with a large number of friends, so much so, that they have begun to doubt not only my wisdom but even my honesty. Now I hold my wisdom in not such a treasure which I cannot afford to lose; but my honesty is a precious treasure to me and I can ill-afford to lose it. I seem however to have lost it for the time being.

Friend of the Empire

Such occasions arise in the life of the man who is pure seeker after truth and who would seek to serve the humanity and his country to the best of his lights without fear or hypocrisy. For the last fifty years I have known no other way, I have been a humble servant of humanity and have rendered on more than one occasion such service as I could to the empire, and here let me say without fear of challenge that throughout my career never have asked for any personal favour. I have enjoyed the privilege of friendship as I enjoy it today with Lord Linlithgow. It is a friendship which has outgrown official relationship. Whether Lord Linlithgow will bear me out, I do not know, but there is a personal bond between him and myself. He introduced me to his daughter. His son-in law, the A.D.C. was drawn towards me. He fell in love with Mahadev more than with me and Lady Anna and he came to me. She is an obedient and favorite daughter. I take interest in their welfare. I take the liberty to give out these personal and sacred tit-bits only to give you an earnest of the personal bond which exists between us; and yet let me declare here that that personal bond will never interfere with the stubborn struggle on which, if it falls to my lot, I may have to launch against Lord Linlithgow, as the representative of the Empire. I will have to resist the might of that Empire with the might of the dumb millions with no limit but of non-violence as policy confined to this struggle. It is a terrible job to have to offer resistance to a Viceroy with whom I enjoy such relations. He has more than once trusted my word, often about my people. I would love to repeat that experiment, as it stands to his credit. I mention this with great pride and pleasure. I mention it as an earnest of my desire to be true to the empire when the Empire forfeited my trust and the Englishman who was its Viceroy came to know it.

Charlie Andrews

Then there is the sacred memory of Charlie Andrews which wells up within me. At this moment the spirit of Andrews hovers me. For me he sums up the brightest traditions of English culture. I enjoyed his confidence. There were no secrets between us. We exchanged our hearts every day. Whatever was in his heart, he would blurt out without the slightest hesitation or reservation. It is true he was a friend of Gurude-4 but he looked upon Gurudev with awe. He had that peculiar humility. But with me he became the closest friend. Years ago he came to me with a note of introduction from Gokhale. Pearson and he were the first rank specimens of Englishjman. I know that his spirit is listening to me.

Voice of Conscience

With all this background, I want to declare to the world, although I may have forfeited the regard of many friends in the West and I must bow my head low; but even for their friendship or love I must not suppress the voice of conscience the promptings of my inner basic nature today. There is something within me impelling me to cry out my agony. I have known humanity. I have studied something of psychology. Such a man knows exactly what it is. I do not mind how you describe it. That voice within tells me, "You have to stand against the whole world although you may have to stand alone. You have to stare in the face the whole world although the world may look at you with bloodshot eyes. Do not fear. Trust the little voice residing within your hearts." It says: "Forsake friends, wife and all; but testify to that for which you have lived and for which you have to die." I want to live my full span of life. And for me I put my span of life at 120 years. By that time India will be free, the world will be free.

Real Freedom

Let me tell you too that I do not regard England or for that matter America as free countries. They are free after their own fashion, free to hold in bondage coloured races of the earth. Are England and America fighting for the liberty of these races today? If not, do not ask me to wait until after the war. You shall not limit my concept of freedom. The English and American teachers, their history, their magnificent poetry have not said that you shall not broaden the interpretation of freedom. And according to my interpretation of that freedom I am constrained to say they are strangers to that freedom which their teachers and poets have described. If they will know the real freedom they should come to India. They have come not with pride or arrogance but in the spirit of real earnest seekers of truth. It is a fundamental truth which India has been experimenting with for 22 years.

Congress and Non-violence

Unconsciously from its very foundations long ago the congress has been building on non-violence known as constitutional methods. Dadabhai and Pherozeshah who had held the congress India in the palm of their hands became rebels. They were lovers of the Congress. They were its masters. But above all they were real servants. They never countenanced murder, secrecy and the like. I confess there are many black sheep amongst us Congressmen. But I trust the whole of India today to launch upon a non-violent struggle. I trust because of my nature to rely upon the innate goodness of human nature which perceives the truth and prevails during the crisis as if by instinct. But even if I am deceived in this I shall not swerve. I shall not flinch. From its very inception the Congress based its policy on peaceful methods, including Swaraj and the subsequent generations' added non-violence. When Dadabhai entered the British Parliament, Salisbury dubbed him as a black man; but the English people defeated Salisbury and Dadabhai went to the Parliament by their vote. India was delirious with joy. These things however India has outgrown.

I will go Ahead

It is, however, with all these things as the black ground

that I want Englishmen, Europeans and all the United Nations to examine in their hearts what crime had India committed in demanding Independence. I ask, is it right for you to distrust such an organization with all its blackground, tradition and record of over half a century and misrepresent its endeavours before all the world by every means at your command? It is right that by hook or by crook, aided by the foreign press, aided by the President of the U.S.A., or even by the Generalissimo of China who has yet to win his laurels, you should present India's struggle in shocking caricature? I have known him through Madame Shek who was my interpreter; and though he seemed inscrutable to me, not so Madame Shek; and he allowed me to read his mind through her. There is a chorus of disapproval and righteous protest all over the world against us. They say we are erring, the move is inopportune. I had great regard for British diplomacy which has enabled them to hold the Empire so long. Now it stinks in my nostrils, and others have studied that diplomacy and are putting it into practice. They may succeed in getting, through these methods, world opinion on their side for a time; but India will speak against all the organized propaganda. I will speak against it. Even if all the United Nations opposed me, even if the whole of India forsakes me, I will say, "You are wrong. India will wrench with non-violence her liberty from unwilling hands." I will go ahead not for India's sake alone, but for the sake of the world. Even if my eyes close before there is freedom, non-violence will not end. They will be dealing a mortal blow to China and to Russia if they oppose the freedom of non-violent India which is pleading with bended knees for the fulfillment of debt long overdue. Does a creditor ever go to the debtor like that? And even when, India is met with such angry opposition, she says, "We won't hit below the belt, we have learnt sufficient gentlemanliness. We are pledged non-violence." I have been the author of non-embarrassment policy of the Congress and yet today you find me talking this strong language. I say it is consistent talking this strong language. If a man holds me by the neck and wants to drown me, may I not struggle to free myself directly? There is no inconsistency in our position today.

Appeal to United Nations

There are representatives of the foreign press assembled here today. Through them I wish to say to the world that the United Powers who somehow or other say that they have need for India, have the opportunity now to declare India free and prove their bona fides. If they miss it, they will be missing the opportunity of their lifetime, and history will record that they did not discharge their obligations to India in time, and lost the battle. I want the blessings of the whole world so that I may succeed with them. I do not want the united Powers to go beyond their obvious limitations. I do not want them to accept nonviolence and disarm today. There is a fundamental difference between fascism and this imperialism which I am fighting. Do the British get from India all they want? What they get today is from India which they hold in bondage. Think what difference it would make if India was to participate as a free ally. That freedom, if it is to come, must come today. It will have no taste left in it if today come today. It will have no taste left in it if today you who have the power to help cannot exercise it. If you can exercise it, under the glow of freedom what seems impossible, today will become possible tomorrow. If India feels that freedom, she will command that freedom for China. The road for running to Russia's help will be open. The Englishmen did not die in Malaya or on Burma soil. What shall I go, and where shall I take the forty crores of India? How is this vast mass of humanity to be aglow in the cause of world deliverance, unless and until it has touched and felt freedom. Today they have no touch of life left. It has been crushed out of them. If luster is to be put into their eyes, freedom has to come not tomorrow, but today.

Do or Die

I have pledged the Congress and the Congress will do or die.

□

Indian Economic Liberalisation*

—Manmohan Singh

Sir, I rise to present the budget for 1991-92. As I rise, I am overpowered by a strange feeling of loneliness. I miss a handsome, smiling, face listening intently to the Budget Speech. Shri Rajiv Gandhi is no more. But his dream lives on; his dream of ushering India into the twenty-first century; his dream of a strong, united, technologically sophisticated but humane India. I dedicate this budget to his inspiring memory.

The new Government, which assumed office barely a month ago, inherited an economy in deep crisis. The balance of payments situation is precarious. International confidence in our economy was strong until November 1989 when our Party was in office. However, due to the combined impact of political instability witnessed thereafter, the accentuation of fiscal imbalances and the Gulf crisis, there was a great weakening of international confidence. There has been a sharp decline in capital inflows through commercial borrowing and non-resident deposits. As a result, despite large borrowings from the International Monetary Fund in July 1990 and January 1991, there was a sharp reduction in our foreign exchange reserves. We have been at the edge of a precipice since December 1990 and more so since April 1991. The foreign exchange crisis constitutes a serious threat to the

* *Budget 1991-92 Speech, as Minister af Finance (Government of India), Loksabha, Parliament House, New Delhi, 24th July, 1991*

sustainability of growth processes and orderly implementation of our development programmes. Due to the combination of unfavourable internal and external factors, the inflationary pressures on the price level have increased very substantially since mid-1990. The people of India have to face double digit inflation which hurts most the poorer sections of our society. In sum, the crisis in the economy is both acute and deep. We have not experienced anything similar in the history of independent India.

The origins of the problem are directly traceable to large and persistent macro-economic imbalances and the low productivity of investment, in particular the poor rates of return on past investments. There has been an unsustainable increase in Government expenditure. Budgetary subsidies, with questionable social and economic impact, have been allowed to grow to an alarming extent. The tax system still has many loopholes. It lacks transparency so that it is not easy to assess the social and economic impact of various concessions built into its structure. The public sector has not been managed in a manner so as to generate large investible surpluses. The excessive and often indiscriminate protection provided to industry has weakened the incentive to develop a vibrant export sector. It has also accentuated disparities in income and wealth. It has worked to the disadvantage of the rural economy. The increasing difference between the income and expenditure of the Government has led to a widening of the gap between the income and expenditure of the economy as a whole. This is reflected in growing current account deficits in the balance of payments.

The crisis of the fiscal system is a cause for serious concern. The fiscal deficit of the Central Government, which measures the difference between revenue receipts and total expenditure, is estimated at more than 8 percent of GDP in 1990-91, as compared with 6 percent at the beginning of the 1980s and 4 percent in the mid-1970s. This fiscal deficit had to be met by borrowing. As a result, internal public debt of the Central Government has accumulated to about 55 percent of Gross Domestic Product (GDP). The burden of servicing this debt has now become onerous. Interest payments alone are about 4 percent of GDP and constitute almost 20 percent of the total expenditure of the Central Government. Without decisive action now, the situation will move beyond the possibility of corrective action.

The balance of payments situation is most difficult. The current account deficit, which was about 2 percent of GDP for several years, is estimated to be more than 2.5 percent of GDP in 1990-91. These persistent deficits, which were inevitably financed by borrowings from abroad, have led to a continuous increase in external debt which, including non-resident Indian (NRI) deposits, is estimated at 23 percent of GDP at the end of 1990-91. Consequently, the debt service burden is estimated at about 21 percent of current account receipts in 1990-91. These strains were stretched to a breaking point on account of the Gulf crisis last year. The balance of payments has lurched from one liquidity crisis to another since December 1990. The current level of foreign exchange reserves, in the range of Rs. 2500 crores, would suffice to finance imports for a mere fortnight.

The price situation, which is of immediate concern to the vast mass of our people, poses a serious problem as inflation has reached a double digit level. During the fiscal year ending 31st March 1991 the wholesale price index registered an increase of 12.1 percent, while the consumer price index registered an increase of 13.6 percent. The major worrisome feature of the inflation in 1990-91 was that it was concentrated in essential commodities. The prices of these commodities rose inspite of the three good monsoons in a row and hence the three successive bumper harvests. Inflation hurts everybody, more so the poorer segments of our population whose incomes are not indexed.

There is no time to lose. Neither the Government nor the economy can live beyond its means year after year. The room for maneuver, to live on borrowed money or time, does not exist any more. Any further postponement of macroeconomic adjustment, long overdue, would mean that the balance of payments situation, now exceedingly difficult, would become unmanageable and inflation, already high, would exceed limits of tolerance. For improving the management of the economy, the starting point, and indeed the centre-piece of our strategy, should be a credible fiscal adjustment and macro-economic stabilisation during the current financial year, to be followed by continued fiscal consolidation thereafter. This process would, inevitably, need at least three years, if not longer, to complete. But there can be no adjustment without pain. The people must be prepared to make necessary sacrifices to preserve our economic independence and restore the health of our economy.

In the macro-management of the economy, over the medium-term, it should be our objective to progressively reduce the fiscal deficit of the Central Government, to move towards a significant reduction of the revenue deficit, and to reduce the current account deficit in the balance of payments. It is only such prudent management that would enable us to curb the exponential growth in internal and external debt and limit the burden on debt servicing, for the Government and the country, to manageable levels. Indeed, we must make a conscious effort to reduce the internal debt of the Government and the external debt of the nation, so that we rely more and more on our own resources to finance the process of development. During the period of transition, it shall be our endeavour to minimise the burden of adjustment on the poor. We are committed to adjustment with a human face. It will also be our endeavour that the adjustment process does not adversely affect the underlying growth impulses in our economy. We do not have time to postpone adjustment and stabilisation. We must act fast and act boldly. If we do not introduce the needed correctives, the existing situation can only retard growth, induce recession and fuel inflation, which would hurt the economy further and impose a far greater burden on the poor.

Macro-economic stabilisation and fiscal adjustment alone cannot suffice. They must be supported by essential reforms in economic policy and economic management, as an integral part of the adjustment process, reforms which would help to eliminate waste and inefficiency and impart a new element of dynamism to growth processes in our economy. The thrust of the reform process would be to increase the efficiency and international competitiveness of industrial production, to utilise for this purpose foreign investment and foreign technology to a much greater degree than we have done in the past, to increase the productivity of investment, to ensure that India's financial sector is rapidly modernised, and to improve the performance of the public sector, so that the key sectors of our economy are enabled to attain an adequate technological and competitive edge in a fast changing global economy. I am confident that, after a successful implementation of stabilisation measures and the essential structural and policy reforms, our economy would return to a path of a high sustained growth with reasonable price stability and greater social equity.

Thanks to the efforts of Pandit Jawaharlal Nehru, Indira Gandhi and Rajiv Gandhi, we have developed a well diversified industrial structure. This constitutes a great asset as we begin to implement various structural reforms. However, barriers to entry and limits on growth in the size of firms, have often led to a proliferation of licensing and an increase in the degree of monopoly. This has put shackles on segments of Indian industry and made them serve the interests of producers but not pay adequate attention to the interests of consumers. There has been inadequate emphasis on reduction of costs, upgradation of technology and improvement of quality standards. It is essential to increase the degree of competition between firms in the domestic market so that there are adequate incentives for raising productivity, improving efficiency and reducing costs. In the pursuit of this objective, we have announced important changes in industrial policy which will bring about a significant measure of deregulation in the domestic sector, consistent with our social objectives and the binding constraints on the balance of payments.

The policies for industrial development are intimately related to policies for trade. There can be no doubt that protection was essential in the initial phase of our industrial development, so that we could go through the learning period without disruption. The past four decades have witnessed import substitution which has not always been efficient and has some times been indiscriminate. The time has come to expose Indian industry to competition from abroad in a phased manner. As a first step in this direction, the Government has introduced changes in importexport policy, aimed at a reduction of import licensing, vigorous export promotion and optimal import compression. The exchange rate adjustments on 1st and 3rd July, 1991 and the enlargement and liberalisation of the replenishment licence system constitute the two major initial steps in the direction of trade policy reform. They represent the beginning of a transition from a regime of quantitative restrictions to a price based mechanism.

After four decades of planning for industrialisation, we have now reached a stage of development where we should welcome, rather than fear, foreign investment. Our entrepreneurs are second to none. Our industry has come of age. Direct foreign investment would provide access to capital, technology and markets. It would expose our industrial sector to competition from abroad in a phased manner. Cost, efficiency, and quality would begin to receive the attention they deserve. We have, therefore, decided to liberalise the policy regime for direct foreign investment in the following manner. First, direct foreign investment in specified high priority industries, with a raised limit for foreign equity at 51 percent, would be given prompt approval, if equity inflows are sufficient to finance the import of capital goods at the stage of investment and if dividends are balanced by export earnings over a period of time. Second, foreign equity upto 51 percent would be allowed for trading companies primarily engaged in export activities. Third, a special board would be constituted to negotiate with a number of large international firms and approve direct foreign investment in selected areas; this would be a special regime to attract substantial investment that would provide access to high technology and to world markets.

For the founding fathers of our Republic, a public sector that would be vibrant, modern, competitive and capable of generating large surpluses was a vital element in the strategy of development. The public sector has made an important contribution to the diversification of our industrial economy. But there have been a number of shortcomings. In particular, the public sector has not been able to generate internal surpluses on a large enough scale. At this critical juncture, it has therefore become necessary to take effective measures so as to make the public sector an engine of growth rather than an absorber of national savings without adequate return. This has been widely accepted, but thought and action in this regard are still far apart. To bridge this gap, the portfolio of public sector investments would be reviewed so as to concentrate the future operations of the public sector in areas that are strategic for the nation, require high technology for the economy, and are essential for the infrastructure. In order to raise resources, encourage wider public participation and promote greater accountability, upto 20 percent of government equity in selected public sector undertakings would be offered to mutual funds and investment institutions in the public sector, as also to workers in these firms. Public enterprises which are chronically sick and which cannot be turned around, will be referred to the Board for Industrial and Financial Reconstruction (BIFR), or to a similar high-powered body to be set up, for the formulation of revival or rehabilitation schemes; a social security mechanism will be created to fully protect the interests of the workers likely to be affected by the rehabilitation packages of the BIFR. Autonomy in management, and corresponding accountability, would be provided through a system of memorandums of understanding between the Government and public sector enterprises.

Our banking system and financial institutions are at the very core of the financial infrastructure in the economy. The widening and deepening of our financial system have helped the spread of institutional finance over a vast area and have contributed significantly to the augmentation of our savings rate, particularly financial savings. This has been a most commendable achievement, but our financial system has developed certain rigidities and some weaknesses which we must address now. The objective of reform in the financial sector would be to preserve its basic role as an essential adjunct to economic growth and competitive efficiency, while improving the health of its institutions. In this task, it is essential to ensure capital adequacy, introduce prudential norms and improve profitability of our commercial banks and financial institutions. There are no magic solutions. These are complex issues which need careful consideration. Therefore, I propose to appoint a high level committee to consider all relevant aspects of structure, organisation, functions and procedures of the financial system. This committee would advise the Government on appropriate measures that would be needed to enhance the viability and health of our financial sector so that it can better serve the needs of the economy without any sacrifice of the canons and principles of a sound financial system.

Interest rates are a crucial dimension of the financial sector. In the formative stages of the development of credit markets, administrative intervention in interest rates is both necessary and desirable. At the present stage of our development, however, we can begin to relax the degree of intervention and impart a greater flexibility to the structure of interest rates. The Reserve Bank of India has already taken an important step in this direction, by stipulating a floor rate of interest and providing freedom to commercial banks to charge interest rates above the floor level based on their perceptions of risk. The Government proposes to extend a similar freedom to term-lending financial institutions, where the minimum interest rate would be 15 percent, and these institutions would be free to charge an interest rate in accordance with their perception of the creditworthiness of borrowers. With the exception of tax free bonds for the public sector, it is also proposed to remove all restrictions on interest rates for debentures, both convertible and nonconvertible, floated in the capital market. The interest rate on such debt instruments will hereafter be governed by market forces, and the credit rating of such debt instruments will become an integral part of the capital market process. In consultation with the Reserve Bank of India, the Government would continue to watch the structure of interest rates. Recently, interest rates payable on bank deposits have been increased. I now propose to do a similar thing with regard to interest rates payable under the small savings schemes. Our ultimate objective is to achieve a significant reduction both in the nominal and the real interest rates. This would be possible if the rate of inflation is reduced significantly over the next three years.

While presenting the budget for 1987-88, our former Prime Minister the late Shri Rajiv Gandhi had assured this House that for a healthy growth of capital markets, for protecting the rights of investors and for preventing trading malpractices the Government would set up a separate Board for the regulation and orderly functioning of the Stock Exchanges and the securities industry. Although the Board was set up, legislation to give the Board adequate powers was unfortunately not enacted. This shall now be done forthwith and full statutory powers will be given to the Securities and Exchange Board of India for administering the relevant provisions of the Securities Contracts (Regulation) Act and the Companies Act. Transferring these powers from the Controller of Capital Issues and the Government to an independent body would enable it to effectively regulate, promote and monitor the working of the Stock Exchanges in the country. A comprehensive package of reforms relating to trading on the Stock Exchanges, including a system of national clearing and settlement and setting up of a central depository, is also under active consideration.

In regard to Mutual Funds, some progress towards evolving a competitive structure has been made in the last few years with encouraging results. For many investors, mutual funds are a more suitable investment vehicle than direct ownership of shares. The Government is already giving tax incentives for equity-linked savings schemes offered through mutual funds. The Government has now decided to further promote the development of mutual funds by throwing the field open to the private sector and joint sector mutual funds. In order to safeguard the interests of the investing public, and to encourage a healthy growth of the capital markets, a comprehensive set of guidelines is being evolved for the operation of all mutual funds. Consideration will also be given to enactment of legislation for this purpose.

A comprehensive review of policies and procedures bearing on Non-resident Indian investments shall be carried out and further relaxations made in order to remove all procedural difficulties and impediments to the setting up of industrial and other ventures by Non-resident Indians. New sectors shall be made available to NRIs for investment on a non-repatriation basis, including housing, infrastructure and real estate development. For example, at present, NRIs of foreign nationality are required to obtain specific permission under section 31 of the Foreign Exchange Regulation Act (FERA) to acquire residential property. It is now proposed to provide general exemption from this provision to such persons. However, rental income and proceeds from the sale of such housing will be non-repatriable. For facilitating interaction with the Central Government, to serve as a focal point for NRIs, Government proposes to establish a Chief Commissioner for Non-resident Indians. I would urge State Governments, also, to establish an office of a Commissioner for Non-Resident Indians.

I believe that the time has come to evolve a more transparent institutional mechanism for fixing tariffs and domestic prices in sectors where there might still be need for protecting Indian industry against foreign competition and for the determination of administered prices, particularly in the area of public utilities. For this purpose, we propose to restructure the Bureau of Industrial Costs and Prices and to transform it into a Tariff Commission.

As we enter the last decade of the twentieth century, India stands at the cross-roads. The decisions we take and do not take, at this juncture, will determine the shape of things to come for quite some time. It should come as no surprise, therefore, that an intense debate rages throughout the country as to the path we should adopt. In a democratic society it could not be otherwise. What can we learn from this debate? The most important thing that comes out clearly is that we cannot realise our goal of establishing a just society, if we abandon the planning process. But India's future development depends crucially on how well the planning process is adapted to the needs of a fast changing situation. I believe that without an intelligent and systematic coordinated resource use in some major sectors of our economy, development will be lopsided. It will violate deeply cherished values of equity and it will keep India well below its social, intellectual and moral potential. But our planning processes must be sensitive to the needs of a dynamic economy. Over centralisation and excessive bureaucratisation of economic processes have proved to be counter productive. We need to expand the scope and the area for the operation of market forces. A reformed price system can be a superior instrument of resource allocation than quantitative controls. But markets can only serve those who are part of the market system. A vast number of people in our country live on the edges of a subsistence economy. We need credible programmes of direct government intervention focussing on the needs of these people. We have the responsibility to provide them with quality social services such as education, health, safe drinking water and roads. In the same way, the development of capital and technology intensive sectors, characterised by long gestation periods, such as transport and communications and energy will need to be planned with much greater care than ever before. The control of land and water degradation, which threatens the livelihood of millions of poor people in this country, will also require effective Government leadership and action.

The challenge that we are facing is without precedent. In its initial stages, the Industrial Revolution in the western world concentrated on the creation of wealth, unmindful of the social misery and inequity which characterised this process. The democratisation of the polity came much later. The socialist experiment in charting a new path for accelerated industrial transformation of an underdeveloped economy and polity did achieve considerable success in developing technological and military capabilities, accumulation of capital for rapid industrial growth and human resources development, in countries such as the USSR. But recent developments have shown that this approach too suffered from major weaknesses, particularly in its allocative efficiency, in the management of technical change, control of environmental degradation and in harnessing the vast latent energy and talents of individuals. In India, we launched an experiment under the leadership of Pandit Jawaharlal Nehru, an experiment which sought to unite the strengths and merits of different approaches to accelerated development of our backward economy. We have achieved considerable success in the field of development, modernisation and greater social equity. However, we are yet far from realising our full potential in all these areas. We have to accomplish the unfinished task, while remaining steadfast in our allegiance to the values of a democratic system.

At the same time, we must restore to the creation of wealth

its proper place in the development process. For, without it, we cannot remove the stigma of abject poverty, ignorance and disease. But we cannot accept social misery and inequity as unavoidable in the process of creation of wealth. The basic challenge of our times is to ensure that wealth creation is not only tempered by equity and justice but is harnessed to the goal of removal of poverty and development for all.

For the creation of wealth, we must encourage accumulation of capital. This will inevitably mean a regime of austerity. We have also to remove the stumbling blocks from the path of those who are creating wealth. At the same time, we have to develop a new attitude towards wealth. In the ultimate analysis, all wealth is a social product. Those who create it and own it, have to hold it as a trust and use it in the interest of the society, and particularly of those who are under-privileged and without means. Years ago, Gandhiji expounded the philosophy of trusteeship. This philosophy should be our guiding star. The austerity that Gandhiji practised and preached is a necessary condition for accelerated economic development in the framework of a democratic polity. The trusteeship that he prescribed for the owners of wealth captured the idea of social responsibility.

In highlighting the significance of reform, my purpose is not to give a fillip to mindless and heartless consumerism we have borrowed from the affluent societies of the West. My objection to the consumerist phenomenon is two-fold. First, we cannot afford it. In a society where we lack drinking water, education, health, shelter and other basic necessities, it would be tragic if our productive resources were to be devoted largely to the satisfaction of the needs of a small minority. The country's needs for water, for drinking and for irrigation, rural roads, good urban infrastructure, and massive investments in primary education and basic health services for the poor are so great as to effectively preclude encouragement to consumerist behaviour imitative of advanced industrial societies. Our approach to development has to combine efficiency with austerity. Austerity not in the sense of negation of life or a dry, arid creed that casts a baleful eye on joy and laughter. To my mind, austerity is a way of holding our society together in pursuit of the noble goal of banishing poverty, hunger and disease from this ancient land of ours.

Let me now turn to fiscal adjustment during the current financial year. The beginning of any attempt to correct the fiscal imbalance in the economy must be directed at a reduction in expenditure and an increase in income of the Government, so as to reduce the fiscal deficit. In the medium-term, however, our fiscal regime would be sustainable only if revenue receipts not only meet revenue expenditure but also provide a sufficient surplus to finance capital expenditure that does not yield direct economic returns as such, as in defence or in social sectors. Even this would not suffice if investment expenditures in the budget do not earn an adequate return. The elimination of structural imbalances in our fiscal system would require a reduction both in the fiscal deficit and in the revenue deficit as a proportion of GDP. The Union Budget for 1991-92 is an essential first step in this direction.

It must be recognised that the necessary reduction in the fiscal deficit, during 1991-92, is a stupendous task. The interim budget presented to Parliament in March 1991 estimated the fiscal deficit at Rs. 38475 crores. But this estimate was based on assumptions about certain decisions that have not been implemented. The postponement of the regular budget has made a formidable task even more difficult because almost four months of the financial year have now elapsed without any effort at fiscal correction. Indeed, past trends in revenue and expenditure suggest that, without any corrective action on our part, the fiscal deficit during 1991-92 could well reach a level of more than Rs. 52000 crores. The difference between the two sets of figures provides the real measure of the fiscal correction needed during the current financial year.

According to provisional data available, the more narrowly defined budget deficit, as measured by borrowing through short term Treasury bills, for 1990-91 at Rs. 11430 crores was significantly higher than the revised estimate of Rs. 10722 crores, largely due to a substantial revenue shortfall, particularly in corporation tax revenues. This highlights the handicap with which we begin. Let me now present the scenario for 1991-92.

The increasing levels of non-plan expenditure, financed through borrowing, have led to an exponential increase in interest payments by the Government. The revised estimates for interest payments during 1990-91, at Rs. 21850 crores, accounted for as much as 38 percent of the net revenue receipts of the Central Government. Interest payments during 1991-92, estimated at Rs. 27450 crores, constitute 42 percent of the net revenue receipts of the Central Government at existing rates of taxation. If the present trends continue without any correction, then interest payments could well account for more than 50 percent of the net revenue receipts of the Central Government by 1994-95. These magnitudes and proportions only serve to highlight the gravity of the situation and the acute need for a substantial adjustment in non-plan expenditure over the next three years.

The revised estimate for total non-plan expenditure in 1990-91 was Rs. 76761 crores. In the normal course, even with the strictest scrutiny but in the absence of specific measures for reducing expenditure, this non-plan expenditure would have increased to a level of Rs. 89000 crores in 1991-92. Any attempt at fiscal correction during the current financial year can be meaningful only if nonplan expenditure is reduced by at least 10 percent from the level it would otherwise reach.

The single largest component of non-plan expenditure is interest payments. Even if there is a drastic reduction in Government borrowing during this year, interest payments would still be in the range of Rs. 35000 crores in the next financial year. The exponential increase in interest payments can be brought under some measure of control, by 1994-95, only through a strict discipline on government borrowing for a period of three years.

The second largest component of non-plan expenditure is the allocation for the defence sector, where the provision in the revised estimates for 1990-91 was Rs. 15750 crores. No attempt at containing non-plan expenditure can succeed if defence is to be excluded. At the same time, it is absolutely essential to ensure that a quest for economy in expenditure does not in any way compromise national security. We must, therefore, seek to limit expenditure without diluting the efficiency and effectiveness of our defence services. Keeping in view all these considerations, it has been decided to provide an outlay of Rs. 16350 crores for defence in the current year.

Honourable Members are aware that export subsidies have been abolished with effect from 3rd July, 1991. The export sector is being adequately compensated through the adjustments in the exchange rate and the expansion of the Replenishment Licensing System which were implemented at the beginning of July. Consequently, it is now necessary to provide only Rs. 1224 crores for export subsidies in the budget estimates for 1991-92, as compared with the earlier estimated requirement of Rs. 4200 crores, yielding a saving of as much as Rs. 3000 crores during the remainder of this year.

In so far as fertiliser subsidies are concerned, with effect from this evening, low analysis fertilisers such as calcium ammonium nitrate, ammonium chloride, ammonium sulphate and sulphate of potash will be free from price and movement controls. There will be an increase of 40 percent, on an average, in the price of all other fertilisers. In addition, in respect of single super phosphate, there shall also be a ceiling on the subsidy per tonne payable to producers so as to move towards total deregulation in the next few years; this should act as an incentive for all high cost units to reduce costs and improve efficiency. The necessary notifications in this regard are being issued separately, today, by the Ministry of Agriculture.

The economic rationale for an increase in the price of fertilisers is so obvious that it does not need to be stated. Nevertheless, I would like to draw the attention of the House to the fact that there has been no increase in fertiliser prices since July 1981. In these ten years, there has been a continuous increase in the procurement prices of paddy and wheat, as also in the market prices of other crops, received by the agricultural sector. Farmers will be compensated for the proposed increase in the price of fertilisers through suitable increases in procurement prices.

We would continue to ensure that 50 percent of the plan resources are invested in the agricultural and rural sector. The provision for the continuing schemes for assistance to small and marginal farmers for dug wells and shallow tubewells would be doubled. The ceilings on assistance in difficult areas, where the watertable is very low, would be removed. Similarly, the provision for assistance for fresh water and brackish water aqua-culture and for oilseeds and pulses production would be substantially stepped up. New schemes are being drawn up to popularise small tractors and matching implements, drip and sprinkler irrigation in areas where water is scarce, and quality seeds in low yield areas. Another new scheme that would be implemented from this kharif season is for providing assistance to State Governments, cooperative societies, and farmers' groups to provide blanket plant protection cover on payment of a small fee in large identified areas under cotton or pulses. It would also be possible to demonstrate the advantages of integrated pest management in these areas. In order to safeguard any possible loss in production because of increase in fertiliser prices, and any decline in consumption, the credit structure would be strengthened to ensure adequate availability of credit particularly to the small and marginal farmers. Simultaneously, soil testing laboratories and farm advisory services all over the country would be strengthened to ensure efficient use of fertilisers and popularise the use of bio-fertilisers. We would also identify a few irrigation projects that can be completed in this very year and ensure that these are provided the necessary funds. The other new initiatives, also, would not be starved of funds. As far as possible our emphasis will be on provision of quality services to our farmers and not on hand outs and subsidies.

The sugar subsidy which is costing the exchequer about Rs. 350 crores per annum is indeed an aberration, which crept into the system from January 1990, when the increase in the levy price paid to producers was not matched by a simultaneous increase in the issue price for consumers in the public distribution system. Small quantities of sugar are made available, mostly in metropolitan and urban areas, under the public distribution system at Rs. 5.25 per kg. whereas the price that most people pay in the market is around Rs. 10 per kg. Government has decided that this subsidy should be abolished forthwith. Consequently, the issue price of sugar under the public distribution system will be increased by 85 paise per kg. to Rs. 6.10 per kg. with effect from this evening. At the same time, the public distribution system is being strengthened to serve more effectively the weaker sections of our population, particularly the rural poor, having special regard to their basic needs for foodgrains such as rice and wheat. The provision for food subsidies in the current year is being stepped up to Rs. 2600 crores, as compared with only Rs. 1800 crores provided in the interim budget and Rs. 2450 crores provided in the revised estimates for 1990-91.

As a result of the exchange rate adjustments, at the beginning of July 1991, there would be an increase in the rupee value of the import bill for crude oil and petroleum products. It is, therefore, necessary to raise the prices of petroleum products for domestic consumers. This would also help to restrain the growth in consumption of petroleum products. The price of motor spirit, domestic LPG and aviation turbine fuel for domestic use would be raised by 20 percent. The prices of other petroleum products, excluding diesel and kerosene for non-industrial use, would be raised by 10 percent. The price of kerosene, for non-industrial use, would be reduced by 10 percent which means a 50 percent roll-back in relation to the increase in the price that came into effect on 15th October, 1990. Even in a most difficult financial situation, this is being done to protect the poor for whom kerosene is an essential source of light and fuel. While there will be no increase in the price of diesel, I would endeavour to protect the interests of the farmers who use diesel. For this purpose, I shall hold discussions with State Governments. The proposed increases in the prices of petroleum products will come into effect from this evening, and the necessary notification in this regard is being separately issued by the Ministry of Petroleum and Natural Gas.

For non-plan expenditure, excluding interest payments, defence, and major subsidies, the total provision in the budget estimates for 1991-92 is Rs. 28,073 crores, reflecting a reduction of Rs. 1538 crores compared with the provision in the revised estimates for 1990-91. If we take into account the fact that no separate provision has been made for the payment of additional installments of dearness allowance by Ministries and Departments in the current year, the total reduction in such other non-plan expenditure will exceed Rs. 2000 crores. In recent years, it has been the usual practice to issue instructions to Ministries that such additional requirements should be accommodated within the approved budget estimates. This has invariably resulted in some programmes on the plan side being deprived of adequate resources. It is my intention to effect maximum possible economies in the non-plan administrative expenditure. Therefore, all Ministries have been requested to prioritise their activities so that those which figure at the bottom of the list can be abridged, while those which have outlived their utility can be abandoned altogether. This exercise has already been initiated by all Ministries and is expected to be completed by the end of August 1991. With this approach, the proposed reduction in other non-plan expenditure, which I am promising to the House, would be brought about in a more meaningful manner without leading to a reduction in the provision for plan programmes.

There is one large component of non-plan expenditure that is a burden on the exchequer. I refer to the Government's obligation under the Rural Debt Relief Scheme. Unfortunately, there was a gross under-estimation of the total fiscal liability under this scheme which was introduced last year. In addition to the sum of Rs. 1500 crores provided in the revised estimates for last year, we have to provide Rs. 1500 crores in the current year. But this is not all. We may need a similar provision in the next year.

As a result of the major adjustments in the sphere of expenditure, which I have outlined in my speech, the budget estimate for total non-plan expenditure in 1991-92 stands at Rs. 79,697 crores. It is simply not possible to reduce interest payments in the short term. The provision for non-plan expenditure, excluding interest payments, in the current year represents a reduction of 4.9 percent compared with the provisions in the revised estimates for 1990-91, and a reduction of almost 15 percent in relation to what we would have had to provide this year, but for the specific correctives that are being introduced. We have, thus, more than fulfilled our commitment to reduce non-plan expenditure by 10 percent, which was stated in our Party's election manifesto.

The election manifesto of the Congress Party identifies areas for special emphasis in our strategy of development. These include a substantial augmentation of employment programmes, the construction of dwelling units for the weaker sections of our society, an expansion of the programme for irrigation wells and so on. This would need a change in, and some reorientation of, plan priorities, with a shift towards investment in rural areas and expenditure on programmes designed for the benefit of the poor. Our strategy would, of course, be reflected in the Eighth Five Year Plan, which would now commence on 1st April, 1992. It shall be our endeavour to finalise the Eighth Plan document by the end of this calendar year, so that the annual plans for 1992-93, as well as the budgets of the Centre and the States for that year, reflect the changed priorities.

As the Vote on Account had earlier been taken only to cover the expenditure in the first four months, this budget has had to be presented before the end of July, 1991. We have, thus, not had the time to re-orient the Annual Plan for 1991-92 to reflect fully our various concerns. Moreover, this year's annual plan has had to be situated in the context of the massive fiscal correction that we have to put through. In fact, it was first felt that it would be necessary to effect a substantial reduction in budget support for the Central Plan and Central Plan assistance for the States. I am, however, happy to inform the House that with the substantial cuts proposed in non-plan expenditure, it is now possible to protect the flow of Central Plan assistance to States and Union Territories at the level of Rs. 14710 crores, as reflected in the interim budget for 1991-92. The Central plan outlay would, however, show a modest increase at Rs. 42969 crores with a budget support of Rs. 19015 crores.

I am aware that in basic infrastructure areas such as power, coal, communications and petroleum, we will have to set our sights much higher. In the present situation, characterised by an acute shortage of foreign exchange, it is, in particular, imperative to augment substantially the domestic production of coal, crude oil, natural gas and electrical energy. Efforts will also have to be made on a crash basis for promoting utmost economy in use of energy through more efficient technologies in industry, agriculture, transport and domestic sectors. The transmission and distribution line losses would also have to be brought down drastically from the present high level of 22 percent. We shall address ourselves to all these tasks once we are through with taking stock of the situation. It is my earnest hope that, by then, thanks to the fiscal corrections now being put through, the resources position would improve, giving us the necessary flexibility. For the present, it has been my endeavour to maintain essential investment through appropriate support for the Central Plan despite binding constraints on the exchequer.

In preparing this budget, I have sought to ensure that the burden of fiscal adjustment does not fall on State Governments. It is my belief that the Central Government must set an example by introducing fiscal correctives, and it is my hope that the State Governments would move in this direction as soon as possible. In particular, I would urge them to ensure prompt payment of dues owed by the State Electricity Boards to the National Thermal Power Corporation, Coal India and the Indian Railways. We cannot allow State level enterprises to become an instrument of unplanned and unauthorised transfer of resources from the Centre to the States. That is neither fair nor equitable. This practice must, therefore, stop forthwith. Simultaneously, State Governments must take effective steps to improve their fiscal performance and streamline the working of their public enterprises. They should not expect me to reward fiscal laxity by permitting them to have recourse to unauthorised overdrafts from the Reserve Bank of India. I want them to be an active partner in the accomplishment of the difficult task of restoring the fiscal health of the country.

The process of macro-economic adjustment, which is being initiated with this budget, would take at least three years to complete. This adjustment must have a human face. Therefore, during the period of transition, we shall do everything that is possible to minimise the burden of adjustment on the poor. To some extent, the poor would be protected as the rate of inflation comes down. We shall make determined efforts to control inflation and the price rise. The fiscal strategy of this budget will make a major contribution in this regard. In addition, it will be our endeavour to provide protection to the poor in the form of enhanced outlays in the social sectors. Employment creation and poverty eradication in rural India will continue to receive the highest priority. At the same time, Government is committed to the uplift of the weakest and the most vulnerable sections of our society.

The plan outlay for the Ministry of Rural Development is being stepped up from Rs. 3115 crores last year to Rs. 3508 crores this year. Within this, the outlay for employment programmes alone is Rs. 2100 crores. The various employment oriented programmes should make it possible to provide nearly 900 million mandays of employment. If, this year, we are not aiming at the target of 1000 million man-days mentioned in our manifesto it is because the season when there is maximum need for such employment is already over. The Eighth Plan now under formulation will spell out a comprehensive strategy and programmes to achieve the long term employment objectives, and targets such as those relating to the construction of irrigation wells, urban night shelters and Sulabh Shauchalayas, dwelling units for poor backward classes, scheduled castes and scheduled tribes in the villages, mentioned in our Party's election manifesto.

The provision for the rural water supply scheme is being stepped up to Rs. 758 crores, so as to make it possible to set aside Rs. 250 crores for ensuring complete coverage of 'no-source problem villages' by the end of 1992-93. The earlier expectation was that these villages would be covered only by the end of the Eighth Plan period. The late Shri Rajiv Gandhi had attached great priority to this programme and had set up a Technology Mission for this purpose. The programme, which is now being named after Shri Rajiv Gandhi, will be accelerated. We will ensure that resource constraints do not stand in the way of achieving the target.

It is a matter of deep concern that we have still not been able to put an end to the dehumanising practice of manual removal of night-soil. The allocation for this programme has in the past been less than adequate. It has now been decided not only to accelerate the programme for the conversion of dry-latrines but also to step up the allocation for the rehabilitation and retraining of scavengers. Towards this end, the allocation for the programme has been increased by Rs. 25 crores and more funds, to the extent necessary, would be provided during the course of the year. Inclusive of the increased provision for this programme, the total outlay for the programmes of the Ministry of Welfare, which is concerned with the welfare of scheduled castes, scheduled tribes and other weaker sections of our society, is being stepped up from Rs. 364 crores in 1990-91 to Rs. 479 crores in 1991-92. The outlay for the Department of Women and Child Development, dealing with perhaps the two most disadvantaged segments of our population among the poor, is being enhanced from Rs. 330 crores last year to Rs. 400 crores this year. For Health and Family Welfare, I am providing a plan outlay of Rs. 1051 crores in 1991-92 as compared with Rs. 950 crores in 1990-91.

The allocation of resources for investment in social sectors is of utmost importance for the development of human resources. In this context, there is no need for me to emphasise the importance of education, in particular, elementary education. Our efforts to restructure and revitalise the economy can succeed only if we invest in our people. Particular attention has to be paid to the provision of quality education to children belonging to the scheduled castes, the scheduled tribes and other economically and socially backward classes. Children who belong to the category of first generation learners need special care and attention. If the equality of opportunity is to acquire its true significance, quality education must not remain the exclusive privilege of the children of the rich. The Government is committed to ensure that, whatever be our constraints, the programmes of education will not be allowed to suffer for want of financial support. Every effort will be made to ensure that the constitutional directive of providing free and compulsory education upto the age of 14 years becomes a reality before we enter the twenty first century. In the sphere of higher education and technical education, more resources are needed for modernisation and diversification, but, at the same time, an effort must be made to secure optimum results from the existing investments in these institutions. The requirements of education are vast and we shall have to seek innovative ways of finding resources. Budget support provided by the Central Government and the State Governments are an important source, but cannot continue to remain the only source. I am raising the allocation for education from Rs. 865 crores in 1990-91 to Rs. 977 crores in 1991-92. This allocation is not commensurate with my deep commitment to education and the priority that is attached by the Government to the education sector. I would have liked to do more but we must learn to live with the constraints on the exchequer.

We have the third largest number of scientists and technologists in the world. Yet, technology development in our country has not been commensurate either with this number or the investments that we have been making in the science and technology sectors in our successive Five Year Plans. This gap would have to be bridged through a suitable reorientation of the Science and Technology Policy and the way paved for relating science and technology more intimately to the requirements of our development, as well as for better upgradation, absorption, adaptation and assimilation of new technologies. This task has become imperative as we prepare ourselves to be an internationally competitive economy.

Government has also decided on five new initiatives. The first of these is the establishment of a Corporation for the welfare of the backward classes, a task that the Congress manifesto has included for completion within the first 100 days. The details of the structure and duties of this Corporation are being finalised by the Ministry of Welfare and will be announced before the end of this session.

Government will establish a National Renewal Fund, with a substantial corpus. The main objective of this fund will be to ensure that the cost of technical change and modernisation of the productive apparatus does not devolve on the workers. This fund will provide a social safety net which will protect the workers from the adverse consequences of the technological transformation. I visualise that this fund will grow in size and State governments will also contribute to its corpus in due course. The fund will not merely provide ameliorative measures for the workers affected in the course of technical change but, more importantly, provide retraining to them, so that they are in a position to remain active productive partners in the process of modernisation.

The third programme relates to the care of children of families affected by communal riots. These riots are a blot on the fair name of our Republic. Our Government is deeply committed to the protection and advancement of all religious and cultural minorities. Effective steps will be taken to prevent recurrence of communal violence. At present there are arrangements to provide compensation of varying amounts to the riot affected families. But experience shows that such compensation does not always protect the interests of children of the riot affected families. These children then grow up into disgruntled and disorganised adulthood. They become an easy prey to the propaganda of anti-social elements and the obscurantist, fundamentalist forces of reaction. To protect the interests of such children, look after their welfare and in particular their education, the Government proposes to set up a National Foundation for Communal Harmony as an autonomous non-government organisation. The Central Government will make a significant contribution to this Foundation in 1991-92. I invite State Governments as well as industry and trade to make liberal contributions for this noble cause.

The fourth programme is to promote national integration through a scheme for enabling the youth of each part of the country to go in large numbers and work for short periods in other parts of the country, giving them an opportunity to mingle with people of different regions and languages. A similar step in this direction has already been taken in the Navodaya Vidyalaya Programme. This will now be strengthened and extended on a national basis.

The fifth programme relates to promotion of South-South cooperation. We as a nation are committed to close cooperation and sharing our development experience, knowledge and expertise with non-aligned and other developing countries. There is immense scope for Indian scientists, technicians, engineers, teachers, social workers and farmers to contribute to the development process in the third world. Our experience in various fields can be of great relevance and assistance to many developing countries particularly in Asia and Africa. It is our hope to arrange for participation of at least 500 volunteers in different nation building tasks, in selected developing countries, in the coming year. The details of the programmes will be worked out and announced before the end of the session.

The House will also be pleased to learn that in acceptance of a recommendation of the South Commission presided over by Dr. Julius K. Nyerere, the former President of Tanzania, we propose to set up a National Committee under the chairmanship of the Prime Minister for mobilising public opinion in support of South-South cooperation and for advising our Government for devising concrete action programmes in this regard. This committee will consist of representatives of Government, trade and industry, trade unions and members of learned professions.

The Rajiv Gandhi Foundation has been established to perpetuate the memory of the great leader and to promote the ideals and objectives for which he lived and laid down his life. This Foundation, among other things, will lay particular emphasis on research and action programmes relating to the application of science and technology for development, propagation of literacy, the protection of the environment, the promotion of communal harmony and national integration, the uplift of the under-privileged, women and handicapped persons, administrative reforms and India's role in the global economy. As a homage to the late Shri Rajiv Gandhi and in support of the laudable objectives of the Foundation, Government has decided to contribute Rs. 100 crores to the Foundation at the rate of Rs. 20 crores per annum for a period of five years beginning from the current year.

Pending determination of the exact amounts that will be necessary for each of these new initiatives, a lump sum provision of Rs. 250 crores has been included in the plan outlay of the Ministry of Finance.

The budget provision for total expenditure in 1991-92 is Rs. 113422 crores, of which Rs. 79697 crores is non-plan expenditure and Rs. 33725 crores is plan expenditure.

In the sphere of revenue receipts, at the existing rates of taxation, gross tax revenues are estimated at Rs. 66218 crores during the current financial year, compared to Rs. 58916 crores in the revised estimates of last year. The payment to States of their share of taxes is placed at Rs. 15643 crores in 1991-92 as against Rs. 14535 crores in the revised estimates for 1990-91. Thus, the net revenue receipts of the Centre, including non-tax revenue, are estimated to increase from Rs. 57381 crores in 1990-91 to Rs. 65524 crores in 1991-92.

In the sphere of capital receipts, market borrowings are placed at Rs. 7500 crores this year, which is lower than Rs. 8000 crores last year; this is part of a conscious effort to reduce the borrowing of the Central Government which would, in keeping with the past trends, have gone up by about 10 percent. The net collections on account of small savings are estimated at Rs. 8000 crores, which are at the same level as the revised estimates for last year. In addition, the Government has decided to disinvest upto 20 percent of its equity in selected public sector undertakings in favour of mutual funds and investment institutions in the public sector, which is expected to yield Rs. 2500 crores to the exchequer during the current financial year. This disinvestment would broad-base the equity, improve the management and enhance the availability of resources in these enterprises.

The net receipts on account of external assistance, excluding grants, are placed at Rs. 3510 crores compared to Rs. 3984 crores in the revised estimates of 1990-91. While the increase in the loan repayment and interest payment liabilities, as a consequence of the recent exchange rate adjustments, is fully reflected in the budget estimates, the likely increase in the rupee value of external assistance following the exchange rate adjustments is still under assessment. To the extent that these receipts increase, there will also be a corresponding increase in expenditure when the assistance is passed on to the concerned projects or schemes for which such assistance is received. These changes, which will thus be budget deficit neutral, will be incorporated at the stage of revised estimates.

Taking into account other changes in receipts and expenditure, total receipts at the existing rates of taxation are estimated at Rs. 103698 crores, while total expenditure is estimated at Rs. 113422 crores. Therefore, without additional resource mobilisation, the budget deficit is estimated at Rs. 9724 crores, the revenue deficit at Rs. 15859 crores, and the fiscal deficit at Rs. 39732 crores.

Honourable Members would have observed that expenditure adjustment constitutes the core of the proposed fiscal correction during the current financial year. But the process of fiscal adjustment cannot be complete without revenue measures to increase the income of the Government. I now seek the indulgence of the House to present the reliefs, the incentives and the levies in the sphere of direct taxes.

The revenue from direct taxes, both as a proportion of GDP and as a percentage of total tax revenues, has registered a steady decline over time. This trend has to be reversed, so as to restore equity in, and balance to our fiscal system. Resources for development must be raised from those who have the capacity to pay. For this purpose, we must place greater emphasis on direct taxes. This calls for increased rates wherever necessary and a better tax compliance. At the same time, rationalisation of the system, which reduces the maximum marginal rate of tax, simplifies the procedures, reduces the plethora of concessions, and brings the average rates of income tax at various levels of income to more appropriate levels, is necessary. The time available before presenting the budget was simply not enough to formulate basic structural changes. Yet, I have made a conscious effort to move one step forward in this direction.

Nobody can deny the existence of large scale tax evasion, both in terms of income and in terms of wealth. Unless I find substantial improvement in tax compliance in the next few months, Government will have no choice but to take strong measures to make the tax evader pay a sufficiently high price for such delinquency. Before coming down heavily on tax evaders,

I would like to give them a last opportunity to come clean. The black money so mobilised will be utilised for the achievement of social objectives such as slum clearance and low cost housing for the rural poor.

I propose to institute a scheme, under which any person would be allowed to make a deposit with the National Housing Bank on or before close of business on 30th November, 1991. Thereupon, forty percent of such deposit would be deducted and set apart as a special levy, which would form the corpus of a fund in the National Housing Bank. This fund will be utilised for financing slum clearance and low cost housing for the poor, in accordance with guidelines and priorities laid down by the Government. The depositor would be allowed to draw the balance amount in one or more installments through account payee cheques for any stated purpose of his choice. There will be no lock-in period for this deposit. Persons making such deposits will not be required to disclose the source of funds from which the deposits are made. In other words, the monies deposited would be provided complete immunity from enquiry and investigation. The provisions of Direct Tax Laws would, however, apply to the net deposits after deduction of the special levy, from the date of the deposit. The levy itself would not be an allowable deduction in the computation of income of the person concerned. Necessary legislation in this regard will be introduced shortly, in this session of Parliament. The details of the scheme and its date of commencement will also be announced soon.

The Income-tax Act contains a provision under which tax payers can avail of the facility of waiver of penalty and interest on the amount disclosed once in a life-time. To those who have already availed of this facility, I propose to give just one more opportunity to disclose their unaccounted incomes. The Finance Bill contains a proposal for making suitable amendments to section 273A of the Incometax Act for this purpose.

The Settlement Commission was set up to provide an opportunity to assessees to declare their undisclosed income and wealth. Under the existing procedures, the Commissioner of Income Tax can, on certain grounds, objects to admission of an application by the Settlement Commission. This results in unnecessary delay. This provision is, therefore, being deleted. The Settlement Commission will, however, continue to call for and take into account the Commissioner's report, provided it is furnished within a period of six months.

Our election manifesto has promised that we will promote reinvestment of profits, by suitable tax exemptions, in areas where there is crying need for massive investment such as low and middle income group housing, highways, roads and bridges, non-conventional energy, school buildings and supply of drinking water. I, therefore, propose to make a provision in the Income-tax Act to provide deduction, in computing taxable profits of a taxpayer carrying on a business or profession, of the entire amount paid for financing projects or schemes promoting social and economic welfare. To ensure optimum use of scarce resources, I propose to set up a National Committee of eminent persons to identify areas requiring support and for recommending specific projects and schemes. A similar deduction will be allowed also in the case of taxpayers not carrying on any business or profession.

As a token of my commitment to education and research and in recognition of the significant role they have to play in our development process, I propose to extend certain tax concessions that will help in the funding of social science research and provide some incentive to authors and publishers.

At present, only taxpayers carrying on a business or profession get deduction for sums paid to any approved university, college or other institutions for research in social sciences related to the class of business carried on by them. I consider that there is a case for providing more tax incentives for social science research. I, therefore, propose to allow the same100 percent deduction in respect of sums paid for research in these areas whether related to business or not. I also propose to allow this deduction to taxpayers not carrying on any business or profession.

The role of books, particularly in the context of our National Literacy Mission as well as the National Education Policy cannot be overemphasized. To encourage publication of better and less expensive books and to give a fillip to the publishing industry, I propose to revive, with effect from the current accounting period, the deduction of twenty percent of profits from publication of books for a period of 5 years. To encourage the publication of quality text books in various Indian languages I also propose to revive the 25 percent deduction from professional income of authors of text books in Indian languages. This will also be available for a period of five years, beginning with the current income-earning period.

Offshore country funds are emerging as important channels for attracting foreign institutional investment particularly from non resident Indians. India made a beginning in this direction in 1989. Of late, however, there are signs of diminishing interest of foreign institutional investors in off-shore India country funds. The comparative national tax structure is one of the key factors affecting the direction of international financial flow. I, therefore, propose to substantially reduce the rate of tax on dividend income received by the off-shore funds from the units of UTI or other mutual funds and on long-term capital gains from such units. On dividend income the proposed rate of tax will be 10 percent as against the existing rate of 25 percent. On long-term capital gains, I propose to have the same rate of 10 percent as against the effective rate of about 45 percent at present.

In the light of our deep emotional involvement with the struggle of the Black majority in South Africa and as a further affirmation of our commitment to South-South cooperation, I propose that donations to the AFRICA FUND be entitled to 100 percent deduction under section 80G of the Income-tax Act.

The Government is committed to the welfare of our unfortunate handicapped citizens. In an effort to mitigate in some small measure their hardship, I propose to increase the deduction available under Section 80 U of the Income-tax Act in respect of totally blind or physically handicapped persons, from fifteen thousand rupees to twenty thousand rupees. The benefit of this tax concession is also proposed to be extended to partially blind persons.

Promotion of housing activity ranks high in Government's socioeconomic priorities. Towards this objective, I propose to extend the benefit of tax rebate under section 88 of the Income-tax Act also to contractual schemes floated by public housing corporations like HUDCO and State Housing Boards along the lines of the Home Loan Account Scheme of the National Housing Bank. Further, the tax rebate under section 88 will also be available in relation to installment/repayment of loans towards cost of land and also in cases where the house was purchased or constructed before 1st April, 1987.

Our software industry has made considerable progress in recent years. However, there is still a vast unexploited potential for growth. It is time we make all-out efforts to capture the overseas software market. With this objective, I propose to extend the tax concession under section 80HHC of the Income-tax Act to export of software. With this concession, the exports of this industry should register rapid growth.

I also propose to extend the concession under section 80HHC to the export of processed minerals.

I consider that scientific, technical and professional skills, knowledge and experience possessed by our professionals in various fields like architecture, accounting etc. have an increasing capacity to earn foreign exchange for the country. Many of them carry on their professions as individuals or partnership firms. To enable them to benefit from the tax concession available under section 80-O, I propose to extend, to the non-corporate assessees, the concession presently available only to the corporate sector.

In order to encourage development of tourist infrastructure in regions where such facilities are almost non-existent today, I propose to exempt from Expenditure Tax for a period of ten years expenditure incurred in new approved hotels set up in hilly and other remote areas. I also propose to allow to such hotels a deduction of 50 percent from their profits instead of the normal 30 percent under section 80-I, subject to certain conditions.

As a token of my appreciation of the role of a healthy capital market in the development of our economy, I propose to raise the basic deduction of Rs. 10,000 now available under section 48 of the Income-tax Act in respect of long-term capital gains to Rs. 15,000.

As indicated earlier, I wish to take some positive steps to reverse the trend of decline in the proportion of direct tax revenues to total revenues. I therefore propose to raise additional resources this year through a greater reliance on direct taxes. I now turn to my proposals for ensuring better tax compliance and moblising revenues through the imposition of additional taxes.

To enable the Government to identify income earners, most of whom would not otherwise declare their income or would not declare their full income, I propose to extend the scheme of tax deduction at source to cover new areas of payments in the nature of commissions, interest paid by banks on time deposits and withdrawals from the National Savings Scheme. To minimise the inconvenience for small depositors, tax will be deducted at source only in respect of payments in excess of Rs. 2500 per year. Those receiving payments in excess of the limit but not having taxable income will have the facility of collecting payment with no tax deduction by filing a declaration in the prescribed manner.

The present provision for offsetting short-term capital losses against income leads to tax avoidance. I, therefore, propose that any loss on transfer of a capital asset will be set off only against gain from transfer of another capital asset. This is only logical. It should also stop the practice of buying short-term capital losses being resorted to by some unscrupulous tax payers.

Over the years, those with an instinct for gambling have increasingly patronised the races. I propose to withdraw the income-tax exemption of Rs. 5000 in respect of earnings from races, including horse races. I am sure that persons who place bets will now also have the added pleasure of sharing their earnings from races with the Government.

Professor Kaldor once observed that no civilised society should have a maximum marginal rate of income tax higher than 45 percent. We are firmly committed to a tax system which is simple, credible, yet progressive, in which people realise that honesty is the best policy. I expect to make a beginning in this direction as soon as we can overcome the present fiscal difficulties. I am confident that this process can be completed before the end of the five year term of our Government. Tax payers can help to accelerate the process of tax reform if all of them resolve to pay their income-tax dues fully and promptly. In the midst of a fiscal crisis however, such a change is not feasible. We must wait for better times. The best I can do under the circumstances, is what I propose to do this year : keep the personal income-tax rate structure including the surcharge unchanged. That I have not added to the burden of the taxpayer is, in itself, a relief.

I have received several representations that wealth-tax rates need to be rationalised. I see considerable merit in these representations. However, taking into account the needs of revenue and also for want of time, I propose to make no change in the rates of wealth-tax.

For the purposes of levy of wealth-tax, the rules of valuation of assets aim at capturing their market value, or near about, as on the valuation date. I find that a distortion has crept into these rules. When an individual holds any asset in his name its valuation is at the market value. However, if a group of persons holds its assets through an investment company the taxable value of these assets gets reduced considerably because it is based on the book value and not on the market value. I, therefore, propose to remove this anomaly by providing that in valuing unquoted shares of an investment company, the break-up value of the share will be determined after revaluing the assets of the company at their market value.

I feel disappointed that the phenomenal growth in the output, value added and profits of the corporate sector, in recent years, has not been appropriately reflected in corporate tax collections. The experience of the preceding financial year, in particular, is a matter of serious concern. I am, therefore, raising the corporate tax rate for widely held companies, from 40 to 45 percent. A corresponding increase of 5 percentage points from 45 to 50 percent is being made in the corporate tax rate for closely held companies. I also propose to continue the existing surcharge of 15 percent.

The traditional distinction in corporate tax rates between trading companies and industrial companies has outlived its utility. I therefore propose to remove this distinction.

I recognise that in the medium term the rates and structure of corporate taxation have to be consistent with the needs of an economy aiming to become internationally competitive. I shall attend to this task as soon as we have overcome the present fiscal crisis.

As indicated earlier, I wish to take some positive steps to reverse the trend of decline in the proportion of direct tax revenues to total revenues. I therefore propose to raise additional resources this year through a greater reliance on direct taxes. I now turn to my proposals for ensuring better tax compliance and moblising revenues through the imposition of additional taxes.

To enable the Government to identify income earners, most of whom would not otherwise declare their income or would not declare their full income, I propose to extend the scheme of tax deduction at source to cover new areas of payments in the nature of commissions, interest paid by banks on time deposits and withdrawals from the National Savings Scheme. To minimise the inconvenience for small depositors, tax will be deducted at source only in respect of payments in excess of Rs. 2500 per year. Those receiving payments in excess of the limit but not having taxable income will have the facility of collecting payment with no tax deduction by filing a declaration in the prescribed manner.

The present provision for offsetting short-term capital losses against income leads to tax avoidance. I, therefore, propose that any loss on transfer of a capital asset will be set off only against gain from transfer of another capital asset. This is only logical. It should also stop the practice of buying short-term capital losses being resorted to by some unscrupulous tax payers.

Over the years, those with an instinct for gambling have increasingly patronised the races. I propose to withdraw the income-tax exemption of Rs. 5000 in respect of earnings from races, including horse races. I am sure that persons who place bets will now also have the added pleasure of sharing their earnings from races with the Government.

Professor Kaldor once observed that no civilised society should have a maximum marginal rate of income tax higher than 45 percent. We are firmly committed to a tax system which is simple, credible, yet progressive, in which people realise that honesty is the best policy. I expect to make a beginning in this direction as soon as we can overcome the present fiscal difficulties. I am confident that this process can be completed before the end of the five year term of our Government. Tax payers can help to accelerate the process of tax reform if all of them resolve to pay their income-tax dues fully and promptly. In the midst of a fiscal crisis however, such a change is not feasible. We must wait for better times. The best I can do under the circumstances, is what I propose to do this year : keep the personal income-tax rate structure including the surcharge unchanged. That I have not added to the burden of the taxpayer is, in itself, a relief.

I have received several representations that wealth-tax rates need to be rationalised. I see considerable merit in these representations. However, taking into account the needs of revenue and also for want of time, I propose to make no change in the rates of wealth-tax.

For the purposes of levy of wealth-tax, the rules of valuation of assets aim at capturing their market value, or near about, as on the valuation date. I find that a distortion has crept into these rules. When an individual holds any asset in his name its valuation is at the market value. However, if a group of persons holds its assets through an investment company the taxable value of these assets gets reduced considerably because it is based on the book value and not on the market value. I, therefore, propose to remove this anomaly by providing that in valuing unquoted shares of an investment company, the break-up value of the share will be determined after revaluing the assets of the company at their market value.

I feel disappointed that the phenomenal growth in the output, value added and profits of the corporate sector, in recent years, has not been appropriately reflected in corporate tax collections. The experience of the preceding financial year, in particular, is a matter of serious concern. I am, therefore, raising the corporate tax rate for widely held companies, from 40 to 45 percent. A corresponding increase of 5 percentage points from 45 to 50 percent is being made in the corporate tax rate for closely held companies. I also propose to continue the existing surcharge of 15 percent.

The traditional distinction in corporate tax rates between trading companies and industrial companies has outlived its utility. I therefore propose to remove this distinction.

I recognise that in the medium term the rates and structure of corporate taxation have to be consistent with the needs of an economy aiming to become internationally competitive. I shall attend to this task as soon as we have overcome the present fiscal crisis.

In our economy, labour is abundant and capital is scarce. These economic realities have to be reflected in our fiscal policy. Yet, over the years, the Indian economy has witnessed a disturbing shift towards greater capital intensity in production. This has led to distortion and avoidable hardship in cases where labour is replaced, or employment potential reduced, by resort to capital intensive methods of production, even in cases where such a shift is not justified on other economic and technical considerations. Fiscal incentives have been conducive to such a shift. While there can be no compromise with the imperatives of technological upgradation and continuous modernisation, the tendency towards excessive capital intensity in our industry must be checked.

The rates for depreciation prescribed in 1987, in relation to plant and machinery, are far too generous and provide much more than is needed to compensate for wear and tear. These rates of depreciation do not reflect the true economic life of business assets. An asset would be almost fully written off in six years at the present rate of 33.33 percent applicable to the bulk of plant and machinery. I think an eight year period would be more reasonable taking into account the pace of technological change in India, the true economic life of the business assets, and the need to discourage tax induced replacement of assets. Therefore, I propose to reduce the general rate of depreciation for machinery and plant from 33.33 percent to 25 percent. I also propose to reduce the rate of depreciation for aeroplanes, motor buses, motor taxis and some other equipments from 50 percent to 40 percent, which would mean almost complete recoupment of cost in six, instead of five years. However, to encourage use of energy saving devices and renewable energy devices, I propose to continue to provide 100 percent depreciation on such items of plant and machinery as also some others. Further, I also propose to restrict the rates of depreciation to 50 percent of the normal rates of depreciation in cases where the asset is used for less than 6 months in a year.

Tax support to special institutions may be necessary in their nascent stage. However, it should not be extended in perpetuity. Such institutions must strive to become self-reliant. The Industrial Development Bank of India (IDBI) has been enjoying complete tax exemption in respect of its income since its inception, unlike other public financial institutions. I propose to withdraw this tax exemption, which is no longer necessary.

In 1987, the Government had introduced a tax on ostentatious expenditure. It is in the form of a tax of 20 percent of expenditure incurred in hotels where the room rent exceeds Rs. 400 per day. I propose to extend the coverage of this tax to the expenditure incurred in restaurants providing superior facilities like airconditioning. This tax will be levied at the rate of 15 percent of such expenditure.

In view of the binding fiscal constraints and the need to mobilise resources, I propose to revive the interest-tax which was first introduced in 1974 and withdrawn in 1978, re-introduced in a modified form in 1980 and finally withdrawn in 1985. I am enlarging, slightly, the coverage of this tax. The new tax will be levied on the gross amount of interest received by all banks, financial institutions and nonbanking financial companies in the corporate sector on loans and advances made in India. These institutions would reimburse themselves by making necessary adjustments in the interest rates charged from borrowers. The proposed tax is expected to raise the cost of borrowing and yield revenue to the Government. It should, therefore, have both monetary and fiscal impact.

The proposed tax will be levied at the rate of 3 percent of the gross amount of interest earned by banks, financial institutions and financial companies on loans and advances made in India. Interest received on transactions between the various credit institutions will be exempted from the proposed tax. The proposed tax will operate prospectively and interest accruing before 1st October, 1991 will not be taxed. The proposed tax will be allowed as a deduction in computing taxable income under the Income-tax Act. 99. I do not propose to take up the time of the House with other minor changes in the Direct Tax Laws. 100. My proposals on direct taxes are estimated to yield a net revenue gain of Rs. 2139 crores. Of this amount, Rs. 97 crores will accrue to the States.

Honourable Members of the House are aware that the balance of payments situation is exceedingly difficult. In order to attract larger inflows of foreign exchange, I propose to introduce two schemes.

Under the first scheme, I propose that remittances in foreign exchange can be made to any person in India. Even if the remittance is received as a gift by the donee in India, it would not be subjected to gift tax. The source of funds out of which the remittances are made would not be subject to scrutiny under the Direct Tax Laws and Exchange Control Regulations. In other words, I propose to provide immunity for such remittances under these laws. The provisions of Direct Tax Laws will apply in the normal manner to the rupee proceeds of these remittances. The scheme will come into immediate effect and will be open until close of business on 30th November 1991. The details of the scheme will be announced by the Reserve Bank of India. I also propose to introduce the necessary legislation in this regard as early as possible before this House.

Under the second scheme, the State Bank of India would issue India Development Bonds to be denominated in US dollars. These bonds will be available for purchase by non-resident Indians and their overseas corporate bodies. There will be no ceiling for investment in these bonds which will have a maturity period of five years. The bonds will be fully transferable among non-resident Indians. Interest from the bonds will be exempt from income tax. The bond itself would also be exempt from wealth tax until maturity. For the non-resident holder, the face value of the bond and the interest thereon would be repatriable with exchange rate protection. The bonds can also be gifted to residents, who would be provided with amnesty and immunity, as in the first scheme for inward remittances. Such amnesty and immunity will be available only to the first resident donee. The gift would be exempt from gift tax. The resident donee bond holder would also be entitled to exchange rate protection, and the same exemption from income tax and wealth tax, until maturity, but the proceeds will be paid only in rupees in India and would not be remittable abroad. The bonds will be available for sale at all important branches of the State Bank of India abroad until close of business on 30th November, 1991. The details of the scheme will be announced by the Reserve Bank of India. I would also bring before this House the necessary legislation at the earliest.

In formulating my proposals on indirect taxes, I have kept in mind the wider context. In keeping with the promises made in the election manifesto of our party, we have also to ensure that prices of essential commodities and goods used by the common man are kept well under check. Conspicuous consumption must be curbed and the burden of taxation should be borne by the more affluent sections of the society. In the light of these imperatives, I have attempted to structure the proposals for customs and excise levies in a manner that indigenous industries are encouraged, and, at the same time, imports of items required for export production are not thwarted. In the long term, if revenues are buoyant and tax compliance improves, I expect to bring down the rates of customs and excise levies. Even now, some moderation in import duties is being attempted and a more broad-based effort may be attempted to streamline the structure and reduce the rates in the next budget. I have also tried to ensure that the proposed changes improve competitiveness of the industrial sector, particularly the export oriented industries.

It is my intention to rationalise and simplify the procedures, rules and regulations pertaining to indirect taxes, so that the delays in the system are eliminated, and the interface between the tax collector and the tax payer is reduced to the minimum. Given the paucity of time, it has not been possible to undertake such an exercise in this budget, but we should be able to formulate concrete measures soon as a part of structural reforms in the tax system.

Recent years have witnessed an excessive reliance on indirect taxes for additional resource mobilisation. This escalates costs, fuels inflation and is regressive in its impact. Therefore, I have not relied on indirect taxes as the major source of resource mobilisation. Indeed, the overall impact of my proposals for customs and excise levies is revenue negative in so far as the Central Government is concerned.

In the sphere of customs duties, over time, the objective of protection for infant industries and the need to raise revenues have led to a situation where import duties prescribed for certain items are inordinately high and, in several cases, more than 300 percent. As a measure of reform, I propose to reduce the ad valorem rate of basic plus auxiliary duties of customs to a maximum of 150 percent where it is more than that at present, thereby eliminating the tariff peaks above 150 percent. The only exceptions that would remain hereafter are imported alcoholic beverages and passenger baggage. The revenue loss on this account would be Rs. 132 crores in a full year.

In view of the deterioration in the fiscal situation last year, auxiliary duty of customs was increased across-the-board, with effect from 15th December, 1990, so as to mobilise additional resources. The increase was not quite rational and was asymmetric in its incidence. In some cases, the auxiliary duty went up by 20 percentage points - from 5 percent to 25 percent and from 30 percent to 50 percent, while in some others, by just 5 percentage points i. e., from 45 percent to 50 percent. This steep and uneven increase imposed a very high burden of duties on certain items, and also led to distortions in the overall rate structure. In order to remove the anomalies which had been created and rationalise rates of duties, I propose to give a duty relief of 10 percentage points to almost every item which suffered an increase of 20 percentage points. Moreover, on certain items, which are important from the point of view of environmental protection, export promotion, saving of foreign exchange and so on, I propose to roll back the rates to levels prevailing before 15th December, 1990. These items include waste paper, wood in the rough, jigat used in the manufacture of Agarbattis, ethylene, machinery for fuel injection equipment and certain items of machinery for printing and the newspape industry. These proposals will result in a revenue loss of Rs. 472 crores in a full year.

The prevailing rates of import duty on capital goods for general projects and machinery are, in general, high. While I cannot make a substantial reduction at this stage because of the revenue implications, which are considerable, I propose to reduce the level of duties from 85 percent to 80 percent. In tandem, the rate of duty on their components is also being reduced by 5 percentage points, from the existing levels of 65 or 70 percent. This proposal would mean a revenue loss of Rs. 167 crores in a full year.

A technology upgradation scheme was launched in 1987 by the late Shri Rajiv Gandhi. Under this scheme, fiscal relief was provided on import of capital equipment for the manufacture of power generation equipment, paper machinery, textile machinery and many others to promote domestic production of such machinery. The scheme has been instrumental in bringing about considerable improvement in the quality of machines produced in India. In order to give a further thrust to the scheme, I propose to expand the list of machinery items which will now attract a concessional duty of 50 percent. The revenue loss on this account is estimated at Rs. 5 crores in a full year.

We have recently taken several innovative steps to give an impetus to our exports. I would now like to outline some fiscal measures which will give a further boost to the export effort.

At present 100 percent export oriented undertakings or units in a free trade zone are allowed to divert a certain proportion of their production to the domestic market. However, the present stipulation, that excise duty payable must be equal to the import duty, has proved to be a deterrent. These units have to be fostered if they are to compete effectively in the international market; for this purpose they should not be prevented from creating a niche in the domestic market. Accordingly, I propose to reduce the excise duty on the goods, permitted to be sold in the domestic market under the scheme, to a level which would be equivalent to half the import duty leviable on such goods subject, inter alia, to the condition that the duty would not be less than the excise duty levied on similar items produced in the domestic tariff area.

To promote the growth of the marine products industry, fiscal relief has been given by way of customs duty concession on specified machinery items required by this industry. I propose to extend the duty concession to a few more items of such machinery. Out of my concern for the welfare of our fishermen, I also propose to fully exempt from excise duty specified yarns which are generally used for making fish-nets.

In order to encourage the growth of the finished leather industry and also as a measure of export promotion, I propose to reduce the basic and auxiliary duties of customs on polyurethane film and foil, as well as polyols from 150 percent to 40 percent. The duty on isocyanates is being reduced from 120 percent to 40 percent. The import duty on two important leather preservatives, namely TCMTB and PCMC, is being reduced from over 150 percent to 50 percent. These preservatives will replace certain other chemicals which are suspected to have carcinogenic effects. I also propose to extend the concessional duty, available at present to specified capital goods required by the leather industry to a few more items of such machinery.

Synthetic cubic zirconium, which is the closest imitation of natural diamonds, has the potential to provide job opportunities for a large number of artisans. The jewelry made therefrom also has a significant export potential. In order to encourage indigenous manufacture of cubic zirconium, I propose to reduce the import duty on the raw materials viz. zirconium oxide and yttrium oxide to the level of 40 percent from the present level of over 150 percent.

Our Government attaches the highest priority to agriculture. One of the promises made in our election manifesto is to provide a massive thrust to food processing and other agro-based industries, in an endeavour to increase the income of farmers, create employment opportunities, diversify the rural economy and foster rural industrialisation. As an important step in this direction, I propose to exempt agro-based products such as sauces, ketchup, butter, cheese, skimmed milk powder, vegetable oils, jams, jellies and juices, canned fruits and dried vegetables, certain soya products, starches and preparations of meat and fish from excise duties altogether. I am doing so to promote the diversification of our agricultural economy, to increase the farmers' share of the consumer's income spent on processed agricultural products, to promote rural industrialisation based on agricultural produce and to encourage the adoption of modern post-harvest technologies. The measures I have proposed, I expect, will also lead to some reduction in consumer prices of such products, providing relief to the harassed consumers in a period of rising prices. The revenue loss will be Rs. 84 crores but I am convinced that the overall gain to the economy will more than offset the loss to the exchequer.

As a relief to the agro-based jute industry, which has been beset with chronic problems, I propose to reduce the excise duty on products which contain a minimum of 35 percent of jute fibre from Rs. 660 to Rs. 330 per metric ton.

At present a number of specified bulk pesticides and pesticide intermediates enjoy concessional import and excise duties. I propose to extend the duty concession to a few more bulk pesticides and pesticide intermediates. The proposals involve a revenue loss of about Rs. 11 crores in a full year.

There is a money credit scheme in vogue to encourage the use of minor oils for the manufacture of soaps. I propose to increase the money credit of Rs. 640 per metric ton that is currently available in respect of rice bran oil used in the manufacture of soap to Rs. 1000 per metric ton. In addition, I propose to include some more non-conventional oils and solvent extracted oils in the scheme. This would also help in generating more employment for our tribal women. These proposals involve a revenue sacrifice of about Rs. 10 crores in a full year.

The MODVAT scheme was introduced in 1986 to minimise the cascading effect of indirect taxes. The scheme has been well received by the industry, and there have been persistent demands for its extension to other areas. I propose to reintroduce the scheme in respect of aerated waters, and also to extend it to cover man-made fibres and filament yarns in respect of their inputs. While extending the scheme to fibres and yarns, I do not propose to raise the duty on those fibres and yarns on which the duty was increased as recently as December, 1990. On other fibres and yarns, the duty rates have been adjusted with a view to retaining the collection of excise duties at the earlier level. But duties on polypropylene monofilament and multifilament yarns are being increased to raise additional revenue. In respect of aerated waters also, I do not propose any increase in duty. The proposals involve a revenue loss of about Rs. 230 crores in a full year. I expect that the benefit would be passed on to the consumers in the form of reduced prices.

I propose to rationalise the existing excise duty rates on polyester blended yarns. As an anti-evasion measure, I also propose to charge additional excise duty on cotton fabrics containing 40 percent or less of polyester at the same rates as applicable to cotton fabrics containing more than 40 percent of polyester. The proposals involve a revenue gain of about Rs. 23 crores in a full year.

In our effort to make essential drugs available to the people at affordable prices, I propose to fully exempt five specified anti-epileptic formulations from excise duty. At present, some drug intermediates and bulk drugs carry a concessional rate of import duty. I wish to extend the concession to a few more drug intermediates and bulk drugs, and grant concessions in excise duties to a few more drug intermediates.

In keeping with our commitment to give special priority to cottage, khadi and village industries, I propose to give some excise duty concessions to this sector. At present, footwear of value not exceeding Rs. 100 per pair manufactured in rural areas by registered co-operative societies, women's societies or by institutions recognised by KVIC, are fully exempted. I propose to raise the value limit of exemption to Rs. 150 per pair. Further, I propose to extend to synthetic detergents the benefit of full exemption from excise duty that is presently available to specified products when manufactured in rural areas by registered co-operative societies, women's societies, institutions recognised by KVIC etc.

I would now like to outline some of the steps that I propose for the protection of our environment and for ecological security. In view of our dwindling forest cover, we must conserve our scarce resources. Therefore, as I have stated earlier, the import duty on waste paper and wood in the rough is proposed to be rolled back to the rates that were prevailing before 15th December, 1990. I also propose to fully exempt from excise duty aluminium doors, windows and their frames so as to encourage the use of aluminium in the place of wood in construction activities. Fly ash is a pollutant. It can, however, be put to productive use in the manufacture of bricks and other construction materials. In order to encourage such use, I propose to fully exempt from excise duty various building components containing more than 25 percent of fly ash or phosphogypsum. I also propose to exempt phosphogypsum which is one of the bye-products of the fertilizer industry from excise duty to encourage its use by farmers.

Few would disagree that I am one of the most harassed Finance Ministers in recent times. To perform the onerous task before me, I need support from the Press. As a gesture of goodwill, I propose to exempt standard newsprint from import duty which is, at present, Rs. 450 per metric ton. I have already proposed to bring down the rates of import duty on certain specified machinery and equipment required by the printing and newspaper industry to the levels that were obtaining before 15th December 1990. The monetary limit of duty free import of photographic goods by accredited cameramen of the Press is being raised from the present level of Rs. 30,000 to Rs. 60,000. These proposals involve a revenue loss of over Rs. 9 crores in a full year.

Ever since my appointment as Finance Minister, I have had to spend long hours in office. This has quite naturally made my wife very unhappy. The House will agree that it is not good for the health of our economy if the Finance Minister of the country has strained relations with his own finance minister at home. I propose that the total exemption from payment of excise duty currently available to utensils made of aluminium, copper and stainless steel be extended to certain other household items particularly tiffin boxes.

The same consideration has induced me to propose a reduction in the excise duty on specified tableware produced by semi-automatic process from the present level of 20 percent to 15 percent. Mindful of the need for peace at home and also taking into account the labour intensive nature of the manufacture of glassware by the mouth blown process, I propose to reduce the excise duty on such glassware to 15 percent uniformly. Some people may not applaud my action. But I am sure most housewives harassed by the ever rising price level will appreciate my action.

In keeping with the commitment in our election manifesto, I shall make every effort to ensure that indirect taxes do not unduly add to the prices of essential commodities. Of the items listed in the manifesto, at present, there is no excise duty on salt, cycles, newsprint, post cards, inland letters and envelopes, and certain varieties of stoves. Cotton sarees and dhoties attract only additional excise duty in lieu of sales tax which accrues wholly to the State Governments. I have earlier proposed to fully exempt edible oils from excise duty. Electric bulbs of upto 60 watts, are already exempt from excise duty. I now propose to fully exempt electric bulbs, of higher wattage, which presently attract a duty of Re. 1 per bulb, from the payment of excise duty. Energy efficient chulhas, too, would be exempted from excise duty. I also propose to reduce the excise duty on two wheelers of engine capacity exceeding 50 cc but not exceeding 75 cc from 20 percent to 15 percent.

I recognise that the tax reliefs I have given, by themselves, constitute only a small step towards the realisation of the objective mentioned in our manifesto in regard to prices of essential commodities. In pursuit of this objective, I propose to invite the representatives of industry and trade to sit together with our Government to work out modalities as to how best we can contribute to the realisation of the price objectives listed in our election manifesto, for the benefit of the common man.

In order to promote tourism which is an important means of earning foreign exchange, I propose to reduce the import duty on adventure sports equipment from rates ranging from about 100 to 300 percent to 40 percent.

In keeping with the recent exchange rate adjustments of the rupee, I propose to raise the baggage allowances including duty free limits for bona fide gifts suitably; for instance the general duty free allowance for personal baggage is being raised from Rs. 2000 to Rs. 2400.

Let me now turn to the major proposals for additional revenue mobilisation. 133. At present special excise duty is being levied at the rate of 5 percent of the basic excise duty. I propose to raise it to 10 percent. Since the increase is only a percentage of the basic excise duty, the impact of the additional levy would be minimal on prices. For instance, in respect of any article on which the basic excise duty is say, 20 percent, the increase would be only 1 percent of the value. Tea, coffee, sugar, kerosene, matches, and vanaspati, being items of mass consumption, would remain exempt from special excise duty. In addition, I am ensuring that the increase in special excise duty will not apply to diesel and two wheelers. The proposal involves a revenue gain of Rs. 1010 crores in a full year, a substantial portion of which will accrue to the States.

One of the promises made in our election manifesto is to evolve policies and measures to curb conspicuous consumption. In pursuance of this, I propose to increase the excise duty rates on refrigerators, air-conditioners including compressors, motor cars, audio and video cassette tapes, video cassettes, picture tubes, colour television sets, VCRs and VCPs.

I propose to increase the excise duty on refrigerators by amounts varying from Rs. 200 to Rs. 800 depending upon the capacity, and in the case of airconditioners, by amounts varying from Rs. 2000 to Rs. 30000. I also propose to raise the excise duty on compressors for air conditioners of a capacity not exceeding 7.5 metric ton by Rs. 1800. The expected additional revenue from these proposals is about Rs. 91 crores in a full year.

Motor cars at present attract excise duty at the rate of 50 percent. I propose to increase the excise duty to 60 percent. The duty on taxis at 30 percent will, however, remain unchanged. The proposal will yield an additional revenue of Rs. 150 crores per year.

I propose to increase the excise duty on audio cassette tapes from Rs. 3 to Rs. 5 per sq. metre and on video cassette tapes from Rs. 10.50 to Rs. 15 per sq. metre. The estimated revenue gain from the proposal will be Rs. 29 crores in a full year.

As regards colour television sets, I propose to increase the excise duty by Rs. 500 and Rs. 750 per set, depending on the screen sizes. I propose to raise the excise duty on colour picture tubes as well. I am exempting all black and white television sets from excise duty and shifting the burden to picture tubes. I also propose to increase excise duty on VHS type VCRs and VCPs by Rs. 400 per set and Rs. 250 per set, respectively, and on other types of VCRs and VCPs, from 25 percent to 30 percent. The revenue gain on this account is Rs. 66 crores in a full year.

Every Finance Minister has to do his bit to curb smoking, which is injurious to health. I must also fall in line and add to the tax on cigarettes. In respect of nonfilter cigarettes, I propose to raise the duties by Rs. 10 to Rs. 25 per thousand cigarettes depending upon the length. In respect of filter cigarettes, the increase will be between Rs. 35 and Rs. 125 per thousand cigarettes. However, filter cigarettes exceeding 85 mm will attract the ceiling rate prescribed in the excise tariff. This will give us additional revenue to the extent of Rs. 300 crores in a full year.

The excise duty on hand-made branded biris is Rs. 3.75 per thousand. Although the duties on cigarettes have been increased almost every year, excise duties on biris have remained unchanged since 1986. I feel that biri smokers should not be denied the opportunity of increasing their share of contribution to the national exchequer. I accordingly propose to increase the duty on hand-made branded biris, other than paper rolled biris to Rs. 4.50 per thousand. Paper rolled biris will attract a duty of Rs. 10 per thousand. The present exemption on other hand made biris would, however, continue. The expected additional revenue is Rs. 33 crores in a full year. Pan masala not containing tobacco attracts a specific rate of excise duty. I propose to raise the excise duty on the same by Rs. 5 and Rs. 10 per kg. depending on its value. This involves a revenue gain of Rs. 4 crores in a full year.

The excise duty on sugar, which is levied on a specific basis, has remained unchanged since 1983, with the result that the ad-valorem incidence has come down as the price of sugar has increased considerably over this period. In ad valorem terms, the present incidence of excise duty on levy sugar is more than the incidence on free sale sugar. In order to correct the situation, I propose to increase the excise duty on free sale sugar from the present level of Rs. 50 to Rs. 71 per quintal. This would mean an additional tax burden of 21 paise per kilogram of free sale sugar which costs about Rs. 10 per kg in the market place. This proposal is expected to yield an additional revenue of Rs. 122 crores in a full year. I would like to make it clear that I am not proposing any increase in excise duty on levy sugar which is sold through the public distribution system.

I propose to exclude khandsari sugar from the list of items chargeable to additional excise duty. The State Governments will be free to levy sales tax on khandsari sugar, if they so desire.

Molasses which is a bye-product of the sugar industry is presently subject to excise duty at the rate of Rs. 120 per metric ton. A substantial portion of molasses is used in the manufacture of liquor. In the circumstances, it can bear a higher rate of duty. Accordingly, I propose to increase the excise duty on molasses to Rs. 150 per metric ton. The estimated revenue gain from the proposal is Rs. 13 crores in a year.

The details of the revenue implications of the measures announced are given in the Explanatory Memorandum to the Finance Bill.

I have also proposed certain amendments in the Finance Bill seeking to effect changes in the Customs Act, and excise and customs tariffs. These include certain consequential amendments to the customs tariff based on the amendments to the Harmonised Commodity Description and Coding System which has been adopted by our country in terms of the International Convention on the Harmonised System. The amendments are merely enabling provisions and do not have significant revenue implications. Besides, there are proposals for amendment of some of the existing notifications. In order to save the time of the House, I do not propose to recount them.

The increases in excise duties will lead to a revenue gain of Rs. 1799.00 crores while the reliefs will amount to Rs. 358.06 crores in a full year. The net revenue gain from excise duties is thus Rs. 1440.94 crores in a full year, of which the States will get Rs. 750.04 crores leaving the balance of Rs. 690.90 crores for the Centre. The proposals in regard to changes in the customs duties imply a revenue loss of Rs. 822.52 crores and a revenue gain of Rs.

78.00 crores in a full year. The net impact of the proposals relating to customs duties is a loss of Rs. 744.52 crores in a full year. Thus, as compared with the additional net revenue of Rs. 696.42 crores from customs and excise duties, the States would gain Rs. 750.04 crores, while the Centre would lose Rs. 53.62 crores in a full year.

Copies of notifications giving effect to the changes in customs and excise duties effective from 25th July, 1991, will be laid on the Table of the House in due course.

The proposals I have made in regard to direct taxes will yield Rs. 2139 crores of which Rs. 97 crores will accrue to the States and Rs. 2042 crores to the Centre. My proposals in regard to customs duties will involve a net revenue loss of Rs. 510 crores in the current year while those relating to Union excise duties are estimated to yield a net additional revenue of Rs. 988 crores in the remaining part of the current year of which Rs. 515 crores will be the share of States and Rs. 473 crores will be retained by the Centre. Taking both direct and indirect taxes into account, the net gain to the Centre in the current year is estimated at Rs. 2005 crores and with this, the budgetary deficit of the Centre for the current year is estimated at Rs. 7719 crores, the revenue deficit at Rs. 13854 crores and the fiscal deficit at Rs. 37727 crores.

Sir, I have now nearly come to the end of my labour. Before I conclude, let me end on a personal note. Years ago, in a letter which Jawaharlal Nehru wrote to the young Indira Gandhi, he advised her that in dealing with the affairs of the State one should be full of sentiment but never be sentimental. But the House will forgive me if on an occasion like this I cannot avoid being somewhat sentimental.

I was born in a poor family in a chronically drought prone village which is now part of Pakistan. University scholarships and grants made it possible for me to go to college in India as well as in England. This country has honoured me by appointing me to some of the most important public offices of our sovereign Republic. This is a debt which I can never be able to fully repay. The best I can do is to pledge myself to serve our country with utmost sincerity and dedication. This I promise to the House. A Finance Minister has to be hard headed. This I shall endeavour to be. I shall be firm when it comes to defending the interests of this nation. But I promise that in dealing with the people of India I shall be soft hearted. I shall not in any way renege on our nation's firm and irrevocable commitment to the pursuit of equity and social justice. I shall never forget that ultimately all economic processes are meant to serve the interests of our people. It is only through a commitment to social justice and the pursuit of excellence that we can mobilise the collective will of our people for development, to give it a high moral purpose and to keep alive the spirit of national solidarity. The massive social and economic reforms needed to remove the scourge of poverty, ignorance and disease can succeed only if backed by a spirit of high idealism, self sacrifice and dedication.

The grave economic crisis now facing our country requires determined action on the part of Government. We are fully prepared for that role. Our party will provide an effective Government to our country. Our people are our masters. We see the role of our Government as one of empowering our people to realize their full potential. This budget constitutes a vital component of a comprehensive vision, a well thought out strategy and an effective action programme designed to get India moving once again.

Sir, I do not minimise the difficulties that lie ahead on the long and arduous journey on which we have embarked. But as Victor Hugo once said, "no power on earth can stop an idea whose time has come." I suggest to this august House that the emergence of India as a major economic power in the world happens to be one such idea. Let the whole world hear it loud and clear. India is now wide awake. We shall prevail. We shall overcome.

With these words, I commend the budget to this august House.

□

Shivaji Maharaj Must Be Remembered*

—Mohan Bhagwat

[After working underground during the Emergency, Mohan Madhukar Bhagawat, became 'Pracharak' of Akola in Maharashtra in 1977 and rose within the organization responsible for Nagpur and Vidarbha regions. He became 'Akhil Bharatiya Sharirik Pramukh' (in-charge of physical training) for India, 1991 to 1999. Mohan was further promoted as 'Akhil Bharatiya Pracharak Pramukh,' (in-charge of RSS volunteers working full-time for India).

In 2000, when Rajendra Singh 'Rajju Bhaiya' and H.V. Sheshadri decided to step down as Sarsanghchalak (Supreme Leader) and Sarkaryavaha (General Secretary) respectively due to poor health, K. S. Sudarshan was nominated as the new chief and Mohan Bhagwat became Sarkaryavaha. Bhagwat was chosen as the Sarsanghchalak of the RSS on 21st March 2009. He is one of the youngest leaders to head the Rashtriya Swayamsevak Sangh after Dr. K.B. Hedgewar and M.S. Golwalkar.

Bhagwat gave a thought provoking speech on the occasion of Hindu Samrajya Divas, organized in Nagpur on 24th June, 2010. Although it was a conventional speech for RSS

* *Hindu Samrajya Divas, Nagpur, 24th June, 2010*

follower, in which Bhagwat outlined the RSS dream of India as Hindu Nation, but it intensified his future line of action. In 2014, when Narendra Modi led Bhartiya Janta Party gained the absolute majority power in India, Bhagwat's speech became relevant worldwide, particularly among so called secular Indian ideologues.]

This is a special convention of the Hindu Samrajya Divas that is celebrated every year. The Sangh has completed 84 years and has entered its 85th year. When so much time elapses in any activity, two generations have passed and this is the third generation, it becomes necessary to recapitulate the thought underlying the activities and conventions of the organisation. Without such contemplation, if we act mechanically, there is effort but no result. And as time advances, the knowledge of many things is lost. In this situation, when several types of questions arise in the mind, and answers are not found, then it can also lead to a lack of dedication towards ideal conventions.

Hindu Samrajya Divas, Jyeshta Shukla Trayodashi is the coronation day of Chatrapati Shivaji Maharaj. Those who don't know why this day is celebrated by the Sangh in today's circumstances may be afflicted by several questions. There is no shortage of kings in our country, even of kings who fought for the country and were victorious. It is not as if Shivaji Maharaj's Coronation day is celebrated as Hindu Samrajya Divas because Sangh was first established in Nagpur, and the first activists of Sangh were all from Maharashtra.

If we look at the times of Shivaji Maharaj, we will perceive several similarities between those times and our own circumstances. Just as those times were fraught with dangers, society was afflicted by atrocities and was suffering; our times too are afflicted by dangers, not only foreign and military, but dangers of all kinds. In those days, these dangers were also there, but society had lost its self confidence. This was the biggest danger of all.

These dangers had their inception in the invasion of Mohammad bin Qasim. We fought on, but were repeatedly defeated, were cut down, beaten. And when Vijayanagar Empire vanished, a sense of despair pervaded the society, a type of despair that we see today. If we visit people who ponder about our society, sit with them, listen to them, we will find this sense of despair in all of them. There is no ray of hope, and the first child of despair is the loss of self confidence. Self-confidence has been lost.

Just recently, fanatical miscreants started constructing a mosque without provocation in a fully Hindu neighbourhood in Kolkatta. And what was the first reaction of Hindu society? "Hey Ram! A mosque has come up here! Let us leave this neighbourhood." The Swayamsevaks of the Sangh went there, explained matters, and organised opposition. But this is a different matter. The fact remains that the first response of Hindu society is: They have come! Let us run! The same situation prevailed before the advent of Shivaji. Hindu society had forsaken valour and had sunk into despair. It had come to believe that it was destined to serve foreigners.

This mentality is best reflected in the play 'Shivasambhava' written by Ram Ganesh Gadkariji. It revolves round the conception and birth of Shivaji Maharaj. Jijamata is pregnant, and pregnant women have special desires particularly in matters of food and drink. It is said that these desires reflect the nature of the child in the womb. It us called 'dhohalle' in Marathi. Every pregnant woman has such desires. And her friends inquire about her desires and try to satisfy them. There is an episode in the play where the friends ask Jijamata: "what is your desire". Then Jijamata says, "I want to ride a tiger; I want that I have not two but eighteen hands, and with each hand holding a weapon, I want to go round the earth destroying demons; or I want to sit on a canopied throne with my victories being acclaimed all over the world. These are the kinds of desires welling in my heart." In normal circumstances, listeners would have felt happy that the coming child would be imbued with such valour. But Jijamata's friends say: "What is this? What are you thinking? Don't you know that one king tried to do this, and what befell him? We are Hindu, can we sit on the throne? Can we take up weapons in our hands? What are these characteristics of a beggar that you are describing?" "Bhikeche Dohaalle" is the word used in Marathi. Characteristics of a beggar! That is, if a

Hindu desired to take up arms and fight, or desired to sit on a throne, it was a sign of impending ruin. This was the mentality of the Hindu society of those days.

Once self confidence disappears, all kinds of faults appear. Selfishness enters. Internecine conflicts appear. And foreign powers taking advantage of this, advance, and advance till life becomes difficult for ordinary people.

अन्न नाही, वस्त्र नाही, सौख्य नाही जनामध्ये,
आश्रयो पाहता नाही, बुद्धि दे रघुनायका।।
)Neither food, nor clothes, nor happiness for people;
Even support we will not find on looking, grant us
understanding Raghunayaka(.

माणसा खावया अन्न नाही, अंथरूण पांघरूण ते ही नाही,
घर कराया सामग्री नाही, अखंड चिंतेच्या प्रवाही पडिले लोक।।
)Man has not food to eat; nothing to cover himself with;
No means to construct a house; People are trapped in the
seamless flow of worry.(

This was the situation of those times as described by Ramadasa Swami. Such was the pathetic state of society, devoid of any signs of valour. Then, impelled by Shivaji Maharaj's drive and after a prolonged fight with foreign invaders, for the first time in Indian history, an independent, authoritative, legitimate throne of Hindus was established.

The true message: The coronation of Shivaji Maharaj is not simply a matter of victory of Shivaji Maharaj. Ever since the invasions from Kabul started, till the coronation of Shivaji Maharaj, efforts to achieve an all-round progress of Hindu Rashtra based on its religion, culture and society, failed repeatedly. There were many experiments. Kings fought using different strategies of war; Saints struggled to unify society, to consolidate society, and to keep alive the spirit of devotion in different ways. There were some momentary successes. There were some total failures. But the success that society sought and needed remained elusive. Shivaji Maharaj's coronation was the final successful consummation of all these efforts and experiments.

This is not the victory of Shivaji Maharaj alone. It is a victory of a warring Hindu Rashtra over its enemies. It ushered in a new era, which aimed not at power or loot of property, but which tried to transform mankind, extirpating those refusing to change; protecting the tolerant, peace loving, nonviolent, all embracing, philosophy of India from destructive, anti-religious, divisive invasions; fighting victoriously for the protection of such a philosophy and religion—this was a five hundred year old problem which was resolved by the coronation of Shivaji Maharaj. This is the significance of this day. After seeing the efforts of Shivaji Maharaj, everybody came to believe that only he could find a solution to this problem, and put Hindu society, Hindu religion, culture and nation on the path of progress.

That is why the poet Bhushan kicked off servitude to Aurangzeb and came to the south and sang his Shiv Bhavani before Shivaji Maharaj. Bhushan did not need wealth and fame. He was poet in the court of Aurangzeb. But he was a Hindu. He was a patriot. That is why it was not in his nature to eulogise such irreligious persons who committed all kinds of atrocities on the nation. That is why he used to spend his time with all kinds of love poetry. Once Aurangzeb ordered him to compose a eulogy in his honour. Even though the emperor insisted, Bhushan refused in open court, saying that a poet is not for sale. He would only eulogise that which is bright. He said that the emperor was not fitted for his eulogy, and so rejecting servitude to the emperor, he came to the south.

It is not as if only people from Maharashtra thought that Shivaji Maharaj should become a king. Of course, they thought so. But even saints of India thought that Shivaji Maharaj should become a king to establish Dharma. Jijamata thought that her son was capable of leading the Hindu society. Gaga Bhatt, the descendant of the traditional priests of Kashi Vishweshvar temple, started making inquiries after witnessing the destruction of the temple as to who could stopped such destruction of temples in the county, and heard of Shivaji Maharaj. He came to Maharashtra. From Nasik till the time he reached the court of Shivaji Maharaj, he collected all information directly experienced his rule, and then on meeting Shivaji Maharaj, he said: "You must be enthroned!" That is why the effects of the enthronement of Shivaji Maharaj were not restricted to Maharashtra.

When Shivaji Maharaj went to Agra to meet Aurangzeb, then the eyes of the entire Hindu world, nay the world itself were on him. But the Hindu world was watching this with a special reason. It understood that this was the ultimate test. Would the experiment of Shivaji Maharaj succeed? All were fighters. They wanted Hindu Swarajya. The language might differ. But the this was the real test of whether final success would crown the hitherto successful endeavours of Shivaji Maharaj.

That is why, when Shivaji Maharaj successfully escaped from the court of Aurangzeb, revived his struggles, and enthroned himself, the results were far reaching.

The Rajputs of Rajasthan buried their internecine conflicts and united under the the leadership of Durgadas Rathod, and within some years of the coronation of Shivaji Maharaj created such a situation that foreign invaders had to vacate the lands of Rajasthan. After that, no Moghal or Turk set his foot on the soil of Rajasthan as a ruler, although they may have come as servitors of the Indian rulers. Chatrasal was actually directly inspired by Shivaji Maharaj. The fight against moghals had been going on till the time of his father, Champatrai. After witnessing in person the methods of Shivaji Maharaj, Chatrasal left and finally won against the moghals, and established an empire.

Even the king of Assam, Chakradhvajasimha used to say "I will adopt the same policies as Shivaji and prevent any foreigner from stepping on the soil of Assam." So the foreign marauders had to return from Brahmaputra. Assam never became subservient to the Moghals, to Islam. But Chakradhvajasinha said and wrote that we should adopt policies like Shivaji and drive out the Moghals. And after this, even Raja Rudrasinh who was fighting in cooch-bihar succeeded. He said, "we must drown the hypocrites in the Bay of Bengal just like this". For this, he drew inspiration from Shivaji Maharaj.

All this in history. The coronation of Shivaji Maharaj was a clarion call to the whole Hindu Rashtra, that this is the path to victory. Take this path! This was the purpose of the coronation of Shivaji Maharaj. This was the purpose of all his endeavours.

His endeavours were not for himself. Shivaji never fought for his personal fame, respect and power. This was not in his nature. On his return from a visit to Qutb Shah in the south, Shivaji visited the temple of Shrishaila Mallikarjuna. It is said he became so ecstatic on having a darshan of the Shiva that he prepared to cut off his head and sacrifice his life for Shiva. His ministers and bodyguards who were present saved him from this act. Leave alone personal gain, he was not even attached to his life.

If he was for personal gain, he would have made a vassal of Chatrasal who had come to his court to seek a chance to serve the nation. He did not do so. Instead, he told him: "Are you born for serving? You are born a Kshatriya, will you serve other kings? Carve out your own kingdom!" He did not tell him to carve out a kingdom and then join his empire, or become his vassal, in order to gain his support. He did not say so. That is because this was never his aim. His object was never to elevate his small jagir into a kingdom, and become the most influential king of all.

There is a letter from the Governor of Goa in Lisbon's Portuguese archives. One servant of the Governor of Goa, was a relative of a commander of a fort belonging to Shivaji Maharaj: Raoji Somnath Patki. He asked Raoji "Why is this Shivaji causing such commotion?" Patki asked Shivaji Maharaj: "Maharaj, we have borne a lot of suffering in course of this work, and now Swarajya has become very big. Your jagir at Poona was very small, but now it has expanded a lot. What should we do? How much farther have we to advance?" Shivaji Maharaj replied: " Listen! Our land stretches from the starting point of Sindhu to the southern bank of Kaveri. Our objective is to drive out the foreigners from here and to restore the holy places that they have destroyed." This reply given by Shivaji is recorded in Portuguese Archives. Raoji Somnath related this to his relative, who reported it to the Governor, and the Governor reported this in a letter to Lisbon. This letter is available in the archives.

Shivaji Maharaj had such an broad vision. As we are wont to say in modern terms: All round progress of the nation based on the protection of our sacred Hindu religion, Hindu culture and Hindu society!

This was the viewpoint of Shivaji Maharaj. He did not want anything for himself. He was not driven by a desire for fame. If that was the case he would not borne with disrepute. When Afzal Khan attacked him, finding it difficult to defeat him in open battle, Shivaji retreated into Pratapgarh. The temple of Tuljabhavani was desecrated, as was the temple of Pandharpur. People were chased from their homes, and their crops were destroyed. Whole villages were burnt down. Cows were being slaughtered openly and people asked where Shivaji was with his bombastic talk. Where was his bluster and braggadocio? Shivaji Maharaj shrugged off the infamy because he was not driven by a desire for fame. He was driven by policy, and that is why he added fuel to fire and spread rumors that he was actually scared. This was his subtle strategy. He drew Afzal Khan into the jungle and exterminated his force. He who is afraid of disrepute cannot adopt such a subtle strategy. Such a person has always to please the populace in some way. He is bound to adopt that strategy as will please the mob. He can never accept a strategy which will invite public criticism or opprobrium. Shivaji Maharaj's life was not dictated by a desire for popular acclaim. He was above considerations of self.

Sivaji's self confidence: Confidence Confidence Confidence Shivaji was concerned with the well being of the nation and religion. He strove for it. And with what self-confidence! This has been highlighted in Revered Sri Guruji's Baudhik class. You must have read that people entertain thoughts of martyrdom for the country, and God blesses them: "So be it! Be a martyr for your country." Many such people attain martyrdom. This is in itself is a great thing. But a temperament driven by valour and the spirit of conquest says that I will fight for the nation, and after defeating all enemies, will achieve victory.

What was the state of affairs in those days? North India was ruled by the emperor, while there were five sultanates in the south. Even a powerful empire like Vijayanagara had vanished. But Shivaji Maharaj declares: I will establish Hindu Swarajya here. He adds : "Hindu swarajya is desired by the Lord! This is a divine task. It is bound to succeed. Its victory is assured. We have to strive for it." You must have read historical accounts of all previous battles and conflict, or heard of them. I say here that all previous endeavours merge into the endeavours of Shivaji Maharaj which is the culmination of all previous efforts.

For instance, the ministerial council of eight of Shivaji Maharaj was customary in ancient India, and it had been forgotten in the intervening period. Only the Vijayanagara empire had a ministry of eight and no other sovereign Hindu kings had a ministerial council of eight. The custom had been forgotten. How did Shivaji Maharaj revive this custom? He was very observant in his trips abroad. He was very inquisitive. He inquired a lot. When he went to Bangalore Shahji Raje was with him. He used to learn a lot. He learnt a lot by asking questions about everything. He learnt about history, and met saints like Tukaram Maharaj and Swami Ramdas. Samartha Ramdas had toured the country. He had stayed for three days in Hampi, where even now we can see an idol of Hanuman installed by him. It seemed as if the spirit of valour and conquest was dead. But the collective memory of the society does not vanish. Social leadership may lose self confidence, but the inner flame of social consciousness keeps on burning.

After finding out what was happening in the society of his times, learning from it, collecting the experiences of the past, correcting their mistakes, Shivaji Maharaj decided to strive and took a step forward. Such self confidence had he! I will win. I must win. This task is divinely ordained. And that is why; he first took steps to raise the self confidence of society. He did not plunge into battle instantaneously.

He first went to Poona to take charge of his jagir. Earlier Shahji Raje used to look after it from Poona. He had fought the Nizam for freedom. He had not checked whether his alliance would break or endure. It did not endure, but split, and in order to teach a lesson to the Hindus fighting under Shahji Raja, Poona was burnt down. The land was ploughed by ploughshares drawn by donkeys, and finally, a crowbar was hammered into the ground and a torn slipper was hung on it. The people of Poona would surreptitiously peep out of their doors in daytime, and their hearts would sink at the thought that this would be the fate of those who fought for their country and for their religion. Then came Shivaji Maharaj. The first step he took was to discover and establish a temple of Ganesa, a symbol of our tradition, culture and pride. He had the fields of Poona ploughed ritually with ploughshares of gold. The Hindu society saw that where a slipper hung on a crowbar, a valiant young man had come and ploughed the fields with ploughshares of gold. This gave them hope that change was possible. Much of their self confidence must have been restored. By providing good governance in his jagir, Shivaji Maharaj made his subjects able. He united them for other tasks.

Shivaji–the strategist: Shivaji Maharaj knew that one leader and one power centre could not change the fortunes of the society for good. Momentary victories would only lead to a repetition of history. Hence, the spirit of valour had to be first aroused. The self confidence of society had to be roused. Society had to be organised. He united all types of people. His followers were of diverse types. As they say in Marathi: 'athara pagad jaati.' People who tied eighteen different types of turbans: big leaders of eighteen classes of people, from priests to the lowest, even those considered to be inferior and mean into those days, even people of such groups were friends of Shivaji Maharaj in life and speech. They were ready to lay down their lives for him, and not for him alone, for self rule and their religion as well. Shivaji Maharaj did not have weapons at that time. He did not have many means. He did not have horses and elephants.

But when he roused his heroes, tales of freedom were woven round them. One such folk tale runs that Shivaji himself went once to meet Qutb Shah. The latter is believed to have asked sarcastically: "How many elephants do you have?" He knew that Shivaji Maharaj did not have elephants. Shivaji Maharaj replied:

"We have many elephants."

"Did you not bring them?"

"We have brought them."

"Where are they?"

"They are standing behind me."

Behind Shivaji Maharaj were his Mavla soldiers. Mockingly,

Qutb Shah asked: "Will they fight with our elephants?"

Shivaji said: "Let us put them on the field tomorrow."

The next day, Qutb Shah had his most ferocious elephant brought, and fielded him in the grounds of Golconda. Shivaji Maharaj asked one of his men, Yesaaji Kank, to fight with the elephant. Yesaaji threw his blanket on the ground, and jumped into the arena with a sword in hand. He cut off the trunk of the elephant and killed him.

Thus, Shivaji raised an army of heroes with courage in their hearts, ready to fight rutting elephants for the pride of their country and religion, and filled the entire society with enthusiasm. That is why, even after the demise of Shivaji Maharaj, when Rajaram Maharaj had to go to live in the south, and was relegated to a life in fort, without a king, without a treasure, without an army, without a general, the people of Maharashtra fought with spades, crowbars and sickles for twenty years and the forces of Aurangzeb which came to destroy Swarajya were buried on the soil of Maharashtra.

Shivaji nurtured this strength of the society and directed it into action. He never thought of his own life. His life of fifty years, was a life of immeasurable industry. He never restricted himself to command positions while directing his men in battle; he would himself plunge into the struggle, demonstrate by example, and later by precept. He faced Shaista Khan personally to punish him. When fighting the forces of Kartalab Khan, Shivaji Maharaj was present, fully armed and in heroic splendour. He would be in the forefront of battles and give testimony to his courage. This would raise the spirits of his followers. He also had sense. His battle plans were based on equanimity and enthusiasm.

It was on the basis of courage, equanimity and enthusiasm that he fought and defeated Afzal Khan. When Afzal Khan attacked, Shivaji Maharaj accepted disrepute and stayed put in Pratapgarh. He went to meet him, and bore all insults with fortitude. And when the opportune moment arose, he destroyed Afzal Khan, lock, stock and barrel. Afterwards, his war efforts took Swarajya outside the territories of Bijapur in just four months. He understood well when to show courage, when to display fortitude, when to be aggressive, and when to remain silent.

Until then, the war strategy in Bharat was straightforward and religious. We used to fight religious wars. Shivaji Maharaj redefined war policy. He said that when the enemy resorts to cunning and subterfuge, he has to be replied to in kind. For the victory of dharma, we have to act like Lord Krishna in Mahabharata. For this reason, when the court of Bijapur arrested Shahaji Raja, he wrote to Aurangzeb that we are your sincere servants and are looking after your borders. Adil Shah is harassing us. Please put in a word with him. After this letter was written, a missive went to Adil Shah and Shahaji Maharaj was released. But in the meantime, Shivaji Maharaj also looted two villages belonging to the Mughal Empire.

He handled all his enemies in like manner, sometimes extending a hand of friendship, sometimes displaying the strength of weapons. This is not honest, but honesty could play no role when faced with dishonest enemies. There must have been a clamour after Afzal Khan's assassination. Shivaji Maharaj was asked: you are treacherous, you had taken an oath with tulasi and bilva leaves in hand, and then you treacherously killed Afzal Khan. You betrayed his trust. Sivaji's reply was: "He had come to take me dead or alive, should I have died? I do not want to live for myself alone. This is fledgling Swarajya, it has to grow, but before it does grow into a banyan tree should I allow it to be cut down? I had to be perfidious to him because he had perfidy in his heart. He was deceitful. I replied in kind. Give me one instance when I have betrayed a friend."

Thus, Shivaji Maharaj fully retouched India's policy response to invasion. With his unerring ability to plan, he moved from victory to victory. He even converted momentary defeats into victories. When he went to meet Aurangzeb, he revived the waning spirit of freedom among the Rajputs of Rajasthan. He breathed strength into their self confidence. It is not as if he only successfully escaped from Moghal custody. In Delhi, he won over people in many places, and after returning from Aurangzeb's court, recovered the wealth looted from him, and expanded his kingdom.

He was the first king in contemporary India to combine in a common strategy: navy, cavalry and infantry. This master strategist, courageous and far sighted Shivaji Maharaj did not become king merely to possess power. That is because; he had a vision of a protected Hinduism, Hindu culture, Hindu society and a valiant, prosperous, Hindu Rashtra.

Shivaji's good governance: Many deeds of Shivaji are such, that even today they would be considered progressive. In those days when socialism was not even dreamt of, Shivaji Maharaj abolished zamindari and vatandari. We can be trustees of social wealth, not its owners. Land is society's property, it should be in the custody of the state that looks after social order, it cannot be given to individuals. Individuals can be entrusted to look after it. They will have status not power. He abolished vatandari system.

In those days, chieftain jagirdars used to have private armies. Shivaji Maharaj changed this, and by beginning the practice of paying soldiers from the coffers of central administration of Swarajya, he converted private loyalties of soldiers into patriotism. All horses of the army were owned by central administration in his kingdom.

He enforced a two tiered tax revenue system based on the type and crop yield of the lands of poor peasants. He dug lakes and wells, planted trees, built hospices, temples and roads.

Shivaji contemplated on the changes necessary in his contemporary society, and enforced them. He was fearless in this regard. He brought back Netaji Palkar and Bajaji Nimbalkar into the fold of Hindu Dharma. Not only did he reconvert them, but in order to establish their social status, he brought them into relationship with himself. He had discernment. He had vision.

The force of the sword was driving Islamisation. What was the vision of Shivaji Maharaj? He picked out foreign muslims and drove them out. In order to absorb those who had become muslim from our own society, he started a rational process of owning them. He gave an assurance of peace to Qutub Shah on two conditions. The first was that the first two ministers of that kingdom would be Hindus. It was due to this that Venkanna and Madanna were appointed ministers. The second condition was that there would be no atrocities on the Hindu populace. When he realised that the Portuguese Governors aimed to convert the Hindu populace on the strength of arms, he attacked Goa.

Absorbing those of other religions did not mean a wobbly attitude to our own religion. He attacked directly. He went to Chiploon. He re-established the Parashuram temple. When, the Kashi Vishweshwar temple was broken on the orders of Aurangzeb, he wrote a letter to Aurangzeb stating: "You have become a king due to divine beneficence and the grace of God. And in the eyes of God all people are equal. God does not discriminate between Hindu and Muslim. Rule over them justly. If you engage in attacking and breaking temples, I will have to come to the north, sword in hand."

Shivaji Maharaj's kingdom did not extend to the north. It was small. It was in the south. No one could prophecy that in his life time, his kingdom would extend to Kashi. Nevertheless Shivaji Maharaj wrote this letter because Kashi Vishveshvar is a holy place in our country. This is my national duty. But what is to be done about those have converted to Islam while I am doing this? Bind them with love. Bring them back as much as possible. This vision can be discerned in his deeds.

He had a wonderful sense of the direction of time and what needed to be done. Hence, he brought from Europe a printing press which was based on old pegs. After importing it, he studied it and tried to make a similar press, and tried to start the practice of printing. He obtained good cannon and swords from foreigners and contemplated making such weapons domestically. For the security of Swarajya, he set up an effective communication system through the medium of an extensive network of spies.

The sealine is closely associated with the nation's security. It provides the direct line for invasion, and since ships are being built to traverse the ocean, we need our own navy. He established a navy. After studying the European art of shipbuilding and comparing it with the knowledge in our own books, he encouraged scholars to develop an art of shipbuilding suitable to our country and built ships in the light of this knowledge. He established sea fortresses like Sindhudurg, Suvarnadurg, Padmadurg and Vijayadurg.

How expansive was his vision, and what a foresight he had! His thoughts were not hemmed in by his times. His object was not just to defeat one emperor and establish Swarajya. He aimed to protect it. He aimed to modernise his society and bring it to the forefront of the world.

These were not just words. His actions spoke louder. There are many such examples. That is why his kingdom was marked by good governance. The country's decisions were made after consulting and discussing with administrators and ministers. In order to run the administration in the language of the people, he had a dictionary made of administrative language and stopped the use of Persian. He banned cow slaughter. He established the rule of one-own religion and self-administration.

His edict is famous. It is rich with so many details. What do we mean when we call his rule as good governance? It was people friendly. He told the army that when you go and establish a camp, then you must bear in mind that you do not take anything from the neighbouring fields without their owners' consent. Even a piece of rope, if taken, should be paid a just price. One must not leave trash, ropes etc. lying around because they could lead to an accidental fire due to the sparks from a smoker's pipe. These details reveal wisdom and people friendliness.

His administration was known for its justice. There is an anecdote of the time when he had just taken charge of his Poona jagir. The head of a village name Ranjha, intoxicated by his power, raped a helpless woman from his own village. Shivaji Maharaj sent his soldiers to fetch him trussed in ropes and cut off his hands and legs as punishment. Since that time oppression by the power-mad vanished. There was no instance of a complaint by people that was not investigated by the administration. There was discrimination between the appropriate and the inappropriate, and the inappropriate was punished. The punishment of the powerful was harsher, while if there was some redeeming feature even in the transgressions of ordinary people, they were accorded due consideration.

The story of the cowherdess Hirkani is famous. She used to come to Raigarh fort to sell milk. One day she stayed back late in the fort. According to the rules, all doors of the fort were closed at dusk. How was she to return to the village? She fretted about the fate of her child left in her house at the foot of a mountain. In her anxiety, she jumped from a steep unscalable boulder on the edge of the fort and went out. Shivaji Maharaj came to know of this. On the one hand, he called the cowherdess Hirkani to the court and felicitated her bravery. On the other hand, he had the boulder broken, the side made more unscalable, and built a bastion over it to close passage. Even today, that bastion is called the "Hirkani bastion".

History tells us that while making forts or strengthening old forts he used to organise competitions inviting ordinary people to find out secret or difficult ways of scaling the fort. After the competitors had located all the paths, he used to retain one and blow up the other paths. The best competitors would be rewarded. Such was his people friendly, wise, and just government.

There was no discrimination between subjects. There was consideration. There was toughness. It was a people-friendly and compassionate government. But compassion did not mean that it was wobbly and weak. It was very strict. The status of a person did not mitigate the crime. He did not forgive his own son. Even Sambhaji Maharaj was punished. He did not spare his friend. When Kanhoji Jedhi complained to him that Khandoji Khopade had committed a crime, but that he had good relations with him, and consequently should be forgiven in consideration of friendship, he spared him his life, but cut off his hands and legs. His explanation was that in view of you entreaty, I did not kill him, but cut his hands that were treacherous and his legs that took him. Thus, he did not forgive and was very strict.

His administration was strict, just, in popular interest, wise, people friendly, and compassionate. Shivaji Maharaj was himself an ideal leader. His character was unimpeachable, beyond the reproach of even his enemies. The story of the daughter-in-law of a subedar of Kalyan is very famous. There are many such instances in the life of Shivaji Maharaj.

In spite of being an extremely popular and all powerful king, he was very humble before gentlemen. He respected the arts.

He was artist. He would himself perform and then ask others to do so. He was courageous, had faith in his victory, and was a strategist. He was skilful in work, and had the Gurumantra to perform every task with excellence. Even an extremely discerning person like Samartha Ramadasa Swami praised Shivaji Maharaj as follows.

"शिवरायाचे आठवावे रूप, शिवरायाचा आठवावा प्रताप,
शिवरायाचा आठवावा साक्षेप भूमंडली,
शिवरायाचे कैसे चालणे, शिवरायाचे कैसे बोलणे,
शिवरायाचे सलगी देणे, कैसे असे.
यशवंत, नीतिवंत, सामर्थ्यवंत, वरदवंत,
पुण्यवंत, कीर्तिवंत, जानता राजा श्रीमंत योगी।।"

("Remember the form of Sivaraj, Remember the valour of Sivaraj,
Remember the earthly abilities of Sivaraj,
How Sivaraj walked, How Sivaraj talked,
How Sivaraj counseled.
The famous, strategist, capable, blessed,
Merited, well known, knowledgeable king, honoured yogi.")

Such was Chatrapati Shivaji Maharaj, whose personal vision of an ideal king, and ideal citizen of Hindu society, an ideal leader of Hindu society, lives on as an ideal even today; whose self-confidence and spirit of conquest kindled the self-confidence of the entire society, whose endeavours took with him the entire society, whose leadership led to the establishment of the throne of Hindu Rashtra; the victory of that Shivaji Maharaj was the decisive victory in the first stage in the long war for Hindu Rashtra. If we had followed Shivaji's policy in the second stage of this war, we would have achieved the same kind of decisive victory. We did not follow him, and so we got Pakistan.

Exemplary message in contemporary context: Circumstances remain the same today. Today's need is the same. We have to rouse the same spirit of conquest, self-confidence, and endeavour in today's society. Every individual needs to emulate Shivaji Maharaj's character, his virtues. And living in Hindu society, become an able leader of Hindu society, not for self, but for the allround progress of Hindu Rashtra; raise the self-confidence of the entire society to new heights, helping the society to establish a Hindu rule, that is, a rule in people's interest: wise, compassionate, egalitarian, and driven by tough policies.

This is the remedy for today's ills and it will emerge from the organisation of the society. It will emerge on the foundations of the society's virtues, endeavours and self-confidence. We have a living example in the endeavours of Shivaji Maharaj in similar circumstances in the past. In those days, he had become an living example to all people. Bringing together all past experiments, correcting their mistakes, and putting them to practice in this final successful experiment was the Shivaji Maharaj's achievement, and that is why his coronation day is a memorable day.

We in the Sangh do not observe his birthday or death anniversary. That is because, many are born and many die – what is important is what they have achieved in the world.

His coronation was the successful consummation of the efforts of Shivaji Maharaj for an integral state. That is why we do not call this the anniversary of Shivaji's Empire. We call it the Hindu Empire Day (Hindu Samraajya Diwas). That is why, our first three Sarasanghachalakas said several times – Doctorji used to say, Guruji said, and Balasahebji said, that our ideal is the abstract principle, the saffron flag, but many a time, the ordinary person does not understand abstract formless principles. He requires a concrete form and such a concrete form with characteristics is present in the person of Chatrapati Shivaji Maharaj, whose every aspect enlightens us. We need today that character, that policy, that skill, and the sanctity of that ideal.

It is with this understanding that our Sangh has decided to observe this Jyestha Shukla Trayodashi, the day of the coronation of Shivaji Maharaj as the Hindu Samrajya Divas. That is why, in today's circumstances, we will observe it all over India. Shivaji Maharaj's dedication to work, his virtues, the inspiration from his character, provide us with guidance in circumstances that are similar to his. They are exemplary even today. Understanding the importance of the Hindu Samrajya Divas, let us celebrate it every year. Let its message properly reach not only the Swayamsevaks, but the entire society, let it reach their minds, and from there enter their hearts. Let it inspire from their hearts and manifest in the behaviour of every individual. Let us all understand the object of Sangh and participate in its efforts to achieve it.

[Shivaji was crowned king of the Marathas in a lavish ceremony at Raigad on 6th June, 1674. In the Hindu calendar it was on the 13th day (trayodashi) of the first fortnight of the month of Jyeshtha in the year 1596. Pandit Gaga Bhatt officiated, holding a gold vessel filled with the seven sacred waters of the rivers Yamuna, Indus, Ganges, Godavari, Krishna and Kaveri over Shivaji's head, and chanted the coronation mantras. After the ablution, Shivaji bowed before his mother Jijabai and touched her feet. Nearly fifty thousand people gathered at Raigad for the ceremonies. Shivaji was bestowed with the sacred thread 'jaanva', with the Vedas and was bathed in Panchamrita (a mixture of five foods used in Hindu worship and puja, usually honey, sugar, milk, yogurt and ghee/clarified butter). Shivaji was entitled Shakakarta—the founder of an era, Kshatriya Kulavantas—the head of Kshatriyas, the ruling and military elite, and Chhatrapati—the paramount sovereign).

Shivaji established a competent and progressive civil rule with the help of disciplined military and well-structured administrative organisations. He innovated military tactics, pioneering the guerrilla warfare methods (Shiva sutra or ganimi kava), which leveraged strategic factors like geography, speed, and surprise and focused pinpoint attacks to defeat his larger and more powerful enemies. From a small contingent of 2,000 soldiers inherited from his father, Shivaji created a force of 100,000 soldiers; he built and restored strategically located forts both inland and coastal to safeguard his territory. He revived ancient Hindu political traditions and court conventions and promoted the usage of Marathi and Sanskrit, rather than Persian, in court and administration.

Shivaji's legacy was to vary by observer and time but began to take on increased importance with the emergence of the Indian independence movement, as many elevated him as a proto-nationalist and hero of the Hindus. Particularly in Maharashtra, debates over his history and role have engendered great passion and sometimes even violence as disparate groups have sought to characterise him and his legacy. Anyhow, today Shivaji is considered as a national hero in India.

In 1895, Tilak founded the Shri Shivaji Fund Committee for celebration of 'Shiv Jayanti', the birth anniversary of Chhatrapati Shivaji. The project also had the objective of funding the reconstruction of the tomb (Samadhi) of Shivaji at Raigad Fort. Nineteenth century Hindu revivalist Swami Vivekanada considered Shivaji a hero and paid glowing tributes to his wisdom. When Tilak organised the birthday celebrations of Shivaji, Vivekananda agreed to preside over the festival in Bengal in 1901. He was of the view about Shivaji, "Shivaji is one of the greatest national saviours who emancipated our society and our Hindu dharma when they were faced with the threat of total destruction. He was a peerless hero, a pious and God-fearing king and verily a manifestation of all the virtues of a born leader of men described in our ancient scriptures. He also embodied the deathless spirit of our land and stood as the light of hope for our future." Following the path of Tilak, RSS founder modeled Shivaji Maharaj to be ideal king of his dream India—the Hindu Rashtra. Now, RSS celebrate Sivaji's coronation day as Hindu Samrajya Divas, to revive the idea and ideals of Shivaji style of Governance.

As political tensions rose in India in the early 20th century, some Indian leaders came to re-work their earlier stances on Shivaji's role. Jawaharlal Nehru had in 1934 noted "Some of the Shivaji's deeds, like the treacherous killing of the Bijapur general, lower him greatly in our estimation." Following public outcry from Pune intellectuals, some Congress leader T.R. Deogirikar noted that Nehru had admitted he was wrong regarding Shivaji, and now endorsed Shivaji as great nationalist.

However, Shivaji remains a political icon in modern India, and particularly in the state of Maharashtra. His image adorns literature, propaganda and icons of the Maratha-centric Shiv Sena (Army of Shivaji) party, the Hindu nationalist Bharatiya

Janata Party, and also of the Maratha caste dominated Congress parties in Maharashtra. Past Congress party leaders in the state such as Yashwantrao Chavan were considered political descendants of Shivaji.]

□

Learning From the West

—N.R. Narayana Murthy

Ladies & Gentlemen:

It is a pleasure to be here at the Lal Bahadur Shastri Institute of Management. Lal Bahadur Shastri was a man of strong values and he epitomized simple living. He was a freedom fighter and innovative administrator who contributed to nation-building in full measure. It is indeed a matter of pride for me to be chosen for the Lal Bahadur Shastri Award for Public Administration and Management Sciences. I thank the jury for this honour.

When I got the invitation to speak here, I decided to speak on an important topic on which I have pondered for years – the role of Western values in contemporary Indian society. Coming from a company that is built on strong values, the topic is close to my heart. Moreover, an organisation is representative of society, and some of the lessons that I have learnt are applicable in the national context. In fact, values drive progress and define quality of life in society.

The word 'community' joins two Latin words 'com' ('together' or 'with') and 'unus' ('one'). A community, then, is both one and many. It is a unified multitude and not a mere group of people. As it is said in the Vedas: Man can live individually, but can survive only collectively. Hence, the challenge is to form a progressive community by balancing the interests of the individual and that of the society. To meet this, we need to develop a value system where people accept modest sacrifices for the common good.

What is a value system? It is the protocol for behaviour that enhances the trust, confidence and commitment of members of the community. It goes beyond the domain of legality– it is about decent and desirable behaviour. Further, it includes putting the community interests ahead of your own. Thus, our collective survival and progress are predicated on sound values.

There are two pillars of the cultural value system – loyalty to family and loyalty to community. One should not be in isolation to the other because successful societies are those which combine both harmoniously. It is in this context that I will discuss the role of Western values in contemporary Indian society.

Some of you here might say that most of what I am going to discuss are actually Indian values in old ages, and not Western values. I live in the present, not in the bygone era. Therefore, I have seen these values practised primarily in the West and not in India. Hence, the title of the topic.

I am happy as long as we practise these values – whether we call it Western or old Indian values. As an Indian, I am proud to be part of a culture, which has deep-rooted family values. We have tremendous loyalty to the family. For instance, parents make enormous sacrifices for their children. They support them until they can stand on their own feet. On the other side, children consider it their duty to take care of aged parents.

We believe: Mathru devo bhava—mother is God, and pithru devo bhava—father is God. Further, brothers and sisters sacrifice for each other. In fact, the eldest brother or sister is respected by all the other siblings. As for marriage, it is held to be a sacred union – husband and wife are bonded, most often, for life. In joint families, the entire family works towards the welfare of the family. There is so much love and affection in our family life.

This is the essence of Indian values and one of our key strengths. Our families act as a critical support mechanism for us. In fact, the credit to the success of Infosys goes, as much to the founders as to their families, for supporting them through the tough times. Unfortunately, our attitude towards family life is not reflected in our attitude towards community behaviour.

From littering the streets to corruption to breaking of contractual obligations, we are apathetic to the common good. In the West– the US, Canada, Europe, Australia, New Zealand– individuals understand that they have to be responsible towards their community.

The primary difference between the West and us is that there people have a much better societal orientation. They care more for the society than we do. Further, they generally sacrifice more for the society than us. Quality of life is enhanced because of this. This is where we need to learn from the West.

I will talk about some of the lessons that we Indians can learn from the West. In the West, there is respect for the public good. For instance, parks free of litter, clean streets, public toilets free of graffiti – all these are instances of care for the public good. On the contrary, in India, we keep our houses clean and water our gardens everyday – but, when we go to a park, we do not think twice before littering the place.

Corruption, as we see in India, is another example of putting the interest of oneself, and at best that of one's family, above that of the society. Society is relatively corruption-free in the West. For instance, it is very difficult to bribe a police officer into avoiding a speeding ticket.

This is because of the individual's responsible behaviour towards the community as a whole. On the contrary, in India, corruption, tax evasion, cheating and bribery have eaten into our vitals. For instance, contractors bribe officials, and construct low-quality roads and bridges. The result is that society loses in the form of substandard defence equipment and infrastructure, and low-quality recruitment, just to name a few impediments. Unfortunately, this behaviour is condoned by almost everyone.

Apathy in solving community matters has held us back from making progress, which is otherwise within our reach. We see serious problems around us, but do not try to solve them. We behave as if the problems do not exist or is somebody else's. On the other hand, in the West, people solve societal problems proactively. There are several examples of our apathetic attitude. For instance, all of us are aware of the problem of drought in India.

More than 40 years ago, Dr. K.L. Rao, an irrigation expert, suggested creation of a water grid connecting all the rivers in North and South India, to solve this problem. Unfortunately, nothing has been done about this. The story of power shortage in Bangalore is another instance. In 1983, it was decided to build a thermal power plant to meet Bangalore's power requirements. Unfortunately, we have still not started it. Further, the Milan subway in Bombay is in a deplorable state for the last 40 years, and no action has been taken.

To quote another example, considering the constant travel required in the software industry; five years ago, I had suggested a 240-page passport. This would eliminate frequent visits to the passport office. In fact, we are ready to pay for it. However, I am yet to hear from the Ministry of External Affairs on this.

We, Indians, would do well to remember Thomas Hunter's words: Idleness travels very slowly, and poverty soon overtakes it. What could be the reason for all this? We were ruled by foreigners for over thousand years. Thus, we have always believed that public issues belonged to some foreign ruler and that we have no role in solving them.

Moreover, we have lost the will to proactively solve our own problems. Thus, we have got used to just executing someone else's orders. Borrowing Aristotle's words: We are what we repeatedly do. Thus, having done this over the years, the decision-makers in our society are not trained for solving problems. Our decision-makers look to somebody else to take decisions. Unfortunately, there is nobody to look up to, and this is the tragedy.

Our intellectual arrogance has also not helped our society. I have travelled extensively, and in my experience, have not come across another society where people are as contemptuous of better societies as we are, with as little progress as we have achieved. Remember that arrogance breeds hypocrisy. No other society gloats so much about the past as we do, with as little current accomplishment.

Friends, this is not a new phenomenon, but at least a thousand years old. For instance, Al Barouni, the famous Arabic logician and traveller of the 10th century, who spent about 30 years in India from 997 AD to around 1027 AD, referred to this trait of Indians. According to him, during his visit, most Indian pundits considered it below their dignity even to hold arguments with him. In fact, on a few occasions, when a pundit was willing to listen to him, and found his arguments to be very sound, he invariably asked Barouni: which Indian pundit taught these smart things!

The most important attribute of a progressive society is respect for others who have accomplished more than they themselves have, and learn from them. Contrary to this, our leaders make us believe that other societies do not know anything! At the same time, everyday, in the newspapers, you will find numerous claims from our leaders that ours is the greatest nation. These people would do well to remember Thomas Carlyle's words: The greatest of faults is to be conscious of none.

If we have to progress, we have to change this attitude, listen to people who have performed better than us, learn from them and perform better than them. Infosys is a good example of such an attitude. We continue to rationalise our failures. No other society has mastered this part as well as we have. Obviously, this is an excuse to justify our incompetence, corruption and apathy. This attitude has to change. As Sir Josiah Stamp has said: It is easy to dodge our responsibilities, but we cannot dodge the consequences of dodging our responsibilities.

Another interesting attribute, which we Indians can learn from the West, is their accountability. Irrespective of your position, in the West, you are held accountable for what you do. However, in India, the more 'important' you are, the less answerable you are. For instance, a senior politician once declared that he 'forgot' to file his tax returns for 10 consecutive years – and he got away with it. To quote another instance, there are over 100 loss-making public sector units (central) in India. Nevertheless, I have not seen action taken for bad performance against top managers in these organisations.

Dignity of labour is an integral part of the Western value system. In the West, each person is proud about his or her labour that raises honest sweat. On the other hand, in India, we tend to overlook the significance of those who are not in professional jobs.

We have a mindset that reveres only supposedly intellectual work.

For instance, I have seen many engineers, fresh from college, who only want to do cutting-edge work and not work that is of relevance to business and the country. However, be it an organisation or society, there are different people performing different roles. For success, all these people are required to discharge their duties. This includes everyone from the CEO to the person who serves tea – every role is important. Hence, we need a mindset that reveres everyone who puts in honest work.

Indians become intimate even without being friendly. They ask favours of strangers without any hesitation. For instance, the other day, while I was travelling from Bangalore to Mantralaya, I met a fellow traveller on the train. Hardly 5 minutes into the conversation, he requested me to speak to his MD about removing him from the bottom 10% list in his company, earmarked for disciplinary action. I was reminded of what Rudyard Kipling once said: A westerner can be friendly without being intimate while an easterner tends to be intimate without being friendly.

Yet another lesson to be learnt from the West is about their professionalism in dealings. The common good being more important than personal equations, people do not let personal relations interfere with their professional dealings. For instance, they don't hesitate to chastise a colleague, even if he is a personal friend, for incompetent work.

In India, I have seen that we tend to view even work interactions from a personal perspective. Further, we are the most 'thin-skinned' society in the world – we see insults where none is meant. This may be because we were not free for most of the last thousand years. Further, we seem to extend this lack of professionalism to our sense of punctuality. We do not seem to respect the other person's time.

The Indian Standard Time somehow seems to be always running late. Moreover, deadlines are typically not met. How many public projects are completed on time? The disheartening aspect is that we have accepted this as the norm rather than the exception. In the West, they show professionalism by embracing meritocracy. Meritocracy by definition means that we cannot let personal prejudices affect our evaluation of an individual's performance. As we increasingly start to benchmark ourselves with global standards, we have to embrace meritocracy.

In the West, right from a very young age, parents teach their children to be independent in thinking. Thus, they grow up to be strong, confident individuals. In India, we still suffer from feudal thinking. I have seen people, who are otherwise bright, refusing to show independence and preferring to be told what to do by their boss. We need to overcome this attitude if we have to succeed globally.

The Western value system teaches respect to contractual obligation. In the West, contractual obligations are seldom dishonoured. This is important – enforceability of legal rights and contracts is the most important factor in the enhancement of credibility of our people and nation.

In India, we consider our marriage vows as sacred. We are willing to sacrifice in order to respect our marriage vows. However, we do not extend this to the public domain. For instance, India had an unfavourable contract with Enron. Instead of punishing the people responsible for negotiating this, we reneged on the contract – this was much before we came to know about the illegal activities at Enron.

To quote another instance, I had given recommendations to several students for the national scholarship for higher studies in US universities. Most of them did not return to India even though contractually they were obliged to spend five years after their degree in India.

In fact, according to a professor at a reputed US university, the maximum default rate for student loans is among Indians – all of these students pass out in flying colours and land lucrative jobs, yet they refuse to pay back their loans. Thus, their action has made it difficult for the students after them, from India, to obtain loans. We have to change this attitude.

Further, we Indians do not display intellectual honesty. For example, our political leaders use mobile phones to tell journalists on the other side that they do not believe in technology! If we want our youngsters to progress, such hypocrisy must be stopped. We are all aware of our rights as citizens. Nevertheless, we often fail to acknowledge the duty that accompanies every right. To borrow Dwight Eisenhower's words: People that value their privileges above their principles soon lose both. Our duty is towards the community as a whole, as much as it is towards our families.

We have to remember that fundamental social problems grow out of a lack of commitment to the common good. To quote Henry Beecher: Culture is that which helps us work for the betterment of all. Hence, friends, I do believe that we can make our society even better by assimilating these Western values into our own culture – we will be stronger for it.

Most of our behaviour comes from greed, lack of self-confidence, lack of confidence in the nation, and lack of respect for the society. To borrow Gandhi's words: There is enough in this world for everyone's need, but not enough for everyone's greed. Let us work towards a society where we would do unto others what we would have others do unto us. Let us all be responsible citizens who make our country a great place to live. In the words of Churchill: Responsibility is the price of greatness. We have to extend our family values beyond the boundaries of our home.

Finally, let us work towards maximum welfare of the maximum people– *Samasta janaanaam sukhino bhavantu*. Thus, let us – people of this generation– conduct ourselves as great citizens rather than just good people so that we can serve as good examples for our younger generation.

□

The First Parliamentary Speech*

—Narendra Modi

[In the last nine months during 2013-14 Lok Sabha election campaign, Narendra Modi made millions in India run through an entire gamut of emotions: anger, aversion, pluck, mirth, amazement and much more. In all these speeches, he looked like a man in control of his emotions. But on 20th May, 2014, after being elected leader of the BJP parliamentary party—in other words, the PM elect—he choked with emotions. Modi wept. Before him, his senior L.K. Advani had wept. In fact, he triggered the emotions in Modi. Years from now those present at Parliament's historic Central Hall on that day, may or may not remember what Modi said. But few, if any, will ever forget the moment when tears welled up in the BJP leader's voice and eyes revealing a carefully concealed softer side.

Responding to Advani's speech where he had said that Modi had done the party a kripa (favour), he said, "Advaniji ne ek shabda kahaa. Main Advanji se prarthna karoonga ki woh iss shabd ka istemaal na karen. Unhone kaha ki Narendra bhai ne kirpa ki (Advaniji said that I have done a favour to BJP. I will request him not to use this term)."

At this juncture, the BJP leader broke down. He paused

* *As Leader of BJP Parliamentary Party (Prime Minister Elect), Central Hall of Parliament, New Delhi 20th May, 2014*

to sip water and took a moment to gather himself before continuing. "Kya maa ki seva kabhi kirpa ho sakti hai? Katai nahin ho sakti hai. Jaise Bharat meri maa hai, waise hi BJP bhi meri maa hai. Aur isliyee beta kabhi maa par kirpa nahin karta, sirf samarpit bhav se maa ki sewa karta hai (Can a son do any favour by serving the mother? Not at all. Like India, BJP is also my mother. A son never does any favour. He only serves his mother in a dedicated manner)," he said.

Like a gifted artist who makes the audience sway with the emotion, Modi appeared to be making others emotional. It was evident right from the very beginning that it was day of emotional drama. While entering the Parliament building, Modi knelt and placed his forehead on the green carpeted steps like a devotee before a temple. "This is the temple of democracy," he said later.

At the start of his speech, Modi was overcome up with feelings while talking about former Prime Minister Atal Bihari Vajpayee, who is unwell. "Had Vajpayeeji been well, his presence would have been 'sone par suhaga' (icing on the cake)." Throughout the speech, Modi underlined the power of the pause during speech. Emotions aside, he not only displayed his command over the Hindi language but also spoke like a man in total control and command of everything he surveys.

Here is the full text of translated Narendra Modi's speech, delivered extempore in Hindi, at the Central Hall of Parliament on 20th May, 2014]

Respected Advaniji, our national president Rajnathji and all Chief Ministers of Bharatiya Janata Party and newly elected members, I am grateful to all of you for having unanimously given me a new responsibility. I am thankful and grateful, particularly to Advaniji and Rajnathji as they have given me blessings.

I was thinking of Atalji's health. Had his health been good, he would have been with us today and his presence would have completed this moment. His blessings are with us and will be with us in future.

We are here in the temple of democracy. We will work with all purity... not for the post but the people of the country. Work and responsibility are the biggest things. I accept the responsibility you have reposed in me.

For me post is not important, I have not considered that post is important in life but in my view responsibility is the bigger thing.

We will have to dedicate ourselves to fulfill this responsibility. In last 13th September, 2013, the BJP parliamentary board gave a responsibility to me and from 15th September. I started my work and with full sense of responsibility of a worker. The parishram yagya, which I began at that time and when the campaigning ended on 10th May, 2014, I rang up my president and wanted to meet him before going to Ahmedabad. He asked if I was not tired and needed a break but I insisted on reporting to him as the responsibility given to me had been completed on 10th May.

And like a disciplined solider I reported to my president that from 13th September to 10th May, I have tried to fulfill my responsibility to the best of my ability. In this campaign, I had to cancel only one event and that too in Ghosi where our district president had died suddenly.

And I told him that as a loyal and committed worker, I am reporting to you on this sacred land. Whatever was given to me, I have tried to do and fulfill the role of a party worker.

After I became Chief Minister, I saw Chief Minister's chamber for the first time. Today also it is the same situation as I have come to this historic Central Hall for the first time.

I salute all freedom fighters and also salute makers of the Constitution of our country as because of them, the world is witnessing the power of democracy. When global leaders called me, I told them about millions of voters of India. They were surprised. It is the power of our Constitution that a poor person belonging to a poor and deprived family is standing here today. This is the power of our Constitution and hallmark of our democratic elections that a common citizen can also reach this height. The BJP's victory and somebody else's loss is a point for debate later. Citizens have realised that this democratic setup can fulfill their aspirations. Their faith in democracy has strengthened further.

A government is a one which thinks about the poor, listens to the poor and which exists for the poor. Therefore, the new government is dedicated to the poor, millions of youth and mothers and daughters who are striving for their respect and honour. Villagers, farmers, Dalits and the oppressed, this government is for them, for their aspirations and this is our responsibility. And this is our responsibility. I have seen new facets of our country in my campaign. I have seen people who had only one piece of clothing on their body but had the BJP's flag. This section is looking at us with hope and aspirations. And therefore, our dream is to fulfill their dreams.

Advaniji has used; I would urge Advaniji not to use that word. He said that Narendra Bhai has done him kripa.

(Breaks down and there is a pause for a few moments)

Please don't use this word. Can a son ever do his mother kripa? It can never be. Like India is my mother, the same way the BJP is also my mother. And therefore, a son can never do kripa, he can only dedicatedly serve his mother. Kripa is by the party, it has done me the favour of giving me an opportunity to serve it.

Various governments in the past tried to do some good work in their own way for which they deserve appreciation. Whatever good has happened, we will carry it forward. We will give something to the country. People should not become pessimistic. I have not seen television and media, everyone has been analysing this verdict... people have voted for hope. This verdict is of hope. I had said earlier that this election is of hope.

A new hope has arisen in the common man. This is the biggest significance of this election results.

But by giving the BJP an absolute majority they have voted for hope and trust. People have voted for hope and faith and I will do everything to fulfill their aspirations. There should be no room for pessimism and because with pessimism nothing can be achieved. The government's motto will be to be with everyone and for everyone's development. This is the time for new hope and strength.

An era of responsibility has begun. In 2019, I will meet the MPs again with a report card. My government is not for myself but for the country. The government is for the poor and we want to do something for them. I will strive my best to fulfill the responsibility you have reposed in me. You will never have to look down on the work it will do.

We were not fortunate to have died for the country, but for every citizen born in independent India, he should dedicate himself to live for the country. Every moment of our lives and every speck of our body should be dedicated to 125 crore people of this country, we have to carry this dream. The country will then progress rapidly.

I am by nature an optimist. It is written in my DNA. Disappointment does not just gel with me. On this occasion, I wish to repeat what I had said in my speech in a college here. Just see this glass of water, some say that it is half filled with water and some say it is half empty. My thinking is of third type. I say this glass is half filled with water and half with air. You may be seeing it half empty but I don't see it that way. That's why I say that I am by nature an optimist. And for traversing a constructive path, it is important and essential to be an optimist. Only an optimistic person can bring and instill hope in the country. Pessimistic persons can never give hope to the country. Adverse times and hardships do come in everybody's life. In 2001 when earthquake struck Gujarat, we were all stricken by death and there was destruction everywhere. Everyone the world over thought it was all over. But in no time, Gujarat once again stood up on its feet. We will have to leave pessimism behind. Who says that such an aware democratic country—the largest in the world cannot move forward? If 125 crore Indians resolve to take one step forward, the entire country will travel 125 crore steps forward.

Which is the other country in the world which has six seasons? This land of ours is blessed; our land is fertile, full of natural resources. People from our country go abroad and earn name and fame, we only have to give opportunity to them here.

In this election, we stressed on two things—sabka saath, sabka vikas. We want everyone's progress and development but it is as important that we take everybody along with us. This election symbolised new hope, I have such able colleagues with me and with guidance from my senior leaders, I have full faith that the responsibility which was given to me on 13th September, 2013 and which was completed on 16th May, 2014 and with the new responsibility given to me today, I assure you that when we meet in 2019, I will place before you my report card. I will try and achieve the pinnacle of perseverance and hard work.

The coming year 2015-16 is important to us all, it will be Pandit Deendayal Updhyaya's centenary year, chairaveti, chairevetimantra was given by him and this led to establishing a system of sacrifice and hard work. We have to think about how to fulfill his dreams and work and strive to fulfill them. Party and the government should also think about this as to how to celebrate this coming event. Antyodaya, the service of the downtrodden, that is what Pandit Deendayal Upadhyaya had stressed. That is why I say that this government is for the poor and deprived. In global perspective also, this election of India and its results are being viewed in a very constructive and positive manner. And the first message that goes out to the world is that it is not important that millions of people have made some party victorious or made someone a prime minister. But it is important that millions have given a good mandate and have held India's position high in the world that is the message of these elections. Who won and who lost is not important. These are the results which will attract the world to India and to its democratic traditions, and capabilities. Hope has been kindled in a common citizen of India and the same hope has arisen in humanitarian forces in the world. This is a very good sign.

Brothers and sisters, once again I express my gratitude to millions of workers who have toiled hard for this victory. Modi which is before you and which you can see is because Modi is hoisted by senior leaders of my party on their shoulders. Whatever we have achieved today, is because of sacrifices made by past five generations. Jan Sangh was not known to the people, some thought it is a social, cultural organisation. Today, I salute all those generations who made sacrifices for nationalist causes. We should not forget that we are here today because of sacrifices made by the past generations. This victory is of millions of our workers. If we think like this, there will not be any opportunity for our society and party to have any complaints. BJP is the party which relies on its strong organisation, that is our strength and none of us is either away or above the organisation.

You have given me this new responsibility, Advaniji has given me blessings. You have reposed faith in me and have expectations from me and I assure you that you will not have any occasion of feeling let down. Once again, I thank you all.

□

Why I Killed Gandhi*

—Nathuram Godse

[Nathuram Godse was arrested immediately after he assassinated Gandhiji, based on a F.I.R. filed by Nandlal Mehta at the Tughlak Road Police staton at Delhi. The trial, which was held in camera, began on 27th May, 1948 and concluded on 10th February, 1949. He was sentenced to death.

An appeal to the Punjab High Court, then in session at Simla, did not find favour and the sentence was upheld. The statement that you are about to read is the last made by Godse before the Court on the 5th May, 1949.

Such was the power and eloquence of this statement that one of the judges, G.D. Khosla, later wrote, "I have, however, no doubt that had the audience of that day been constituted into a jury and entrusted with the task of deciding Godse's appeal, they would have brought a verdict of 'not Guilty' by an overwhelming majority"]

Born in a devotional Brahmin family, I instinctively came to revere Hindu religion, Hindu history and Hindu culture. I had, therefore, been intensely proud of Hinduism as a whole. As I grew up I developed a tendency to free thinking unfettered by any superstitious allegiance to any isms, political or religious.

* *Punjab High Court, Peterhoff (Raj Bhawan—The Governor's Residence), Shimla*

That is why I worked actively for the eradication of untouchability and the caste system based on birth alone. I openly joined RSS wing of anti-caste movements and maintained that all Hindus were of equal status as to rights, social and religious and should be considered high or low on merit alone and not through the accident of birth in a particular caste or profession.

I used publicly to take part in organized anti-caste dinners in which thousands of Hindus, Brahmins, Kshatriyas, Vaisyas, Chamars and Bhangis participated. We broke the caste rules and dined in the company of each other. I have read the speeches and writings of Ravana, Chanakiya, Dadabhai Naoroji, Vivekanand, Gokhale, Tilak, along with the books of ancient and modern history of India and some prominent countries like England, France, America and Russia. Moreover I studied the tenets of Socialism and Marxism. But above all I studied very closely whatever Veer Savarkar and Gandhiji had written and spoken, as to my mind these two ideologies have contributed more to the moulding of the thought and action of the Indian people during the last thirty years or so, than any other single factor has done.

All this reading and thinking led me to believe it was my first duty to serve Hindudom and Hindus both as a patriot and as a world citizen. To secure the freedom and to safeguard the just interests of some thirty crores (300 million) of Hindus would automatically constitute the freedom and the well-being of all India , one fifth of human race. This conviction led me naturally to devote myself to the Hindu Sanghtanist ideology and programme, which alone, I came to believe, could win and preserve the national independence of Hindustan, my Motherland, and enable her to render true service to humanity as well.

Since the year 1920, that is, after the demise of Lokamanya Tilak, Gandhiji's influence in the Congress first increased and then became supreme. His activities for public awakening were phenomenal in their intensity and were reinforced by the slogan of truth and non-violence which he paraded ostentatiously before the country. No sensible or enlightened person could object to those slogans. In fact there is nothing new or original in them. They are implicit in every constitutional public movement. But it is nothing but a mere dream if you imagine that the bulk of mankind is, or can ever become, capable of scrupulous adherence to these lofty principles in its normal life from day to day.

In fact, honour, duty and love of one's own kith and kin and country might often compel us to disregard non-violence and to use force. I could never conceive that an armed resistance to an aggression is unjust. I would consider it a religious and moral duty to resist and, if possible, to overpower such an enemy by use of force. [In the Ramayana] Rama killed Ravana in a tumultuous fight and relieved Sita. [In the Mahabharata], Krishna killed Kansa to end his wickedness; and Arjuna had to fight and slay quite a number of his friends and relations including the revered Bhishma because the latter was on the side of the aggressor. It is my firm belief that in dubbing Rama, Krishna and Arjuna as guilty of violence, the Mahatma betrayed a total ignorance of the springs of human action. In more recent history, it was the heroic fight put up by Chhatrapati Shivaji that first checked and eventually destroyed the Muslim tyranny in India. It was absolutely essentially for Shivaji to overpower and kill an aggressive Afzal Khan, failing which he would have lost his own life. In condemning history's towering warriors like Shivaji, Rana Pratap and Guru Gobind Singh as misguided patriots, Gandhiji has merely exposed his self-conceit. He was, paradoxical as it may appear, a violent pacifist who brought untold calamities on the country in the name of truth and non-violence, while Rana Pratap, Shivaji and the Guru will remain enshrined in the hearts of their countrymen for ever for the freedom they brought to them.

The accumulating provocation of thirty-two years, culminating in his last pro-Muslim fast, at last goaded me to the conclusion that the existence of Gandhi should be brought to an end immediately. Gandhi had done very good in South Africa to uphold the rights and well-being of the Indian community there. But when he finally returned to India he developed a subjective mentality under which he alone was to be the final judge of what was right or wrong. If the country wanted his leadership, it had to accept his infallibility; if it did not, he would stand aloof from the Congress and carry on his own way.

Against such an attitude there can be no halfway house. Either Congress had to surrender its will to his and had to be content with playing second fiddle to all his eccentricity, whimsicality, metaphysics and primitive vision, or it had to carry on without him. He alone was the Judge of everyone and every thing; he was the master brain guiding the civil disobedience movement; no other could know the technique of that movement. He alone knew when to begin and when to withdraw it. The movement might succeed or fail, it might bring untold disaster and political reverses but that could make no difference to the Mahatma's infallibility. 'A Satyagrahi can never fail' was his formula for declaring his own infallibility and nobody except himself knew what a Satyagrahi is. Thus, the Mahatma became the judge and jury in his own cause. These childish insanities and obstinacies, coupled with a most severe austerity of life, ceaseless work and lofty character made Gandhi formidable and irresistible.

Many people thought that his politics were irrational but they had either to withdraw from the Congress or place their intelligence at his feet to do with as he liked. In a position of such absolute irresponsibility Gandhi was guilty of blunder after blunder, failure after failure, disaster after disaster. Gandhi's pro-Muslim policy is blatantly in his perverse attitude on the question of the national language of India. It is quite obvious that Hindi has the most prior claim to be accepted as the premier language. In the beginning of his career in India, Gandhi gave a great impetus to Hindi but as he found that the Muslims did not like it, he became a champion of what is called Hindustani.. Everybody in India knows that there is no language called Hindustani; it has no grammar; it has no vocabulary. It is a mere dialect, it is spoken, but not written. It is a bastard tongue and cross-breed between Hindi and Urdu, and not even the Mahatma's sophistry could make it popular. But in his desire to please the Muslims he insisted that Hindustani alone should be the national language of India. His blind followers, of course, supported him and the so-called hybrid language began to be used. The charm and purity of the Hindi language was to be prostituted to please the Muslims. All his experiments were at the expense of the Hindus.

From August 1946 onwards the private armies of the Muslim League began a massacre of the Hindus. The then Viceroy, Lord Wavell, though distressed at what was happening, would not use his powers under the Government of India Act of 1935 to prevent the rape, murder and arson. The Hindu blood began to flow from Bengal to Karachi with some retaliation by the Hindus. The Interim Government formed in September was sabotaged by its Muslim League members right from its inception, but the more they became disloyal and treasonable to the government of which they were a part, the greater was Gandhi's infatuation for them. Lord Wavell had to resign as he could not bring about a settlement and he was succeeded by Lord Mountbatten. King Log was followed by King Stork. The Congress which had boasted of its nationalism and socialism secretly accepted Pakistan literally at the point of the bayonet and abjectly surrendered to Jinnah. India was vivisected and one-third of the Indian territory became foreign land to us from 15th August, 1947.

Lord Mountbatten came to be described in Congress circles as the greatest Viceroy and Governor-General this country ever had. The official date for handing over power was fixed for 30th June, 1948, but Mountbatten with his ruthless surgery gave us a gift of vivisected India ten months in advance. This is what Gandhi had achieved after thirty years of undisputed dictatorship and this is what Congress party calls 'freedom' and 'peaceful transfer of power'. The Hindu-Muslim unity bubble was finally burst and a theocratic state was established with the consent of Nehru and his crowd and they have called 'freedom won by them with sacrifice'– whose sacrifice? When top leaders of Congress, with the consent of Gandhi, divided and tore the country – which we consider a deity of worship – my mind was filled with direful anger.

One of the conditions imposed by Gandhi for his breaking of the fast unto death related to the mosques in Delhi occupied by the Hindu refugees. But when Hindus in Pakistan were subjected to violent attacks he did not so much as utter a single word to protest and censure the Pakistan Government or the Muslims concerned. Gandhi was shrewd enough to know that while undertaking a fast unto death, had he imposed for its break some condition on the Muslims in Pakistan, there would have been found hardly any Muslims who could have shown some grief if the fast had ended in his death. It was for this reason that he purposely avoided imposing any condition on the Muslims. He was fully aware of from the experience that Jinnah was not at all perturbed or influenced by his fast and the Muslim League hardly attached any value to the inner voice of Gandhi.

Gandhi is being referred to as the Father of the Nation. But if that is so, he had failed his paternal duty inasmuch as he has acted very treacherously to the nation by his consenting to the partitioning of it. I stoutly maintain that Gandhi has failed in his duty. He has proved to be the Father of Pakistan. His inner-voice, his spiritual power and his doctrine of non-violence of which so much is made of, all crumbled before Jinnah's iron will and proved to be powerless. Briefly speaking, I thought to myself and foresaw I shall be totally ruined, and the only thing I could expect from the people would be nothing but hatred and that I shall have lost all my honour, even more valuable than my life, if I were to kill Gandhiji. But at the same time I felt that the Indian politics in the absence of Gandhiji would surely be proved practical, able to retaliate, and would be powerful with armed forces. No doubt, my own future would be totally ruined, but the nation would be saved from the inroads of Pakistan. People may even call me and dub me as devoid of any sense or foolish, but the nation would be free to follow the course founded on the reason which I consider to be necessary for sound nation-building.

After having fully considered the question, I took the final decision in the matter, but I did not speak about it to anyone whatsoever. I took courage in both my hands and I did fire the shots at Gandhiji on 30th January 1948, on the prayer-grounds of Birla House. I do say that my shots were fired at the person whose policy and action had brought rack and ruin and destruction to millions of Hindus. There was no legal machinery by which such an offender could be brought to book and for this reason I fired those fatal shots. I bear no ill will towards anyone individually but I do say that I had no respect for the present government owing to their policy which was unfairly favourable towards the Muslims.

But at the same time I could clearly see that the policy was entirely due to the presence of Gandhi.

I have to say with great regret that Prime Minister Nehru quite forgets that his preachings and deeds are at times at variances with each other when he talks about India as a secular state in season and out of season, because it is significant to note that Nehru has played a leading role in the establishment of the theocratic state of Pakistan, and his job was made easier by Gandhi's persistent policy of appeasement towards the Muslims. I now stand before the court to accept the full share of my responsibility for what I have done and the judge would, of course, pass against me such orders of sentence as may be considered proper. But I would like to add that I do not desire any mercy to be shown to me, nor do I wish that anyone else should beg for mercy on my behalf. My confidence about the moral side of my action has not been shaken even by the criticism levelled against it on all sides. I have no doubt that honest writers of history will weigh my act and find the true value thereof some day in future.

□

The Crisis of Civilization*

—Rabindranath Tagore

[In 1880 Rabindranath Thakur, anglicised to 'Tagore' returned to Bengal degree-less, resolving to reconcile European novelty with Brahmo traditions, taking the best from each. In 1890 Tagore began managing his vast ancestral estates in Shelaidaha (today a region of Bangladesh) and released his 'Manasi' poems, among his best-known work. In 1901 Tagore moved to Santiniketan to found an ashram with a marble-floored prayer hall—TheMandir—an experimental school, groves of trees, gardens, a library. He gained Bengali and foreign readers alike. In November 1913, Tagore learned he had won that year's Nobel Prize in Literature: the Swedish Academy appreciated the idealistic—and for Westerners—accessible nature of a small body of his translated material focussed on the 1912 Gitanjali: Song Offerings. In 1915, the British Crown granted Tagore a knighthood. He renounced it after the 1919 Jallianwala Bagh massacre.

Tagore, visiting Santa Barbara in 1917, conceived a new type of university, to make Santiniketan the connecting thread between India and the world [and] a world center for the study of humanity somewhere beyond the limits of nation and geography. The school, which he named Visva-

* *Last Public Pronouncement Delivered During His 80th Birthday Celebrations, Shantiniketan, 7th May, 1941*

Bharati, had its foundation stone laid on 24th December, 1918 and was inaugurated precisely three years later. Tagore employed a Brahmacharya system: Gurus gave pupils personal guidance—emotional, intellectual, and spiritual. Teaching was often done under trees. He staffed the school, he contributed his Nobel Prize monies, and his duties as steward-mentor at Santiniketan kept him busy: mornings he taught classes; afternoons and evenings he wrote the students' textbooks. Between 1878 and 1932, Tagore set foot in more than thirty countries on five continents. He fundraised widely for the school in Europe and the United States between 1919 and 1921.

Tagore mourned the perennial poverty of Kolkata and the socioeconomic decline of Bengal. He detailed these newly plebeian aesthetics in an unrhymed hundred-line poem whose technique of searing double-vision foreshadowed Satyajit Ray's film 'Apur Sansar'. Fifteen new volumes appeared. Experimentation continued in his prose-songs and dance-dramas. His respect for scientific laws and his exploration of biology, physics, and astronomy informed his poetry, which exhibited extensive naturalism and verisimilitude. Tagore wrote eight novels and four novellas. 'Ghare Baire' (The Home and the World), through the lens of the idealistic zamindar protagonist Nikhl, excoriates rising Indian nationalism, terrorism, and religious zeal in the Swadeshi movement. The novel ends in Hindu-Muslim violence and Nikhil's—likely mortal—wounding. 'Gora' raises controversial questions regarding the Indian identity. As with Ghare Baire, matters of self-identity (jati), personal freedom, and religion are developed in the context of a family story and love triangle. In 'Jogajog' (Relationships), Tagore flaunts his feminist leanings and depicts the plight and ultimate demise of women trapped by pregnancy, duty, and family honour.

Tagore was a prolific composer with 2,230 songs to his credit. His songs are known as 'rabindrasangit' (Tagore Song), which merges fluidly into his literature, most of which—poems or parts of novels, stories, or plays alike—were lyricised. Influenced by the 'thumri' style of Hindustani music, they ran the entire gamut of human emotion, ranging from his early dirge-like Brahmo devotional hymns to quasi-erotic compositions. In 1971, 'Amar Shonar Bangla' became the national anthem of Bangladesh. It was written—ironically—to protest the 1905 Partition of Bengal along communal lines: lopping Muslim-majority East Bengal from Hindu-dominated West Bengal was to avert a regional bloodbath. Tagore saw the partition as a ploy to upend the independence movement, and he aimed to rekindle Bengali unity and tar communalism. 'Jana Gana Mana' was written in shadhu-bhasha, a Sanskritised register of Bengali, and is the first of five stanzas of a Brahmo hymn that Tagore composed. It was first sung in 1911 at a Kolkata session of the Indian National Congress and was adopted in 1950 by the Constituent Assembly of the Republic of India as its national anthem.

At sixty, Tagore took up drawing and painting; successful exhibitions of his many works—which made a debut appearance in Paris upon encouragement by artists he met in the south of France—were held throughout Europe. He was likely red-green color blind, resulting in works that exhibited strange colour schemes and off-beat aesthetics.

For his 80th birthday in 1941, Tagore wrote this speech—The Crisis of Civilisation. Some sources suggest that the speech was delivered in Santiniketan in Tagore's presence to mark the Bengali New Year on 14th April, 1941. However, as the speech begins literally "Today, my age has completed eighty years", it seems more likely that it was delivered during the celebrations of his 80th birthday on 7th May, 1941. At the height of the Second World War, this speech turned out to be his last public pronouncement. For these reasons it is a profoundly moving and powerful speech. It seems that he thought it to be his final testament as man disillusioned by history. He died on 7th August, 1941.]

Today I complete eighty years of my life. As I look back on the vast stretch of years that lie behind me and see in clear perspective the history of my early development, I am struck by the change that has taken place both in my own attitude and in the psychology of my countrymen–a change that carries within it a cause of profound tragedy.

Our direct contact with the larger world of men was linked up with the contemporary history of the English people whom we came to know in those earlier days. It was mainly through their mighty literature that we formed our ideas with regard to these newcomers to our Indian shores. In those days the type of learning that was served out to us was neither plentiful nor diverse, nor was the spirit of scientific enquiry very much in evidence. Thus their scope being strictly limited, the educated of those days had recourse to English language and literature. Their days and nights were eloquent with the stately declamations of Burke, with Macaulay's long-rolling sentences; discussions centred upon Shakespeare's drama and Byron's poetry and above all upon the large-hearted liberalism of the nineteenth-century English politics.

At the time though tentative attempts were being made to gain our national independence, at heart we had not lost faith in the generosity of the English race. This belief was so firmly rooted in the sentiments of our leaders as to lead them to hope that the victor would of his own grace pave the path of freedom for the vanquished. This belief was based upon the fact that England at the time provided a shelter to all those who had to flee from persecution in their own country. Political martyrs who had suffered for the honour of their people were accorded unreserved welcome at the hands of the English.

I was impressed by this evidence of liberal humanity in the character of the English and thus I was led to set them on the pedestal of my highest respect. This generosity in their national character had not yet been vitiated by imperialist pride. About this time, as a boy in England, I had the opportunity of listening to the speeches of John Bright, both in and outside Parliament. The large-hearted, radical liberalism of those speeches, overflowing all narrow national bounds, had made so deep an impression on my mind that something of it lingers even today, even in these days of graceless disillusionment.

Certainly that spirit of abject dependence upon the charity of our rulers was no matter for pride. What was remarkable, however, was the wholehearted way in which we gave our recognition to human greatness even when it revealed itself in the foreigner. The best and noblest gifts of humanity cannot be the monopoly of a particular race or country; its scope may not be limited nor may it be regarded as the miser's hoard buried underground. That is why English literature which nourished our minds in the past, does even now convey its deep resonance to the recesses of our heart.

It is difficult to find a suitable Bengali equivalent for the English word 'civilization'. That phase of civilization with which we were familiar in this country has been called by Manu 'Sadachar' (literally, proper conduct), that is, the conduct prescribed by the tradition of the race. Narrow in themselves these time-honoured social conventions originated and held good in a circumscribed geographical area, in that strip of land, Brahmavarta by name, bound on either side by the rivers Saraswati and Drisadvati. That is how a pharisaic formalism gradually got the upper hand of free thought and the ideal of 'proper conduct' which Manu found established in Brahmavarta steadily degenerated into socialized tyranny. During my boyhood days the attitude towards the cultured and educated section of Bengal, nurtured on English learning, was charged with a feeling of revolt against these rigid regulations of society.

A perusal of what Rajnarain Bose has written describing the ways of the educated gentry of those days will amply bear out what I have said just now. In place of these set codes of conduct we accepted the ideal of 'civilization' as represented by the English term.

In our own family this change of spirit was welcomed for the sake of its sheer rational and moral force and its influence was felt in every sphere of our life. Born in that atmosphere, which was moreover coloured by our intuitive bias for literature, I naturally set the English on the throne of my heart. Thus passed the first chapters of my life. Then came the parting of ways accompanied with a painful feeling of disillusion when I began increasingly to discover how easily those who accepted the highest truths of civilization disowned them with impunity whenever questions of national self-interest were involved.

There came a time when perforce I had to snatch myself away from the mere appreciation of literature. As I emerged into the stark light of bare facts, the sight of the dire poverty of the Indian masses rent my heart. Rudely shaken out of my dreams, I began to realize that perhaps in no other modern state was there such hopeless dearth of the most elementary needs of existence. And yet it was this country whose resources had fed for so long the wealth and magnificence of the British people.

While I was lost in the contemplation of the great world of civilization, I could never have remotely imagined that the great ideals of humanity would end in such ruthless travesty. But today a glaring example of it stares me in the face in the utter and contemptuous indifference of a so-called civilized race to the wellbeing of crores of Indian people. That mastery over the machine, by which the British have consolidated their sovereignty over their vast Empire, has been kept a sealed book, to which due access has been denied to this helpless country. And all the time before our very eyes Japan has been transforming herself into a mighty and prosperous nation. I have seen with my own eyes the admirable use to which Japan has put in her own country the fruits of this progress.

I have also been privileged to witness, while in Moscow, the unsparing energy with which Russia has tried to fight disease and illiteracy, and has succeeded in steadily liquidating ignorance and poverty, wiping off the humiliation from the face of a vast continent. Her civilization is free from all invidious distinction between one class and another, between one sect and another. The rapid and astounding progress achieved by her made me happy and jealous at the same time.

One aspect of the Soviet administration which particularly pleased me was that it provided no scope for unseemly conflict of religious differences, nor set one community against another by unbalanced distribution of political favours. That I consider a truly civilized administration which impartially serves the common interests of the people.

While other imperialist powers sacrifice the welfare of the subject races to their own national greed, in the USSR I found a genuine attempt being made to harmonise the interests of the various nationalities that are scattered over its vast area. I saw peoples and tribes, who, only the other day, were nomadic savages being encouraged and indeed trained, to avail themselves freely of the benefits of civilization. Enormous sums are being spent on their education to expedite the process.

When I see elsewhere some two hundred nationalities -which only a few years ago were at vastly different stages of development -marching ahead in peaceful progress and amity, and when I look about my own country and see a very highly evolved and intellectual people drifting into the disorder of barbarism, I cannot help contrasting the two systems of governments, one based on co-operation, the other on exploitation, which have made such contrary conditions possible.

I have also seen Iran, newly awakened to a sense of national self sufficiency, attempting to fulfil her own destiny freed from the deadly grinding-stones of two European powers. During my recent visit to that country I discovered to my delight that Zoroastrians who once suffered from the fanatical hatred of the major community and whose rights had been curtailed by the ruling power were now free from this age-long repression, and that civilized life had established itself in the happy land. It is significant that Iran's good fortune dates from the day when she finally disentangled herself from the meshes of European diplomacy. With all my heart I wish Iran well.

Turning to the neighbouring kingdom of Afghanistan I find that though there is much room for improvement in the field of education and social development, yet she is fortunate in that she can look forward to unending progress; for none of the European powers, boastful of their civilization, has yet succeeded in overwhelming and crushing her possibilities.

Thus while these other countries were marching ahead, India, smothered under the dead weight of British administration, lay static in her utter helplessness. Another great and ancient civilization for whose recent tragic history the British cannot disclaim responsibility, is China. To serve their own national profit the British first doped her people with opium and then appropriated a portion of her territory. As the world was about to forget the memory of this outrage, we were painfully surprised by another event. While Japan was quietly devouring North China, her act of wanton aggression was ignored as a minor incident by the veterans of British diplomacy.

We have also witnessed from this distance how actively the British statesmen acquiesced in the destruction of the Spanish Republic. On the other hand, we also noted with admiration how a band of valiant Englishmen laid down their lives for Spain. Even though the English had not aroused themselves sufficiently to their sense of responsibility towards China in the Far East, in their own immediate neighbourhood they did not hesitate to sacrifice themselves to the cause of freedom.

Such acts of heroism reminded me over again of the true English spirit to which in those early days I had given my full faith, and made me wonder how imperialist greed could bring about so ugly a transformation in the character of so great a race. Such is the tragic tale of the gradual loss of my faith in the claims of the European nations to civilization.

In India the misfortune of being governed by a foreign race is daily brought home to us not only in the callous neglect of such minimum necessities of life as adequate provision for food, clothing, education and medical facilities for the people, but in an even unhappier form in the way people have divided themselves. The pity of it is that the blame is laid at the door of our own society. So frightful a culmination of the history of our people would never have been possible, but for the encouragement it has received from secret influences emanating from high places.

One cannot believe that Indians are in any way inferior to the Japanese in intellectual capacity. The most effective difference between these two eastern peoples is that whereas India lies at the mercy of the British, Japan has been spared the shadow of alien domination. We know what we have been deprived of. That which was truly best in their own civilizations, the upholding of the dignity of human relationships, has no place in the British administration of this country.

If in its place they have established, with baton in hand, a reign of 'law and order', in other words a policeman's rule, such mockery of civilization can claim no respect from us. It is the mission of civilization to bring unity among people and establish peace and harmony. But in unfortunate India the social fabric is being rent into shreds by unseemly outbursts of hooliganism daily growing in intensity, right under the very aegis of 'law and order'.

In India, so long as no personal injury is inflicted upon any member of the ruling race, this barbarism seems to be assured of perpetuity, making us ashamed to live under such an administration.

And yet my good fortune has often brought me into close contact with really large-hearted Englishmen. Without the slightest hesitation I may say that the nobility of their character was without parallel–in no country or community have I come across such greatness of soul. Such examples would not allow me to wholly lose faith in the race which produced them.

I had the rare blessing of having Andrews – a real Englishman, a real Christian and a true man – for a very close friend. Today in the perspective of death his unselfish and courageous magnanimity shines all the brighter. The whole of India remains indebted to him for innumerable acts of love and devotion. But personally speaking, I am especially beholden to him because he helped me to retain in my old age that feeling of respect for the English race with which in the past I was inspired by their literature and which I was about to lose completely. I count such Englishmen as Andrews not only as my personal and intimate friends but as friends of the whole human race. To have known them has been to me a treasured privilege.

It is my belief that such Englishmen will save British honour from shipwreck. At any rate if I had not known them, my despair at the prospect of Western civilization would be unrelieved. In the meanwhile the demon of barbarity has given up all pretence and has emerged with unconcealed fangs, ready to tear up humanity in an orgy of devastation. From one end of the world to the other the poisonous fumes of hatred darken the atmosphere.

The spirit of violence which perhaps lay dormant in the psychology of the West, has at last roused itself and desecrates the spirit of Man. The wheels of Fate will some day compel the English to give up their Indian empire. But what kind of India will they leave behind, what stark misery? 'When the stream of their centuries' administration runs dry at last, what a waste of mud and filth they will leave behind them! I had at one time believed that the springs of civilization would issue out of the heart of Europe. But today when I am about to quit the world that faith has gone bankrupt altogether.

As I look around I see the crumbling ruins of a proud civilization strewn like a vast heap of futility. And yet I shall not commit the grievous sin of losing faith in Man. I would rather look forward to the opening of a new chapter in his history after the cataclysm is over and the atmosphere rendered clean with the spirit of service and sacrifice. Perhaps that dawn will come from this horizon, from the East where the sun rises. A day will come when unvanquished Man will retrace his path of conquest, despite all barriers, to win back his lost human heritage.

Today we witness the perils which attend on the insolence of might; one day shall be borne out the full truth of what the sages have proclaimed: 'By unrighteousness man prospers, gains what appears desirable, conquers enemies, but perishes at the root.'

□

Dream of 21st Century India*

—Rajiv Gandhi

Friends,

This is a moment consecrated by history. One hundred years have passed since the Indian National Congress first met in this great city. Between then and now, India and the world have witnessed profound historical changes-changes that have affected the very structure of human thought and action. In this epoch of radical change, the Indian National Congress brought the world to India and took India to the world. Its non-violent revolution has transformed our nation. Today, it charts the path to India's greatness.

We rejoice in this moment. We rejoice in the great achievements, the great deeds of the people of India. We rejoice in the noble expressions of the human intellect and spirit represented by Mahatma Gandhi, Jawaharlal Nehru and Indira Gandhi. We rejoice in the pledge redeemed. We rejoice that the honour is ours now to carry the torch of freedom and progress.

But our joy is mixed with sorrow. Indiraji should have been here today, speaking to you in her gentle, impassioned voice. One with Bharatmata's immortal spirit, she now shines as a lodestar not only for us but for all humanity.

As I recall the great women and men who have led the Indian

* *Inaugural Speech And Centenary Resolve, Congress Centenary Session, Brabourne Stadium, Bombay, 28th December, 1985*

National Congress - the Parliament of Indian Nationalism - I feel proud and humble. I draw strength from the glorious tradition of our party and from the overflowing affection of the people of India.

May I thank dynamic Bombay and its gracious and hospitable people, for playing host to us, as they played host to our founding fathers in 1885? I, of course, have a sentimental relationship with Bombay. I was born here. Life-giving currents from every part of India flow into Bombay. It is India in microcosm.

Many distinguished delegates have come to this session from far and near, bringing to us the friendship and greetings of their parties and peoples. We appreciate this gesture. Through these honoured guests, we send our good wishes to the people of their countries.

As I stand before you this morning, my mind travels back to those fateful years when the Congress fought for India's freedom. And I think of those giants who made the Indian National Congress. Seldom has the world seen a nobler galaxy of women and men, so selfless in their devotion to the cause of freedom, so exalted in thought, so brave in action, so pure in spirit. To remember them is to live once again in those times 'when the world's great age seemed to begin anew.' A.O. Hume, Woomesh Chandra Bonnerji, Dadabhai Naoroji, Pherozeshah Mehta, Mahadev Govind Ranade, Badruddin Tyabji, Lokmanya Tilak, Gopal Krishna Gokhale, Surendra Nath Bannerjee, Annie Besant, Bepin Chandra Pal, Lala Lajpat Rai, Mahatma Gandhi, Motilal Nehru, Madan Mohan Malaviya, Deshbandhu Chitta Ranjan Das, Srivivasa Iyengar, Sarojini Naidu, M.A. Ansari, Jawaharlal Nehru, Sardar Vallabhbhai Patel, Chakravarti Rajagopalachari, Mazharul Huque, Satyamurthi, Rajendra Prasad, Maulana Abul Kalam Azad, Saifudin Kitchlew, Tristao de Braganza Cunha, Gopabandhu Das, Netaji Subhas Chandra Bose, Gopinath Bordoloi, Govind Ballabh Pant, Purushottam Das Tandon, T. Prakasam, Bidhan Chandra Roy, Acharya Kripalani, Acharya Narendra Dev, Rajkumari Amrit Kaur, Rafi Ahmed Kidwai, Acharya Vinoba Bhave, Jayaprakash Narayan, Indira Gandhi, Kamaraj, Lal Bahadur Shastri, Gurmukh Singh Musafir, Fakhruddin Ali Ahmed and countless others. We bow in reverence to their memory. They awakened the spirit of freedom in the Indian people crushed under the oppressive burden of imperialism. Gurudev Tagore and Shri Aurobindo Ghosh were one with the leaders of our struggle for independence in reawakening India to its true destiny.

It is our fortune that one of our great freedom fighters, Khan Abdul Ghaffar Khan Sahib, is with us today. His life is a saga of sacrifice and non-violence. He has asked nothing for himself and has given his all to the service of his fellow men. We greet him with respect, with love, and pray he may long be with us.

We are blessed with the presence of large number of freedom fighters. We honour them for they made freedom a living reality. Their refusal to submit to the indignity of slavery, the very act of their defiance, and their luminous vision of a united and free India touched the imagination of millions. To the nameless and unsung heroes of our freedom struggle, we offer our humble tribute. Their life-blood nourishes the body of independent India.

How did the miracle of India's rebirth in freedom come about? And what did India do with this new life? The answers are to be found in the story of the Indian National Congress.

How shall we remember Mahatma Gandhi, that eternal pilgrim of freedom? Born of the very spirit of India, steeped in the tradition, the song, the legend of our ancient land - and yet he was revolutionary. Unique among revolutionaries, he marched for freedom, clad in the robe of truth, with non-violence for his staff.

He did not counter the violence of the oppressor with the violence of the oppressed. He met it by changing the oppressed from within. He freed them from fear and hatred. He ignited the greatest peaceful mass movement known to history. At his gentle summons, millions of Indians rose to assert their human dignity and walked upright with the spark of greatness in them.

Gandhiji the revolutionary was concerned with nothing less than the total reconstruction of our society. In Champaran among the impoverished peasants, in Ahmedabad among the textile workers, and in hundreds of thousands of villages of India, he had seen the soul of India seared by the ruthless exploitation of the poor. He saw how India's social system had been vitiated by iniquitous practices - the oppression of the Harijans, of the women and of the poor.

To Mahatma Gandhi, the key to India's progress was the development of its villages. In his unified vision, education, agriculture, village industry, social reform, all came together to provide the basis for a vibrant rural society, free from exploitation and linked to the urban centres as equals our planning incorporates this basic insight.

His crusade against untouchability stirred and ossified system. His radical premise of human dignity and equality electrified millions who lived and struggled at the very margin of social existence. Independent India was to enshrine Mahatma Gandhi's war on untouchability in its Constitution.

The freedom movement transformed the status of women. Women fought along with men as comrades. In the process, the shackles that had bound them fell away. Legal safeguards and tights were to come later but Mahatma Gandhi emancipated women from slavery and oppression. What took centuries in other countries was accomplished in a matter of decades in our freedom struggle.

The mark of true revolutionary is that he sets new standards and values. Gandhiji did. Let us recall his words:

"I will give you a talisman. Whenever you are in doubt or when the self becomes too much with you, apply the following test: Recall the face of the poorest and the weakest man whom you may have seen and ask yourself if the step you contemplate is going to be of any use to him. Will he gain anything by it? Will it restore him to a control over his own life and destiny? In other words, will it lead to swaraj for the hungry and spiritually starving millions? Then you will find your doubts and yourself melting away."

We cannot, and will not, rest until we have won true swaraj for the hungry and spiritually starving millions - until we have wiped out poverty from our land. Then and only then can we claim the privilege of being true disciples of the great mahatma.

Mahatma Gandhi called Jawaharlal Nehru 'the jewel of India'. Panditji added new dimensions to our concept of freedom. To a reawakened India, he brought intimations of mighty historical forces at work on the world stage. As the freedom struggle grew in intensity, he went out among the masses, unfolding his vision of the future: immemorial India rejuvenated by modern science, technology, and the cleansing moral force of socialism, yet retaining her identity and the age old wealth of her spiritual wisdom.

Jawaharlal Nehru destroyed the edifice of imperialism. For he knew he had the greater task of building a new society. He was a treat builder. He gave India the enduring structure of democratic parliamentary institutions buttressed by the rule of law. Fundamental rights, directive principles of State policy, and safeguards for the Scheduled Castes and Scheduled Tribes together make our Constitution one of humanity's great charters of freedom and equality. We have passed through many a crisis, but democracy has continued to flourish-to the consternation of those who believed that democracy was for the rich, not for the poor. In India democracy, with all its claimant contention, is alive and vibrant.

Jawaharlal Nehru fashioned the planning process to reach the ultimate objective of a socialist. Planning is now a part of the national consensus. It was not always so. It used to be described as the road to serfdom. Those who scoffed have stayed to praise. We have a strong economy. We are firmly set on the path of self-reliance, which means more freedom, nor less. Our planning process has succeeded.

Panditji built the infrastructure of science and technology with loving care. Atomic energy and Space stand out as symbols of this achievement, bit no field was left untouched. Let us not forget that it was Panditji who established the great laboratories, the giant irrigation dams, the fertilizer plants and the agricultural universities. This was the foundation of our self-sufficiency.

Immersed as he was in the thick of our freedom struggle, Pandit Nehru foresaw that, in the ultimate analysis, the linkages between modern agriculture and industrialisation offered the only lasting solution to the poverty of India's masses. With independence, the time came to translate into reality the dream of a vigorous, industrialised India. Panditji created the imposing structure of our industry. Leading this mighty effort was the public sector, a strong and dependable lever for development. He envisioned for it the commanding heights of the economy. Under his inspiration, basic industries, infrastructure, machine building, oil exploration, metals and minerals and defence industries were established. In the public sector new technology was absorbed and nurtured. New skills came to those who had never turned a simple lathe. Centres of modern industry blossomed in backward and remote areas. With confidence, the Indian people wrote a new chapter in their long and tumultuous history. Through the instrument of the public sector, Jawaharlal Nehru made the decisive break with India's colonial de-industrialised stagnation.

Panditji was the great unifier of the Indian people. India is the home of many great religions. Her many splendoured mansion of unity rests on the bedrock of secularism. Like a great teacher, he expounded in simple language the philosophy of secularism. He repeatedly warned the nation against communalism. To him, secularism was the beacon light when waves of passion threatened to submerge us.

Panditji looked at the world with the eyes of a humanist, in love with nature and with the works of man. He perceived before many others, that the splitting of the atom had changed for all time to come the universe of discourse among nations. War in nuclear age was no longer policy by other means-it was mass suicide. He saw no meaning in military blocs. They did not guarantee security. They only guaranteed fear. He wanted nations to cooperate, not dominate. He evolved the philosophy of non-alignment. Non-align is the international expression of national resurgence. It is the extension of democracy to international relations. It means independence of thought and action. Panditji abjured entanglement with power blocs, because poser blocs are based on conflict, and erode the independence of countries, which join them. He put forward the positive concept of peaceful co-existence, and, co-operation to build a better, saner world free from anxiety, suspicion and fear. This vision of a cooperative world order even today guides the Non-aligned Movement, representing the vast majority of the family of nations. It is a powerful force for freedom, peace and justice in the world. In its centenary year, the Indian National Congress is proud that India has the honour to lead the Non-aligned Movement.

All this and more is the legacy of Jawaharlal Nehru, his imperishable bequest to us in the Indian National Congress.

The smooth succession of Lal Bahadur Shastri proved the inherent strength of our democratic system. He guided the country with steadfast devotion to the basic policies of the Congress. The Congress has always stood for patriotism, simplicity, selfless service and dedication to the cause of the underprivileged, Shastriji epitomised these values.

With the sudden demise of Shastriji, once more the questions arose with even greater urgency: would a united India survive? Would its democracy endure? Would a food-deficit country be able to preserve its independence? Would the cry of social justice remain unheeded? India's voice for freedom, peace and justice remain as firm and resonant as in the past? Or would neo-colonialism claim yet another victim? Would India once again become a petitioner in the chancelleries of the west?

The world was torn by anxiety and conflict. In Vietnam, war continued to rage. There were no signs of any lessening of East-West tensions. In India, food shortages and inflation bred serious unrest. There were intense pressures to abandon the path of planned development. It was situation to daunt the most stout-hearted.

Never known to flee from challenge, Indira Gandhi took up cudgels on behalf of the masses of India. She placed the removal of poverty at the very centre of the planning process. One radical step followed boldly upon another, establishing beyond doubt where the sympathies of the Indian National Congress lay. The nationalisation of banks, the abolition of privy-purses, the takeover of the coal mines, the promulgation of radical land reforms and the creation of constitutional safety-nets for them, the formulation of a system of guaranteed prices to farmers, the setting up of a country wide public distribution system, the large scale extension on modern technology to agriculture, the establishment of

Monopolies and Restrictive Trade Practices Commission to curb concentration of economic power, the great impetus to the growth of the public sector, the Pokharan test for peaceful purposes, the Space programme and the launching of the massive 20-Point Programme and the Rural landless Labour employment Guarantee Programme- all these electrified the nation.

The Congress in the late sixties reminded one of Panditji's address to the 1936 Lucknow Congress, where he said:

"we have largely lost touch with the masses and, deprived of the life-giving energy that flows from them, we dry up and weaken and our organisation shrinks and loses the power it had."

The people were adrift. The policies of the Congress were in confusion. There was no programme of action. At this point of crisis, Indira Gandhi revitalised the party by restoring its organic link with the masses. The sap of action began to flow one again in the veins of the organisation. The vocabulary and the idiom of Indian politics were never to be same again after her historic call for 'garibi hatao'.

Indiraji transformed the Congress from a party in which vested interest had gradually gained ascendancy into a party which identified itself totally with the hopes and aspirations of the poor. Through her unrelenting struggle against those who opposed radical change in our social and economic structure, she placed her indelible stamp on the history of our party. With unparalleled tenacity, she persuaded millions of Congresswomen and men to pursue the path of socialism to progress. She took the people into confidence on the nature of the issues, which were convulsing the Congress and mobilised them behind her policies. The masses gave her the strength to face with unequalled courage the inner turmoil of the party. They manned the barricades. In 1969, the champions of the status quo had to retreat, relinquishing their control of our great organisations. The triumph of the Congress in the 1971 elections was a big blow to the forces that had thwarted social change from within the party. They were to regroup and challenge her again.

India's unequivocal stand on major international issues had disturbed, even alarmed, forces who were exerting pressures on us to deflect us from our independent policy of non-alignment. The emergence of sovereign Bangladesh and Indira Gandhi's historic role in it were anathema to neo-imperialism. Almost immediately thereafter began the collusion between external and internal forces of destabilisation. The international economic crisis, widespread drought and inflation within the country put an intolerable strain on our system. National stability was in dire peril.

To meet an unprecedented threat to the nation's stability, an emergency was proclaimed in 1975. The process of socio-economic change gathered momentum with the promulgation of the bold and dynamic 20 Point Programme. A democrat to the core of her being, Indiraji called elections in 1977. She accepted the verdict of the people who defeated her and the Congress. She knew it was an angry reaction to some mistakes that had been committed, but that the people were still with her and with the Congress. She stood by the people in their travail as they faced the tragic consequences of the reversal of nationally accepted policies. But many of her colleagues did not have her courage of conviction. Their vision faltered. They parted company with her. The congress again emerged, with youth in the vanguard as the sword arm of the poor. They voted her back in 1980, expressing their unbounded love for her and trust in her commitment to social justice.

In radicalising the Congress, Indira Gandhi also gave new strength and vitality to the democratic parliamentary institutions of the Republic. She realigned our political process with the urges of the toiling masses. By translating the people's aspirations into epoch making legislation, policy innovations and programmes for the uplift o the poor, she made the legislatures watchful guardians of the rights and needs of the people. Elections and the parliamentary process acquired ideological and programmatic clarity, giving direction to national progress. She mobilised immense numbers of people from all strata, filling them with hope and deepening their allegiance to the democratic way of life. In victory as in defeat, Indiraji was the prime mover of the people's emotions and endeavours. She ensured that India's democracy would never be the plaything of vested interests.

Indira Gandhi knew, as did Jawaharlal Nehru, that social justice depended on the production and equitable distribution of wealth. She attended to the growth potential of our economy like a living mother. The first to claim her attention was agriculture. Not just because and overwhelming majority derived their livelihood from agriculture, but because national independence and self-respect demanded that we do not stretch our hands before anyone for food. Many here will still recall the pain and the humiliation of the 'ship-to-mouth' days. She called upon our farmers and our agricultural scientists to apply modern technology to increase food production. Their heart-warming response is a matter of history. Thus were laid the impregnable foundations of self-reliance.

As she had faced not one but two oil crises, Indira Gandhi was determined to take India towards self-sufficiency in energy resources. The prodigious effort to raise oil production, trebling it in the short space of four years, is testimony to her far-sighted vision.

Indiraji had a unique relationship with India's dedicated scientific community. She was their special friend to whom they turned for counsel and encouragement. Together they placed India in the front rank of international scientific communities. A few days ago I was in Kalpakkam to inaugurate the fast breeder test reactor. India is the seventh country in the world to have such a reactor. Indiraji's monumental work in furthering indigenous science and technology has greatly strengthened the base for self-reliance.

Generations will remember with gratitude the decisive direction Indira Gandhi gave to India's industrialisation and technological advance. She set exacting tasks for the public sector, which responded with enthusiasm. Through the exertions of the working class and talented managers and technologists, it became the pivot of India's industrial progress. All branches and sectors of industry grew with speed, placing India among the major industrial nations of the world. The enormous range and depth of industrial progress, centred on the public sector, has served the nation well. Today, if we are poised for faster technological growth, the credit goes to Indiraji who prepared the see-bed of modernisation.

In the international field, Indira Gandhi was the authentic voice of non-alignment, of peace and peaceful coexistence, disarmament and development. She was bold and fearless, refusing to be cowed down by pressures howsoever strong. Where the independence or sovereignty of India was in question, she never vacillated, never hesitated, never compromised. She stood like a rock in the defence of India.

The passion that ruled her was above all the passion for the unity and integrity of India. In the perspective of history, she knew how India had been subjugated because of its inability to rectify internal weaknesses and to unitedly confront external dangers. She turned the searchlight on the internal social malaise that weakened the nation-the deprivation of the scheduled castes and the scheduled tribes, the social and economic backwardness of the minorities, communalism, casteism and narrow regional loyalties. Her effort throughout was to strengthen the national fabric. Her socio-economic programmes are her greatest contribution to national integration.

But she never forgot the threats to India, external and internal, direct and indirect, military and economic. She campaigned relentlessly to alert the nation to these dangers and toiled unremittingly to strengthen our defences. She had seen again and again how the independence and unity of nations had been suborned and subverted. She was determined not to let this happen to India. Nothing would induce her to accept the dilution of an iota of India's unity and sovereignty, even at the cost of her life.

What of the future? Where do we go from here?

There is no rest for us. As Jawaharlal Nehru had said, "We cannot rest, for rest is betrayal of those who have gone and in going handed the torch of freedom to us to keep alight; it is betrayal of the cause we have espoused and the pledge we have taken; it is betrayal of the millions who never rest." We cannot rest.

The history of our party tells us that, at each critical turning point, we took stock of our weaknesses and strengths to decide the direction we must take. The present situation demands a similar unsparing examination. Without self-introspection, without soul searching, movement will not be much avail. We must see ourselves in the mirror of truth. What have we done with the legacy of our great leaders?

To answer this question, I must delve into my own political experience, short though it is. When I started my political work, it was only with the motive of being by the side of my mother. She bore with stoic fortitude the irreparable loss of a son who had been a tower of strength. She gave me no directions, no formulate, no prescriptions. She just said, "Understand the real India, Its people, its problems." So I plunged into work. Millions of faces in varying moods of joy and sorrow, of eager expectation, of triumph and defeat filled my being, till they merged into the face of mother India, proud, defiant, confident but also full of sad perplexity. Always, the unspoken question haunting her face: Whither India?

I was exhilarated by what had been achieved in the short period since Independence. I was also saddened by what might have been but was not, because of weaknesses in government and in the party. I kept my counsel to my-self, as I was an apprentice in the great school of politics.

After two years of incessant travelling, meeting people, reading and reflection, I felt I could go to her with my perceptions. Listening to me, she thought I had gained some understanding of the complexities of our society. And then she began to unburden herself. She spoke of India's enduring strength and of her hopes for India, but also of her apprehensions and anxieties. She analysed with clinical precision how the entire system had been weakened from within, how the party had once again been infiltrated by vested interests who would not allow us to move, how patronage and graft had affected the national institutional framework, how nationalism and patriotism had ebbed, how the pettiness and selfishness of persons in political positions had ruptured social fabric. She was clear that if India had to keep her 'tryst with destiny,' so much had to change. And them, suddenly, she left us. Indiraji's thoughts and reflections on the state of the nation are an abiding influence.

We have cherished our democracy. Democracy is our strength. In 1984, the people of India gave out party its largest ever majority. Their eloquent verdict strengthened then unity and integrity of India. A nation sorrowing over its beloved leader drew from its vast reserves of strength to protect the inheritance of its glorious freedom struggle.

We applied the lessons of the 1984 elections to the complex and difficult problems in Punjab and Assam. Our basic concern was to end any sense of alienation in the larger interests of national unity. We carried forward the process to reach understanding and harmony, to dispel mistrust and suspicion, and to seek the people's mandate for progress through brotherhood. We had no narrow partisan considerations in view. The situation demanded that we rise above mere expediency. The Congress, with its century-old tradition of nationalism, put India first.

We have no illusions that all problems have been resolved. But the democratic way of nation building requires patience, perseverance and a spirit of conciliation. Those who have been entrusted with responsibility have to constantly keep in view the larger perspective of unity. They have to act in the same spirit in which we have acted, the spirit of the nationalism. Enduring unity comes from the willing cooperation of all.

We proclaim celebrate the unity of India. It is a fact of transcending significance. But is it not also a fact that most of us, in our daily lives, do not think of ourselves as Indians? We see ourselves as Hindus, Muslims or Christians, or Malyalees, Maharashtrians, Bengalis. Worse, we think of ourselves as Brahmins, Thakurs, Jats, Yadavas and so on and so forth. And we shed blood to uphold our narrow and selfish denominations. We are imprisoned by the narrow, domestic walls of religion, language, caste, and region, blocking out the clear view of a resurgent nation. Political parties, State Governments and social organisations promote policies, programmes and ideologies which divide brother from brother and sister from sister. Bonds of fraternity and solidarity yield to the onslaughts of meanness of mind and spirit. Is this the India for which Mahatma Gandhi and Indira Gandhi sacrificed their lives?

Turn to the great institutions of our country and you will see that too often, behind, their imposing facades, the spirit and substance lack vitality. The work they do sometimes seem strangely irrelevant to the primary concerns of the masses. Attempts are made to taint the electoral process at its very source. Issues of crucial national importance are frequently subordinated to individual sectional and regional interests. Our legislatures do not set standards for other groups to follow; they magnify manifold the conspicuous lack of a social ethic. A convenient conscience compels individuals to meander from ideology, to ideology seeking power, influence and riches. Political parties twist their tenets, enticed by opportunism. "The best lack all conviction and the worst are full of passionate intensity.

We are amongst the few to have the rule of law and an independent judiciary. But thousands wait for decades while an elaborate and arcane machinery grids ever so slowly. The poor have little hope of timely redress.

We value our free press. It made a magnificent contribution to our freedom struggle. After Independence, the national media have helped consolidate our unity and promote social and economic change. But the question the media need to put to themselves is: Does their contribution to nation building measure up to their role in the freedom struggle?

Our economy owes much to the enterprise of our industrialists. But there are some reputed business and industrial establishments which shelter battalions of law-breakers and tax evaders. We have industrialists untouched by the thrusting spirit of the great risk-takers and innovators. The trader's instinct for quick profits prevails. They flourish on sick industries. Many have not cared learn the fundamental lesson that industrialisation springs from the development of indigenous technology, not from dependence on others. Industrial empire built on the shaky foundations of excessive protection, social irresponsibility, import orientation and corruption may not last long.

The trade have a glorious heritage of nationalism and of socially relevant radicalism. Today, they are a mere shadow of their past. They now protect the few who have, oblivious of millions who have not. They feel little concern of the creation of national wealth, only for a larger and larger share in it. Nothing is considered illegitimate if one marches under the right flag. Power without responsibility, rights without duties have come to be their prerogative. Will productivity arise from such stony soil? Let us not forget that the poor and the unemployed have to sacrifice their development programmes to subsidise inefficient industry.

In the field of education, the nation has much to be proud of. Access to education has been widened immeasurably. Indian scholars are in the front rank of creative endeavour in the best institutions across the world. But the schools, the universities and the academies of the Republic, which should fill our minds with hope for tomorrow, cause us great concern. Teachers seldom teach and students seldom learn. Strikes, mass copying, agitations are more attractive alternatives. Where there should be experiment and innovation, there is obeisance to dead ritual and custom, smothering creativity and quest for knowledge and truth. Where there should be independence and integrity, there is the heavy hand of politics, caste and corruption. Where there should be a new integration between modern science and our heritage, there is a dull repetition of lifeless formulate. Millions are illiterate. Millions of children have never been inside a school.

And what of the iron frame of the system, the administrative and the technical services, the police and the myriad functionaries of the State? They have done so much and can do so much more, but as the proverb says there can be no protection if the fence starts eating the crop. We have Government servants who do not serve but oppress the poor and the helpless, police who do not uphold the law but shield the guilty, tax collectors who do not collect taxes but connive with those who cheat the State and whole legions whose only concern is their private welfare at the cost of society. They have no work, ethic, no feeling for the public cause, no involvement in the future of the nation, no comprehension of national goals, no commitment to the values of modern India. They have only a grasping, mercenary outlook, devoid of competence, integrity and commitment.

How have we come to this pass?

We have looked at others. Now let us look at ourselves. What has become of our great organisation? Instead of a party that fired the imagination of the masses throughout the length and breadth of India, we have shrunk, losing touch with the toiling millions. It is not a question of victories and defeats in elections. For a democratic party, victories and defeats are part of its continuing political existence. But what does matter is whether or not we work among the masses, whether or not we are in tune with their struggles, their hopes and aspirations. We are a party of social transformation, but in our preoccupation with governance we are drifting away from the people. Thereby, we have weakened ourselves and fallen prey to the ills that the loss of invigorating mass contact brings.

Millions of ordinary Congress workers throughout the country are full of enthusiasm for the Congress policies and programmes. But they are handicapped, for on their backs ride the brokers of power and influence, who dispense patronage to convert a mass movement into a feudal oligarchy. They are self-perpetuating cliques who thrive by invoking the slogans of caste and religion and by enmeshing the living body of the Congress in their net of avarice.

For such persons, the masses do not count. Their life style, their thinking - of lack of it, their self-aggrandisement, their corrupt ways, their linkages with the vested interests in society, and their sanctimonious posturing are wholly incompatible with work among the people. They are reducing the Congress organisation to shell from which the spirit of service and sacrifice has been empted.

As we have distanced ourselves from the masses, basic issues of national unity and integrity, social change and economic development recede into the background. Instead, phoney issues, shrouded in medieval obscurantism, occupy the centre of the stage. Our Congress workers, who faced the bullets of British imperialism, run for shelter at the slightest manifestation of caste and communal tension. Is this the path that Gandhiji, Panditji and Indiraji showed to a secular, democratic India?

We talk of the high principles and lofty ideals needed to build a strong and prosperous India. But we obey no discipline, no rule, follow no principle of public weal. Corruption is not only tolerated but even regarded as the hallmark of leadership. Flagrant contradiction between what we say and what we do has become our way of life. At every step, our aims and actions conflict. At every stage, our private self crushes our social commitment.

As action has diverged from precept, the ideology of the Congress has acquired the status of an heirloom, to be polished and brought out on special occasions. It must be a living force to animate the Congress workers in their day-to-day activity. Our ideology of nationalism, secularism, democracy and socialism is the only relevant ideology for our great country. But we are forgetting that we must take it to the masses, interpret its content in changing circumstances, and defend it against the attacks of our opponents.

Mahatma Gandhi visualised the Congress as a fighting machine. Time and again we have demonstrated our fighting qualities - in the great non-cooperation movements of the twenties and thirties, in the Quit India movement of 1942, in the fifties and sixties when we carried the message of socialism to every door, in 1969-71 when the vested interests had to be fought in Parliament, in the courts and in the streets and in 1977-79 when persecution and calumny were answered by thousands of brave satyagrahis throughout the country. This is our tradition. We have to revive this tradition to fight for the poor and the oppressed. Only by doing so shall we gain the strength to create the India of our dreams.

The revitalisation of our organisation is a historical necessity. At this critical juncture, there is no other political party capable of defending the unity and integrity of the country. There is no other party capable of taking the country forward to progress and prosperity. All other parties are shot through with internal contradictions. The sorry, un-edifying spectacle of their total incapacity, corruption, nepotism, hypocrisy has disfigured our political landscape. They have shown a cynical disregard for sensitive issues of national security. Some have not hesitated even to colude with anti-national elements. Their ideological roots are shallow, their political outlook circumscribed by region, caste and religion. Whatever they have come to power, they have retarded social and economic progress. They have no sense of history. Those who campaign for a weak Centre, campaign against the unity and integrity of India. Their slogans of welfare are spurious because true welfare comes from growth, which they have been busy destroying. It is the responsibility of the Congress to ensure that India is not left to the mercy of such forces.

We must once more generate a mass movement based on Congress ideology to fulfil this momentous task. Only with such a movement can we cleanse the party and the nation. The inner strength of our people, their unbounded patriotism, their unshakable commitment to social justice, and their aspiration for a strong and prosperous India will destroy the ugliness and enrich the creative ground of India's greatness.

How will this mass movement of epic proportions arise? What are the essentials of the Build India Movements?

The country needs a politics of service to the poor. The country needs a politics based on ideology and programmes. To bring this about, we must break the nexus between political parties and vested interests. We will change the electoral laws to ensure cleaner elections. We will make political parties accountable for the funds they receive. We will wage an ideological war against those who exploit the poor in the name of caste and religion.

The Congress, the custodian of the national will and the sentinel of India's freedom and unity, will be reorganised and revitalised. It will gather in its fold patriots of all sections and all communities. It will be the shield of the oppressed and the sword of the poor.

The war on corruption will go on without let or hindrance. The country needs a clean social and political environment the Congress is determined to give it.

Any denial of justice to the poor and the weak is in itself a crime. Our judicial institutions and legal systems have to be streamlined and strengthened. Sooner, rather than later. We shall put our best brains to work on this problem.

Our administrative machinery is cumbersome, archaic and

alien to the needs and aspirations of the people. It has successfully resisted the imperative of change. It must learn to serve the people. It must become accountable for results. We need structural changes at all levels. We shall have them.

The India of the future is growing in her schools and universities. But our schools and universities do not relate to the vision of the future. They continue to function in the old grooves. A new blueprint for education is being designed. It will not come out of musty corridors of the educational establishments. It will only come from a movement involving teachers, students, parents, thinkers and philosophers. Not a movement to capture more privileges, but a movement that sees the future in relation to the present and the past, a movement that uses that vast untapped energy of millions to create a design suited to our needs.

As we look back on what we have achieved, one thought keeps coming back to mind. How must faster we would have developed had we succeeded in restricting the growth of our population. Progress would have been greater not in material terms alone, but in the quality of human life. That makes the family planning programme so crucial to our future development. We need a better strategy to achieve the national goal of a stable population, healthier and better educated.

The time has come to infuse new life into the struggle against poverty. Our anti-poverty programmes, notably the 20 Point Programme, have to come out of the grip of bureaucratic sloth and inefficiency. They have to become people's programmes. All the elements - education, health and nutrition, family planning, land reforms and cooperatives, communications, agriculture, animal husbandry, industrial and rural crafts - all have to come together in an integrated programme to wipe out the age - old curse of poverty. The power to shape their own lives must lie with the people, not with bureaucrats and experts. Experts must help the people. Vibrant village panchayats must discuss, deliberate and decide the choices to be made. This is a challenge to the Congress cadres. It is up to us, the workers of this great organisation, spread in every village and every hamlet of India, to mobilise the people, to guide them, to stand by their side when they are denied their due, to fight for them and to see that resources are properly utilized, not frittered away on unproductive projects. This will keep our organisation in touch with the masses and will help us to become the true vehicle of change in rural India.

We are building an independent, self-reliant economy. We have already achieved much. But more hard work is required from everyone - from scientists and technologists, from the public sector, from the private sector, form industrial workers, from farmers, public servants, from traders, housewives and each one of us. We have to work hard to accelerate our agricultural and industrial development on the basis of our own resources. We have to produce more than we are doing today to invest more in future progress, and to support anti-poverty programmes. We must remember that self-reliance and eradication of poverty demands, indeed compel, the present generation to bear hardship and make sacrifices. Those who are employed have a duty to the future of India. They have to be more productive and consume less so that resources can be made available for investment and for programmes to help poor. This is a national duty-a patriotic duty.

Our life styles must change, Vulgar, Conspicuous consumption must go. Simplicity, efficiency and commitment to national goals hold the key to self-reliance. The Congress Ministers, Members of Parliament, Members of State Assemblies, party functionaries and leaders at all levels must set the example. Millions of people will follow them. Austerity and swadeshi will galvanise the masses to grow more, to produce more and to serve more.

Above all, we need to create a mass movement for strengthening India's unity and integrity, for deepening our Indian ness. The Congress, which won freedom for India, the Congress, which has brought India to the threshold of greatness, is pre-eminently the party of India's resurgent nationalism. Our nationalism is based on our rich diversity of cultures, languages and religions. The Congress represents the multi-faceted splendour of India.

Today, communal, casteist and regional forces, sustained by external elements, are undermining our unity.

We have to be on our guard. We have to carry the message of nationalism and unity to all. We have to overcome divisive forces. Let the saga of our freedom struggle be our inspiration. Let thousands and thousands of Congress workers fan out into every village, every urban centre to revive the traditions of our glorious struggle for freedom in which, all differences were transcended. We shall persuade. We shall educate. We shall bind people together. But let the divisive forces understand quite clearly that the Congress, with the strength of the masses behind it, will crush with all its might the designs of anti-national elements.

Friends,

A century of achievement ends. A century of endeavour beckons to us. Our resplendent civilization, with unbroken continuity from the third millennium B.C. looks ahead to peaks of excellence in the third millennium A.D.

It falls to us to work for India's greatness. A great country is not one, which merely has a great past. Out of that past must arise, a glorious future.

Let us build an India.

- Proud of her Independence;
- Powerful in defence of her freedom;
- Strong, self-reliant in agriculture, industry and front-rank technology
- United by bonds transcending barriers of caste, creed and religion;
- Liberated from the bondage of poverty, and of social and economic inequality; An India
- Disciplined & efficient;
- Fortified by ethical and spiritual values;
- A fearless force for peace on earth;
- The School of the world, blending the inner repose of the spirit, with material progress;
- A new civilization, with the strength of our heritage, the creativity of the spring time of youth and the unconquerable spirit of our people.

Great achievements demand great sacrifices–sacrifices, not only from our generation and generations gone by, but also from generations to come.

Civilizations are not built by just one or two generations. Civilizations are built by the ceaseless toil of a succession of generations. With softness and sloth, civilizations succumb. Let us beware of decadence.

We must commit ourselves to the demanding task of making India a mighty power in the world, with all the strength and the compassion of her great culture.

To this cause, I pledge myself.

JAI HIND.

□

Farewell Speech

—Sachin Tendulkar

All my friends, settle down. Let me talk. I will get more and more emotional (crowd gets louder as he composes himself). My life, between 22 yards for 24 years, it is hard to believe that that wonderful journey has come to an end, but I would like to take this opportunity to thank people who have played an important role in my life. Also, for the first time in my life, I am carrying this list, to remember all the names in case I forget someone. I hope you understand. It's getting a little bit difficult to talk, but I will manage.

The most important person in my life, and I have missed him a lot since 1999 when he passed away, my father. Without his guidance, I don't think I would have been standing here in front of you. He gave me freedom at the age of 11, and told me that [I should] chase my dreams, but make sure you do not find shortcuts. The path might be difficult, but don't give up, and I have simply followed his instructions. Above all, he told me to be a nice human being, which I will continue to do and try my best. Every time I have done something special [and] showed my bat, it was [for] my father.

My mother, I don't know how she dealt with such a naughty child like me. I was not easy to manage. She must be extremely patient. For a mother, the most important thing is that her child remains safe and healthy and fit. That was what she was most bothered and worried about. She took care of me for the last 24 years that I have played for India, but even before that, she started praying for me the day I started playing cricket. She just prayed and prayed, and I think her prayers and blessings have given me the strength to go out and perform. So, a big 'thank you' to my mother for all the sacrifices.

In my school days, for four years, I stayed with my uncle and aunt because my school was quite far from my home, and they treated me like their son. My aunt, after having had a hard day's play, I would be half asleep and she would be feeding me food so I could go again and play tomorrow. I can't forget these moments. I am like their son and I am glad it has continued to be the same way.

My eldest brother, Nitin, and his family, have always encouraged me. My eldest brother doesn't like to talk much, but the one thing he always told me is that whatever you do, I know you will always give it 100%, and that I have full faith and confidence in you. His encouragement meant a lot to me. My sister, Savita, and her family, was no different. The first cricket bat of my life was presented to me by my sister. It was a Kashmir willow bat. But that is where the journey began. She is one of those many who still continue to fast when I bat, so thank you very much.

Ajit, my brother, now what do I talk about him? I don't know. We have lived this dream together. He was the one who sacrificed his career for my cricket. He spotted the spark in me. And it all started from the age of 11 when he took me to Achrekar sir, my coach, and from there on, my life changed. You will find this hard to believe, but even last night, he called to discuss my dismissal, knowing that there was a remote chance of batting again, but just the habit we have developed, the rapport we have developed, since my birth, has continued and it will continue. Maybe when I'm not playing cricket, we will still be discussing technique.

Various things we agreed upon, my technique, and so many technical things which I didn't agree with him, we have had arguments and disagreements, but when I look back at all these things in my life, I would have been a lesser cricketer.

The most beautiful thing happened to me in 1990 when I met my wife, Anjali. Those were special years and it has continued and will always continue that way. I know Anjali, being a doctor, there was a wonderful career in front of her. When we decided to have a family, Anjali took the initiative to step back and say that 'you continue with your cricket and I will take the responsibility of the family'.

Without that, I don't think I would have been able to play cricket freely and without stress. Thanks for bearing with all my fuss and all my frustrations, and all sorts of rubbish that I have spoken. Thanks for bearing with me and always staying by my side through all the ups and downs. You are the best partnership I've had in my life. Then, the two precious diamonds of my life, Sara and Arjun. They have already grown up. My daughter is 16, my son is 14. Time has flown by. I wanted to spend so much time with them on special occasions like their birthdays, their annual days, their sports day, going on holidays, whatever. I have missed out on all those things. Thanks for your understanding. Both of you have been so, so special to me you cannot imagine. I promise you [that] for 14 and 16 years I have not spent enough time with both of you, but the next 16 years or even beyond that, everything is for you.

My in-laws, Anand Mehta and Annabel, both have been so, so supportive [and] loving and caring. I have discussed on various things in life, generally with them, and have taken their advice. You know, it's so important to have a strong family who is always with you and who are guiding you. Before you start clapping, the most important thing they did was allowing me to marry Anjali, so thank you very much.

In the last 24 years that I have played for India, I have made new friends, and before that, I have had friends from my childhood. They have all had a terrific contribution. As and when I have called them to come and bowl to me at the nets, they have left their work aside to come and help me. Be it joining me on holidays and having discussions with me on cricket, or how I was a little stressed and wanting to find a solution so I can perform better. All those moments my friends were with me. Even for when I was injured, I would wake up in the morning because I couldn't sleep and thought that my career was over because of injuries, that is when my friends have woken up at 3 o'clock in the morning to drive with me and make me believe that my career was not over. Life would be incomplete without all those friends. Thanks for being there for me.

My cricket career started when I was 11. The turning point of my career was when my brother (Ajit) took me to Achrekar sir. I was extremely delighted to see him up in the stands. Normally, he sits in front of the television and he watches all the games that I play. When I was 11/12, those were the days when I used to hop back on his scooter and play a couple of practice matches a day. The first half of the innings I would be batting at Shivaji Park, the second half at some other match in Azad Maidan. He would take me all over Mumbai to make sure I got match practice.

On a lighter note, in the last 29 years, sir has never ever said 'well played' to me because he thought I would get complacent and I would stop working hard. Maybe he can push his luck and wish me now, well done on my career, because there are no more matches, sir, in my life. I will be witnessing cricket, and cricket will always stay in my heart, but you have had an immense contribution in my life, so thank you very much.

My cricket for Mumbai started right here on this ground, the Mumbai Cricket Association (MCA), which is so dear to me. I remember landing from New Zealand at four o'clock in the morning, and turning up for a game here at eight o'clock just because I wanted to be a part of Mumbai cricket, and not that somebody forced me. That was for the love of Mumbai cricket, and thank you very much. The president is here, so thank you very much, along with your team, for taking care of me and looking after my cricket.

The dream was obviously to play for India, and that is where my association with BCCI started. BCCI was fantastic, right from my debut they believed in my ability and selecting me into the squad at the age of 16 was a big step. So, thanks to all the selectors for having faith in me and the BCCI for giving me the freedom to express myself out in the middle. Things would have been different if you had not been behind me, and I really appreciate your support. Especially when I was injured, you were right with me and making sure that all the treatments were taken care of, and that I got fit and fine and playing [right] back for India.

The journey has been special, the last 24 years, I have played with many senior cricketers, and even before that, there were many senior cricketers with whom I watched on television. They inspired me to play cricket, and to play in the right way. Thanks to all those senior cricketers, and, unfortunately, I have not been able to play with them, but I have high regards for all their achievements and all their contributions.

We see it on the mega-screen, Rahul, Laxman, Sourav, and Anil, who is not here, and my team-mates right here in front of me. You are like my family away from home. I have had some wonderful times with you. It is going to be difficult to not be part of the dressing room, sharing those special moments. All the coaches for their guidance, it has been special for me. I know when M.S. Dhoni presented me the 200th Test match cap on Day One morning, I had a brief message for the team. I would like to repeat that. I just feel that all of us are so, so fortunate and proud to be part of the Indian cricket team and serving the nation.

Knowing all of you guys, I know you will continue to serve the nation in the right spirit and right values. I believe we have been the lucky ones to be chosen by the Almighty to serve this sport. Each generation gets this opportunity to take care of this sport and serve it to the best of our ability. I have full faith in you to continue to serve the nation in the right spirit and to the best of your ability, to bring all the laurels to the country. All the very best.

I would be failing in my duties if I did not thank all the doctors, the physios, the trainers, who have put this difficult body together to go back on the field and be able to play. The amount of injuries that I have had in my career, I don't know how you have managed to keep me fit, but without your special efforts, it would never have happened. The doctors have met me at weird hours. I mean I have called them from Mumbai to Chennai, Mumbai to Delhi, I mean wherever. They have just taken the next flight and left their work and families to be with me, which has allowed me to play. So, a big thank you to all three of you for keeping me in good shape.

My dear friend, late Mark Mascarenhas, my first manager. We, unfortunately, lost him in a car accident in 2001, but he was such a well-wisher of cricket, my cricket, and especially the Indian cricket. He was so passionate. He understood what it takes to represent a nation and gave me all the space to go out and express myself, and never pressurised me to do this ad or promotion or whatever the sponsors demanded. He took care of that and today I miss him. So, thank you Mark for all your contribution.

My current management team, WSG, for repeating what Mark has done, because when I signed the contract I exactly told them what I want from them, and what it requires to represent me. They have done that and respected that.

Someone who has worked closely with me for 14 years is my manager, Vinod Nayudu. He is more like my family and all the sacrifices, spending time away from his family for my work, has been special. So, a big 'thank you' to his family as well for giving up so much time for my work with Vinod.

In my school days, when I performed well, the media backed me a lot. They continue to do that till this morning. Thank you so much to the media for supporting and appreciating my performances. It surely had a positive effect on me. Thank you so much to all the photographers as well for those wonderfully captured moments that will stay with me for the rest of my life. So, a big 'thank you' to all the photographers.

I know my speech is getting a bit too long (crowd roars with 'noooo'), but this is the last thing I want to say. I want to thank all the people here who have flown in from various parts of the world, and have supported me endlessly, whether I scored a 0 or a 100-plus. Your support was so dear to me and meant a lot to me. Whatever you have done for me.

I know I have met so many guys who have fasted for me, prayed for me, done so much for me. Without that, life wouldn't have been like this for me. I want to thank you from the bottom of my heart, and also say that time has flown by rather quickly, but the memories you have left with me will always be with me forever and ever, especially 'Sachin, Sachin' which will reverberate in my ears till I stop breathing. Thank you very much. If I have missed out on saying something, I hope you understand. Goodbye!

□

How and Why I Adopted The Hindu Religion*

—Sister Nivedita

[Sister Nivedita (Margaret Elizabeth Noble) was born on 28th October, 1867 in the town of Dungannon in County Tyrone, Ireland. Her father, who was a priest, gave the valuable lesson that service to mankind is the true service to God. Her father died in 1877 when she was only ten years old. Then she was brought up by her maternal grandfather Hamilton in Northern Ireland. Hamilton was one of the first-ranking leaders of the freedom movement of Ireland. Margaret got her education from Church boarding school in London. She attended Halifax College, run by a member of Congregationalist Church. The headmistress of this college taught her about personal sacrifice. She extensively studied various subjects, including physics, arts, music and literature.

Margaret embraced teaching at the age of seventeen. She first worked in Keswick as a teacher of children. Subsequently she established a school in Wimbledon and followed her own unique methods of teaching. She also participated in Church sponsored activities, being religious in nature. She was also a prolific writer and wrote in the paper and periodicals. In this way she soon became a known name among the intellectuals

* *Hindu Ladies' Social Club, Bombay, 2nd October, 1902*

of London. She was engaged to be married to a Welsh youth who died soon after engagement. The regulated religious life could not give her the necessary peace and she began to study various books on religion.

In November 1895 she met Swami Vivekananda who had come from America to visit London and stayed there for three months. On a cold afternoon, Swami Vivekananda, on an invitation, was explaining Vedanta philosophy in the drawing room of an aristocratic family in London. Lady Isabel Margesson, a friend of Margaret, invited her for this meeting. Margaret described her experience on the occasion. A majestic personage, clad in a saffron gown and wearing a red waist-band, sat there on the floor, cross-legged. As he spoke to the company, he recited Sanskrit verses in his deep, sonorous voice. Margaret being already delved deep into the teachings of the East, found nothing quite new in what she heard on this occasion. What was new to her was the personality of the Swamiji himself. She attended several other lectures of Swami Vivekananda. She raised a lot of questions whose answers dispelled her doubts and established deep faith and reverence for the speaker.

Nivedita wrote in 1904 to a friend about her decision to follow Swami Vivekananada as a result of her meeting him in England in November 1895:

"Suppose he had not come to London that time! Life would have been like a headless dream, for I always knew that I was waiting for something. I always said that a call would come. And it did. But if I had known more of life, I doubt whether, when the time came, I should certainly have recognised it.

"Fortunately, I knew little and was spared that torture ... Always I had this burning voice within, but nothing to utter. How often and often I sat down, pen in hand, to speak, and there was no speech! And now there is no end to it! As surely I am fitted to my world, so surely is my world in need of me, waiting – ready. The arrow has found its place in the bow. But if he had not come! If he had meditated, on the Himalayan peaks!... I, for one, had never been here."

Vivekananda's principles and teachings influenced her and this brought about a visible change in her. Seeing the fire and passion in her, Swami Vivekananda could foresee her future role in India. Swami Vivekananda felt extreme pain by the wretchedness and misery of the people of India under the British rule and his opinion was that education was the panacea for all evils plaguing the contemporary Indian society, especially that of Indian women. Margaret was chosen for the role of educating Indian women.

Responding to the call of Swami Vivekananda, Margaret decided to travel to India leaving behind her family and friends, including her mother. Mombasa, the ship bringing Margaret to India reached Calcutta on 28th January, 1898. On 22nd February Margaret visited Dakshineshwar temple, the place where Ramakrishna did his sadhana. Swami Vivekananda devoted the initial few days in building her character and developing her love for India and its people. He explained to her India's history, philosophy, literature, life of the common mass, social traditions, and also the lives of great personalities, both ancient and modern. A few weeks later, two of Swami Vivekananda's women disciples in America, Sara C. Bull, wife of famous Norwegian violinist and composer Ole Bull and Josephine MacLeod arrived in India. The three became lifelong friends.

On 11th March, 1898, Swami Vivekananda organised a public meeting at Star Theatre to introduce Sister Nivedita to the people of Calcutta. In his speech Swami Vivekananda said– "England has sent us another gift in Miss Margaret Noble." In this meeting Margaret expressed her desire to serve India and its people. On 25th March, 1898, Swami Vivekananda formally initiated Margaret in the vow of Brahmacharya (lifelong celibacy) and gave her the name of 'Nivedita', the dedicated one. She became the first Western woman to be received into an Indian monastic order. Swami Vivekananda said to her– "Go thou and follow Him, Who was born and gave His life for others five hundred times before He attained the vision of the Buddha."

Nivedita travelled to a lot of places in India, including Kashmir, with Swami Vivekananda, Josephine Mcleod and Sara Bull and this helped her in connecting to Indian masses, Indian culture and its history. Nivedita was planning to open a school for girls who were deprived of even basic education. She toured England and America, gave lectures on England and America and raised funds to establish a girl's school. On 13th November, 1898, on the day of Kali Puja, at 16 Bosepara Lane in the Bagbazar area of Calcutta, she started the school.

The school was inaugurated by Sarada Devi, in the presence of Swami Vivekananda and some of the other disciples of Ramakrishna. Sarada Devi blessed and prayed for the school saying – "I pray that the blessings of the Divine Mother may be upon the school and the girls; and the girls trained from the school may become ideal girls." Nivedita went from home to home in educate girls, many of whom were in pitiable condition owing to the socio-economic condition of early 20th century India. In many cases she encountered refusal from the male members of the girl's family. Nivedita had widows and adult women among her students. She taught sewing, elementary rules of hygiene, nursing, etc., apart from regular courses.

During the outbreak of plague epidemic in Calcutta in 1899 Nivedita nursed and took care of the patients, cleaned rubbish from the area, and inspired and motivated many youths to render voluntary service. She inserted appeals for help in the English newspapers and requested for financial support for her plague relief activities. She was friend to many intellectuals and artists in the Bengali community, including Rabindranath Tagore, Jagadish Chandra Bose, Abala Bose, and Abanindranath Tagore. Later she took up the cause of Indian independence. Sri Aurobindo was one of her friends as well.

On 2nd October, 1902 Nivedita was invited to speak to Hindu Ladies' Social Club in Bombay. She was requested to speak on 'The virtues of Indian Womenhood'. She met with some members of audience before her speech, and she was requested to speak on what induced her to change her religion. Through a moving account of Englishwoman's conversion to Hinduism, she upheld the values of Indian womanhood, which is still relevant.]

I am born and bred Englishwoman and unto the age of eighteen, I was trained and educated as English girls are. Christian religious doctrines were of course early instilled into me. I was even from my girlhood inclined to venerate all religious teachings and I devotedly worshiped the child Jesus and loved Him with my whole heart for the self-sacrifice He always willingly underwent, while I felt I could not worship Him enough for His crucifying Himself to bestow salvation on the human race. But after the age of eighteen, I began to harbor doubts as to the truth of the Christian doctrines. Many of them began to seem to me false and incompatible with the truth. These doubts grew stronger and stronger and at the same time my faith in Christianity tottered more and more. For seven years I was in this wavering state of mind, very unhappy, and yet, very-very eager to seek the Truth. I shunned going to the Church and yet sometimes my longing to bring restfulness to my spirit impelled me to rush into Church and be observed in the service to feel at peace within, as I had hitherto done, and as others around me were doing. But alas! No peace, no rest was there for my troubled soul all eager to know the truth.

During seven years of wavering to it occurred to me that in the study of natural science I should surely find the truth I was seeking. So, ardently I began to study how this world was created and all things in it and I discovered that in the laws of Nature at least there was consistency, but it made the doctrines of Christian religion seem all the more inconsistent. Just then I happened to get a life of Buddha and in it I found that here, alas, also was there a child who loved ever so many centuries before the child Christ, but whose sacrifices were no self-abnegating than those of other. This dear child Gautama took a strong hold on me and for three more years I plunged myself into the study of the religion of Buddha; and I became more and more convinced that the salvation he preached was decidedly more consistent with the truth than the preaching's of the Christian religion.

And now came, the turning point for my faith. A cousin of your great Viceroy Lord Ripon invited me to have tea with him and to meet the great Swami form India who, he said, might perhaps help the search my soul was longing for. The Swami I met here was none other than Swami Vivekananda who afterwards became my Guru and whose teachings have given relief my doubting spirit had been longing for so long. Yet it was not during one visit or two that my doubts were dispelled. Oh no! I had several warm discussions with him and I pondered on his teachings for more than a year. Then he asked me to visit India, to see the Yogis and to study the subject in the very country of its birth, and I found at last, a faith I could lean upon and obtain my Mukti through the uplifting of the spirit till it is merged into Ananda. Now I have told you how and why I have adopted this religion of yours. If you care to here more, I would gladly go on.

I love India as the birth place of the highest and best of all religion; as the country that has the grandest mountains, the Himalayas; as the place where the sublimest of mountains are located. The country where homes are simple; where domestic happiness is most to be found; where the women unselfishly, unobtrusively, ungrudgingly, serves the dear ones from early morn to dewy eve; where mother and the grandmother studies, foresees and contributes to the comforts of her belongings, regardless of her own happiness, and in the unselfishness raises womanhood to its highest eminence.

You, my sisters, each of whom I dearly love for being the daughter of this lovely land of India, each of you I urge to study the grand literatures of your East in preference to the literatures of the West. Your literature will uplift you. Cling to it. Cling to the simplicity and sobriety of your domestic lives. Keep its purity as it was in the ancient times and as it is still-existing in your simple homes.

Do not let modern fashion and extravagances of the West and its modern English education spoil your reverential humility, your lovable domestic ties consisting in the loving forethought the elders display for the beloved ones, depending on them, and the resulting respectful deference filially and dutifully accorded by the young to the aged. I make this appeal not to my Hindu sisters only but also to Mohammedan and other sisters of mine too. All are my sisters being the daughters of my land of adoption and where I hope to continue the work of my revered Guru Vivekananda.

[Nivedita was a prolific orator and writer and extensively toured India to deliver lectures, especially on India's culture and religion. She appealed to the Indian youth to work selflessly for the cause of the motherland along the ideals of Swami Vivekananda. Initially Nivedita, like contemporary intellectuals from Europe, was optimistic about British rule in India and believed that it was possible for India and England to love each other. However, in the course of her stay, she came to witness the brutal side of the British rule, the repression and oppression and the division between the ruling elite and the ruled plebeians; she concluded that it was necessary for India to gain independence to prosper. Therefore she devoted herself wholeheartedly to the cause of opposing the British rule.

In 1905 the British Government under Curzon initiated the partition of Bengal which was a major turning point in the Indian independence movement. Nivedita played a pioneering role in organising the movement. She provided financial and logistical support and leveraged her contacts to get information from government agencies and forewarn the revolutionaries. Nivedita provided guarded support to Annie Besant, and was very close to Aurobindo Ghosh (later Sri Aurobindo), one of the major contributors towards early nationalist movement. She edited Karma Yogin, the nationalist newspaper of Aurobindo.

Nivedita died on 13th October, 1911, age 43, in Roy villa in Darjeeling. Today, her memorial is located below the Railway station on the way to the Victoria Falls of Darjeeling.]

□

Give Me Blood and I Promise You Freedom*

—Subhas Chandra Bose

[With a promise to his father that he would appear in the Indian Civil Services (ICS) examination, Subhas Chandra Bose went to study in Fitzwilliam College, Cambridge and matriculated on 19th November, 1919. He came fourth in the ICS examination and was selected, but he did not want to work under an alien government which would mean serving the British. As he stood on the verge of taking the plunge by resigning from the Indian Civil Service in 1921, he wrote to his elder brother Sarat Chandra Bose: "Only on the soil of sacrifice and suffering can we raise our national edifice." He resigned from his civil service job on 23rd April, 1921 and returned to India.

Bose started the newspaper 'Swaraj' and took charge of publicity for the Bengal Provincial Congress Committee. His mentor was Chittaranjan Das who was a spokesman for aggressive nationalism in Bengal. In the year 1923, Bose was elected the President of All India Youth Congress and also the Secretary of Bengal State Congress. He was also editor of the newspaper "Forward", founded by Chittaranjan Das. Bose worked as the CEO of the Calcutta Municipal Corporation for

* *Indian National Army, Burma, 4th July, 1944*

Das when the latter was elected mayor of Calcutta in 1924. In a roundup of nationalists in 1925, Bose was arrested and sent to prison in Mandalay, where he contracted tuberculosis. In 1927, after being released from prison, Bose became general secretary of the Congress party and worked with Jawaharlal Nehru for independence. In late December 1928, Bose organized the Annual Meeting of the Indian National Congress in Calcutta. His most memorable role was as General Officer Commanding (GOC) Congress Volunteer Corps. A little later, Bose was again arrested and jailed for civil disobedience; this time he emerged to become Mayor of Calcutta in 1930.

During the mid-1930s Bose travelled in Europe, visiting Indian students and European politicians, including Benito Mussolini. He observed party organisation and saw communism and fascism in action. In this period, he also researched and wrote the first part of his book 'The Indian Struggle', which covered the country's independence movement in the years 1920–1934. Although it was published in London in 1935, the British government banned the book in the colony out of fears that it would encourage unrest. By 1938 Bose had become a leader of national stature and agreed to accept nomination as Congress President.

He stood for unqualified Swaraj (self-governance), including the use of force against the British. This meant a confrontation with Mohandas Gandhi, who in fact opposed Bose's presidency, splitting the Indian National Congress party. Bose attempted to maintain unity, but Gandhi advised Bose to form his own cabinet. The rift also divided Bose and Nehru. Bose appeared at the 1939 Congress meeting on a stretcher. He was elected president again over Gandhi's preferred candidate Pattabhi Sitaramayya. However, due to the manoeuvrings of the Gandhi-led clique in the Congress Working Committee, Bose found himself forced to resign from the Congress presidency. On 22nd June, 1939 Bose organised the All India Forward Bloc a faction within the Indian National Congress, aimed at consolidating the political left, but its main strength was in his home state, Bengal.

On the outbreak of war, Bose advocated a campaign of mass civil disobedience to protest against Viceroy Lord Linlithgow's decision to declare war on India's behalf without consulting the Congress leadership. Having failed to persuade Gandhi of the necessity of this, Bose organised mass protests in Calcutta calling for the 'Holwell Monument' commemorating the Black Hole of Calcutta, which then stood at the corner of Dalhousie Square, to be removed. He was thrown in jail by the British, but was released following a seven-day hunger strike. Bose's house in Calcutta was kept under surveillance by the CID.

Bose's arrest and subsequent release set the scene for his escape to Germany, via Afghanistan and the Soviet Union. From Moscow, he reached Rome, and from there he travelled to Germany. In Germany, he was attached to the Special Bureau for India under Adam von Trott zu Solz which was responsible for broadcasting on the German-sponsored Azad Hind Radio. He founded the Free India Center in Berlin, and created the Indian Legion out of Indian prisoners of war who had previously fought for the British in North Africa prior to their capture by Axis forces. In all, 3,000 Indian prisoners of war signed up for the Free India Legion. But instead of being delighted, Bose was worried. A left-wing admirer of Russia, he was devastated when Hitler's tanks rolled across the Soviet border. Matters were worsened by the fact that the now-retreating German army would be in no position to offer him help in driving the British from India. When he met Hitler in May 1942, his suspicions were confirmed, and he came to believe that the Nazi leader was more interested in using his men to win propaganda victories than military ones. So, in February 1943, Bose turned his back on his legionnaires and slipped secretly away aboard the German submarine U-180 around the Cape of Good Hope to the southeast of Madagascar, where he was transferred to the I-29 for the rest of the journey to Imperial Japan. This was the only civilian transfer between two submarines of two different navies in World War II.

With Japanese support, Bose revamped the Indian

National Army (INA), and then composed of Indian soldiers of the British Indian army who had been captured in the Battle of Singapore. To these, after Bose's arrival, were added enlisting Indian civilians in Malaya and Singapore. Bose had great drive and charisma—creating popular Indian slogans, such as 'Jai Hind,'—and the INA under Bose was a model of diversity by region, ethnicity, religion, and even gender. INA had a separate women's unit, the Rani of Jhansi Regiment headed by Capt. Lakshmi Swaminathan, which is seen as a first of its kind in Asia.

Even when faced with military reverses, Bose was able to maintain support for the Azad Hind movement. Spoken as a part of a motivational speech for the Indian National Army at a rally of Indians in Burma on 4th July, 1944, Bose's most famous quote was "Give me blood, and I shall give you freedom!" In this, he urged the people of India to join him in his fight against the British Raj. Spoken in Hindi, Bose's words are highly evocative. The troops of the INA were under the aegis of a provisional government, the Azad Hind Government, which came to produce its own currency, postage stamps, court and civil code, and was recognised by nine Axis states—Germany, Japan, Italy, the Independent State of Croatia, Wang Jingwei regime in Nanjing, China, a provisional government of Burma, Manchukuo and Japanese-controlled Philippines. On the Indian mainland, an Indian Tricolour, modelled after that of the Indian National Congress, was raised for the first time in the town in Moirang, in Manipur, in north-eastern India.

When Japanese funding for the army diminished, Bose was forced to raise taxes on the Indian populations of Malaysia and Singapore. When the Japanese were defeated at the battles of Kohima and Imphal, the Provisional Government's aim of establishing a base in mainland India was lost forever. The INA was forced to pull back, along with the retreating Japanese army, and fought in key battles against the British Indian Army in its Burma campaign, notable in Meiktilla, Mandalay, Pegu, Nyangyu and Mount Popa. However, with the fall of Rangoon, Bose's government ceased to be an effective political entity.

A large proportion of the INA troops surrendered under Lt Col Loganathan. The remaining troops retreated with Bose towards Malaya or made for Thailand. Japan's surrender at the end of the war also led to the eventual surrender of the Indian National Army, when the troops of the British Indian Army were repatriated to India and some tried for treason.

In the consensus of scholarly opinion, Subhas Chandra Bose's death occurred from third-degree burns on 18th August 1945 after his overloaded Japanese plane crashed in Japanese-occupied Formosa (now Taiwan). A truck served as ambulance, rushed Bose and the other passengers to the Nanmon Military Hospital south of Taihoku. Bose was conscious and mostly coherent when they reached the hospital, and for some time thereafter. Bose was naked, except for a blanket wrapped around him. Soon, in spite of the treatment, Bose went into a coma. A few hours later, between 9 and 10 PM (local time) he, aged 48, was dead. Bose's body was cremated in the main Taihoku crematorium two days later, 20th August, 1945. On 14th September a memorial service was held for Bose in Tokyo and a few days later the ashes were turned over to the priest of the Renkōji Temple of Nichiren Buddhism in Tokyo. There they have remained ever since.

In India the Indian National Congress's official line was succinctly expressed in a letter Mohandas Karamchand Gandhi wrote to Rajkumari Amrit Kaur. Gandhi said, "Subhas Bose has died well. He was undoubtedly a patriot, though misguided." Many congressmen had not forgiven Bose for quarrelling with Gandhi and for collaborating with what they considered was Japanese fascism. The Indian soldiers in the British Indian army, some two and a half million of whom had fought during the Second World War, were conflicted about the INA. Some saw the INA as traitors and wanted them punished; others felt more sympathetic. The British Raj, though never seriously threatened by the INA, tried 300 INA officers for treason in the INA trials, but eventually backtracked.

But, the honorific 'Netaji (Respected Leader), first applied to Bose in Germany, by the Indian soldiers of the Indische

Legion and by the German and Indian officials in the Special Bureau for India in Berlin, in early 1942, was by 1990 used widely throughout India, and his words still boils the blood of millions of nationalist Indians.]

Friends! Twelve months ago a new programme of 'total mobilisation' or 'maximum sacrifice' was placed before Indians in East Asia. Today I shall give you an account of our achievements during the past year and shall place before you our demands for the coming year. But, before I do so, I want you to realise once again what a golden opportunity we have for winning freedom. The British are engaged in a worldwide struggle and in the course of this struggle they have suffered defeat after defeat on so many fronts. The enemy having been thus considerably weakened, our fight for liberty has become very much easier than it was five years ago. Such a rare and God-given opportunity comes once in a century. That is why we have sworn to fully utilise this opportunity for liberating our motherland from the British yoke.

I am so very hopeful and optimistic about the outcome of our struggle, because I do not rely merely on the efforts of three million Indians in East Asia. There is a gigantic movement going on inside India and millions of our countrymen are prepared for maximum suffering and sacrifice in order to achieve liberty.

Unfortunately, ever since the great fight of 1857, our countrymen are disarmed, whereas the enemy is armed to the teeth. Without arms and without a modern army, it is impossible for a disarmed people to win freedom in this modern age. Through the grace of Providence and through the help of generous Nippon, it has become possible for Indians in East Asia to get arms to build up a modern army. Moreover, Indians in East Asia are united to a man in the endeavour to win freedom and all the religious and other differences that the British tried to engineer inside India, simply do not exist in East Asia.

Consequently, we have now an ideal combination of circumstances favouring the success of our struggle- and all that is wanted is that Indians should themselves come forward to pay the price of liberty. According to the programme of 'total mobilisation,'

I demanded of you men, money and materials. Regarding men, I am glad to tell you that I have obtained sufficient recruits already. Recruits have come to us from every corner of east Asia- from China, Japan, Indo-China, Philippines, Java, Borneo, Celebes, Sumatra, Malaya, Thailand and Burma...

You must continue the mobilisation of men, money and materials with greater vigour and energy, in particular, the problem of supplies and transport has to be solved satisfactorily.

We require more men and women of all categories for administration and reconstruction in liberated areas. We must be prepared for a situation in which the enemy will ruthlessly apply the scorched earth policy, before withdrawing from a particular area and will also force the civilian population to evacuate as was attempted in Burma.

Those of you who will continue to work on the Home Front should never forget that East Asia- and particularly Burma- from our base for the war of liberation. If this base is not strong, our fighting forces can never be victorious. Remember that this is a 'total war'- and not merely a war between two armies. That is why for a full one year I have been laying so much stress on 'total mobilisation' in the East.

There is another reason why I want you to look after the Home Front properly. During the coming months I and my colleagues on the War Committee of the Cabinet desire to devote our whole attention to the fighting front- and also to the task of working up the revolution inside India. Consequently, we want to be fully assured that the work at the base will go on smoothly and uninterruptedly even in our absence.

Friends, one year ago, when I made certain demands of you, I told you that if you give me 'total mobilization,' I would give you a 'second front.' I have redeemed that pledge. The first phase of our campaign is over. Our victorious troops, fighting side by side with Nipponese troops, have pushed back the enemy and are now fighting bravely on the sacred soil of our dear motherland.

Gird up your loins for the task that now lies ahead. I had asked you for men, money and materials. I have got them in generous measure. Now I demand more of you. Men, money and materials cannot by themselves bring victory or freedom. We must have the motive-power that will inspire us to brave deeds and heroic exploits.

It will be a fatal mistake for you to wish to live and see India free simply because victory is now within reach. No one here should have the desire to live to enjoy freedom. A long fight is still in front of us.

We should have but one desire today- the desire to die so that India may live- the desire to face a martyr's death, so that the path to freedom may be paved with the martyr's blood.

Friends! My comrades in the War of Liberation! Today I demand of you one thing, above all. I demand of you blood. It is blood alone that can avenge the blood that the enemy has spilt. It is blood alone that can pay the price of freedom.

Give me blood and I promise you freedom.

[Although it was believed that Netaji Subhas Chandra Bose died in a plane crash, his body was never recovered. There have so many theories been put forward regarding his abrupt desertion. The government of India set up a number of committees to investigate the case and come out with truth. After many inquiries and controversies, in 1999, following a court order, the Indian government appointed retired Supreme Court judge M. K. Mukherjee to probe the death of Bose. The commission perused hundreds of files on Bose's death drawn from several countries and visited Japan, Russia and Taiwan. Though oral accounts were in favour of the plan crash, the commission concluded that those accounts could not be relied upon and that there was a secret plan to ensure Bose's safe passage to the USSR with the knowledge of Japanese authorities and Habibur Rahman. The commission observed that the ashes kept at the Renkoji temple, reported to be Bose's, were of Ichiro Okura, a Japanese soldier who died of cardiac arrest. The Mukherjee Commission submitted its report to on 8th November, 2005. The report was tabled in the Indian Parliament on 17th May, 2006. The Indian Government rejected the findings of the commission without assigning any reason.]

□

Chicago Speeches*

—Swami Vivekananda

[In 1893, the city of Chicago hosted the World Columbian Exposition, an early world's fair. So many people were coming to Chicago from all over the world that many smaller conferences, called Congresses and Parliaments, were scheduled to take advantage of this unprecedented gathering. A number of congresses were held in conjunction with the exposition, including those dealing with anthropology (one of the major themes of Exposition exhibits), labor, medicine, temperance, commerce and finance, literature, history, art, philosophy, and science. One of these was the World's Parliament of Religions. The Parliament of Religions was by far the largest of the congresses held in conjunction with the Exposition.

The 1893 Parliament, which ran from 11th to 27th September, marked the first formal gathering of representatives of Eastern and Western spiritual traditions. Today it is recognized as the occasion of the birth of formal interreligious dialogue worldwide. The Parliament of Religions opened on 11th September, 1893 at the World's Congress Auxiliary Building which is now The Art Institute of Chicago. Vivekananda (12nd January, 1863–4th July, 1902), a

* *World Parliament of Religion, 11th To 27th September 1893, Chicago, USA*

wandering Hindu monk (Parivrajaka) represented India and Hinduism as a delegate.

Vivekananda gave his first lecture on that day. Towards the afternoon his turn came. Though initially nervous, he bowed to Saraswati, the Hindu goddess of learning and he felt he got new energy in his body, he felt someone or something else had occupied his body– The Soul of India, the echo of the Rishis, the voice of Ramakrishna, the mouthpiece of the resurgent Time spirit. Then began his speech with salutation, Sisters and brothers of America! To these words he got a standing ovation from a crowd of seven thousand, which lasted for two minutes. When silence was restored he began his address. He greeted the youngest of the nations on behalf of "the most ancient order of monks in the world, the Vedic order of sannyasins, a religion which has taught the world both tolerance and universal acceptance!"

Vivekananda is perhaps best known for this inspiring speech through which he introduced Hinduism at the opening session of the Parliament on 11th September. After this introductory speech, which was of a general nature stating no religion was superior or inferior to the other, his subsequent lectures were on 15th, 19th, 20th and 26th September were on specific issues of religion. These lectures of Vivekananda shook America and the whole world, and after the Parliament Vivekananda immediately became a hero in America.

Thereafter Vivekananda conducted hundreds of public and private lectures and classes, disseminating tenets of Hindu philosophy in America, England and Europe. In America Vivekananda became India's spiritual ambassador. His mission there was the interpretation of India's spiritual culture and heritage. He also tried to enrich the religious consciousness of Americans through the teachings of the Vedanta philosophy. He established the Vedanta societies in America and England. He was a key figure in the introduction of Indian philosophies of Vedanta and Yoga to the western world and was credited with raising interfaith awareness, bringing Hinduism to the status of a major world religion in the late 19th century.

After a comprehensive tour of four years in the West he returned to India in 1897. Later he became a major force in the revival of Hinduism in India and contributed to the notion of nationalism in colonial India.]

Response to Welcome (11th September, 1893)

Sisters and Brothers of America! It fills my heart with joy unspeakable to rise in response to the warm and cordial welcome which you have given us. I thank you in the name of the most ancient order of monks in the world; I thank you in the name of the mother of religions; and I thank you in the name of millions and millions of Hindu people of all classes and sects. My thanks, also, to some of the speakers on this platform who, referring to the delegates from the Orient, have told you that these men from far-off nations may well claim the honour of bearing to different lands the idea of toleration. I am proud to belong to a religion which has taught the world both tolerance and universal acceptance. We believe not only in universal toleration, but we accept all religions as true. I am proud to belong to a nation which has sheltered the persecuted and the refugees of all religions and all nations of the earth. I am proud to tell you that we have gathered in our bosom the purest remnant of the Israelites, who came to Southern India and took refuge with us in the very year in which their holy temple was shattered to pieces by Roman tyranny. I am proud to belong to the religion which has sheltered and is still fostering remnant Zoroastrian nation. I will quote to you, brethren, a few lines from a hymn which I remember to have repeated from my earliest boyhood, which is every day repeated by millions of human beings: "As the different streams having their sources in different places all mingle their water in the sea, so, O Lord, the different paths which men take through different tendencies, various though they appear, crooked or straight, all lead to Thee."

The present convention, which is one of the most august assemblies ever held, is in itself a vindication, a declaration to the world of the wonderful doctrine preached in the Gita: "Whosoever comes to Me, through whatsoever form, I reach him; all men are struggling through paths which in the end lead to me."

Sectarianism, bigotry, and it's horrible descendant, fanaticism, have long possessed this beautiful earth. They have filled the earth with violence, drenched it often and often with human blood, destroyed civilisation and sent whole nations to despair. Had it not been for these horrible demons, human society would be far more advanced than it is now. But their time is come; and I fervently hope that the bell that tolled this morning in honour of this convention may be the death-knell of all fanaticism, of all persecutions with the sword or with the pen, and of all uncharitable feelings between persons wending their way to the same goal.

Why We Disagree (15th September, 1893)

[In this speech Vivekananda tried to explain the reason of disagreement between each other and different sects and religions.]

I will tell you a little story. You have heard the eloquent speaker who has just finished say, "Let us cease from abusing each other," and he was very sorry that there should be always so much variance.

But I think I should tell you a story which would illustrate the cause of this variance. A frog lived in a well. It had lived there for a long time. It was born there and brought up there, and yet was a little, small frog. Of course the evolutionists were not there then to tell us whether the frog lost its eyes or not, but, for our story's sake, we must take it for granted that it had its eyes, and that it every day cleansed the water of all the worms and bacilli that lived in it with an energy that would do credit to our modern bacteriologists. In this way it went on and became a little sleek and fat. Well, one day another frog that lived in the sea came and fell into the well.

"Where are you from?"

"I am from the sea."

"The sea! How big is that? Is it as big as my well?" and he took a leap from one side of the well to the other.

"My friend," said the frog of the sea, "how do you compare the sea with your little well?"

Then the frog took another leap and asked, "Is your sea so big?"

"What nonsense you speak, to compare the sea with your well!"

"Well, then," said the frog of the well, "nothing can be bigger than my well; there can be nothing bigger than this; this fellow is a liar, so turn him out."

That has been the difficulty all the while.

I am a Hindu. I am sitting in my own little well and thinking that the whole world is my little well. The Christian sits in his little well and thinks the whole world is his well. The Mohammedan sits in his little well and thinks that is the whole world. I have to thank you of America for the great attempt you are making to break down the barriers of this little world of ours, and hope that, in the future, the Lord will help you to accomplish your purpose.

Paper on Hinduism (19th September, 1893)

[In this speech Vivekananda gave a short introduction of Hinduism and spoke on "The meaning of the Hindu religion".]

Three religions now stand in the world, which have come down to us from time prehistoric–Hinduism, Zoroastrianism and Judaism. They have all received tremendous shocks and all of them prove by their survival their internal strength. But while Judaism failed to absorb Christianity and was driven out of its place of birth by its all-conquering daughter, and a handful of Parsees is all that remains to tell the tale of their grand religion, sect after sect arose in India and seemed to shake the religion of the Vedas to its very foundations, but like the waters of the seashore in a tremendous earthquake it receded only for a while, only to return in an all-absorbing flood, a thousand times more vigorous, and when the tumult of the rush was over, these sects were all sucked in, absorbed, and assimilated into the immense body of the mother faith. From the high spiritual flights of the Vedanta philosophy, of which the latest discoveries of science seem like echoes, to the low ideas of idolatry with its multifarious mythology, the agnosticism of the Buddhists, and the atheism of the Jains, each and all have a place in the Hindu's religion. Where then, the question arises, where is the common centre to which all these widely diverging radii converge? Where is the common basis upon which all these seemingly hopeless contradictions rest? And this is the question I shall attempt to answer.

The Hindus have received their religion through revelation, the Vedas. They hold that the Vedas are without beginning and without end. It may sound ludicrous to this audience, how a book can be without beginning or end. But by the Vedas no books are meant. They mean the accumulated treasury of spiritual laws discovered by different persons in different times. Just as the law of gravitation existed before its discovery, and would exist if all humanity forgot it, so is it with the laws that govern the spiritual world. The moral, ethical, and spiritual relations between soul and soul and between individual spirits and the Father of all spirits, were there before their discovery, and would remain even if we forgot them.

The discoverers of these laws are called Rishis, and we honour them as perfected beings. I am glad to tell this audience that some of the very greatest of them were women. Here it may be said that these laws as laws may be without end, but they must have had a beginning. The Vedas teach us that creation is without beginning or end. Science is said to have proved that the sum total of cosmic energy is always the same. Then, if there was a time when nothing existed, where was all this manifested energy? Some say it was in a potential form in God. In that case God is sometimes potential and sometimes kinetic, which would make Him mutable. Everything mutable is a compound, and everything compound must undergo that change which is called destruction. So God would die, which is absurd. Therefore there never was a time when there was no creation.

If I may be allowed to use a simile, creation and creator are two lines, without beginning and without end, running parallel to each other. God is the ever active providence, by whose power systems after systems are being evolved out of chaos, made to run for a time and again destroyed. This is what the Brahmin boy repeats every day: "The sun and the moon, the Lord created like the suns and moons of previous cycles." And this agrees with modern science.

Here I stand and if I shut my eyes, and try to conceive my existence, "I", "I", "I", what is the idea before me? The idea of a body.

Am I, then, nothing but a combination of material substances? The Vedas declare, "No". I am a spirit living in a body. I am not the body. The body will die, but I shall not die. Here am I in this body; it will fall, but I shall go on living. I had also a past. The soul was not created, for creation means a combination which means a certain future dissolution. If then the soul was created, it must die. Some are born happy, enjoy perfect health, with beautiful body, mental vigour and all wants supplied. Others are born miserable, some are without hands or feet, others again are idiots and only drag on a wretched existence. Why, if they are all created, why does a just and merciful God create one happy and another unhappy, why is He so partial? Nor would it mend matters in the least to hold that those who are miserable in this life will be happy in a future one. Why should a man be miserable even here in the reign of a just and merciful God? In the second place, the idea of a creator God does not explain the anomaly, but simply expresses the cruel fiat of an all-powerful being. There must have been causes, then, before his birth, to make a man miserable or happy and those were his past actions.

Are not all the tendencies of the mind and the body accounted for by inherited aptitude? Here are two parallel lines of existence–one of the mind, the other of matter. If matter and its transformations answer for all that we have, there is no necessity for supposing the existence of a soul. But it cannot be proved that thought has been evolved out of matter, and if a philosophical monism is inevitable, spiritual monism is certainly logical and no less desirable than a materialistic monism; but neither of these is necessary here.

We cannot deny that bodies acquire certain tendencies from heredity, but those tendencies only mean the physical configuration, through which a peculiar mind alone can act in a peculiar way. There are other tendencies peculiar to a soul caused by its past actions. And a soul with a certain tendency would by the laws of affinity take birth in a body which is the fittest instrument for the display of that tendency. This is in accord with science wants to explain everything by habit, and habit is got through repetitions. So repetitions are necessary to explain the natural not an endless prison of cause and effect, but that at the head of all these laws, in and through every particle of matter and force, stands One "by whose command the wind blows, the fire burns, the clouds rain, and death stalks upon the earth."

And what is His nature? He is everywhere, the pure and formless One, the Almighty and the All-merciful. "Thou art our father, Thou art our mother, Thou art our beloved friend, Thou art the source of all strength; give us strength. Thou art He that beareth the burdens of the universe; help me bear the little burden of this life." Thus sang the Rishis of the Vedas. And how to worship Him? Through love. "He is to be worshipped as the one beloved, dearer than everything in this and the next life."

This is the doctrine of love declared in the Vedas, and let us see how it is fully developed and taught by Krishna, whom the Hindus believe to have been God incarnate on earth.

He taught that a man ought to live in this world like a lotus leaf, which grows in water but is never moistened by water; so a man ought to live in the world–his heart to God and his hands to work.

It is good to love God for hope of reward in this or the next world, but it is better to love God for love's sake, and the prayer goes: "Lord, I do not want wealth, nor children, nor learning. If it be Thy will, I shall go from birth to birth, but grant me this, that I may love Thee without the hope of reward–love unselfishly for love's sake." One of the disciples of Krishna, the then Emperor of India, was driven from his kingdom by his enemies and had to take shelter with his queen in a forest in the Himalayas, and there one day the queen asked him how it was that he, the most virtuous of men, should suffer so much misery. Yudhishthira answered, "Behold, my queen, the Himalayas, how grand and beautiful they are; I love them. They do not give me anything, but my nature is to love the grand, the beautiful, therefore I love them. Similarly, I love the Lord. He is the source of all beauty, of all sublimity. He is the only object to be loved; my nature is to love Him, and therefore I love. I do not pray for anything; I do not ask for anything. Let Him place me wherever He likes. I must love Him for love's sake. I cannot trade love."

The Vedas teach that the soul is divine, only held in the bondage of matter; perfection will be reached when this bond will burst, and the word they use for it is therefore, Mukti– freedom, freedom from the bonds of imperfection, freedom from death and misery.

And this bondage can only fall off through the mercy of God, and this mercy comes on the pure. So purity is the condition of His mercy. How does that mercy act? He reveals Himself to the pure heart; the pure and the stainless see God, yea, even in this life; then and then only all the crookedness of the heart is made straight. Then all doubt ceases. He is no more the freak of a terrible law of causation. This is the very centre, the very vital conception of Hinduism. The Hindu does not want to live upon words and theories. If there are existences beyond the ordinary sensuous existence, he wants to come face to face with them. If there is a soul in him which is not matter, if there is an all-merciful universal Soul, he will go to Him direct. He must see Him, and that alone can destroy all doubts. So the best proof a Hindu sage gives about the soul, about God, is: "I have seen the soul; I have seen God." And that is the only condition of perfection. The Hindu religion does not consist in struggles and attempts to believe a certain doctrine or dogma, but in realising–not in believing, but in being and becoming.

Thus the whole object of their system is by constant struggle to become perfect, to become divine, to reach God and see God, and this reaching God, seeing God, becoming perfect even as the Father in Heaven is perfect, constitutes the religion of the Hindus.

And what becomes of a man when he attains perfection? He lives a life of bliss infinite. He enjoys infinite and perfect bliss, having obtained the only thing in which man ought to have pleasure, namely God, and enjoys the bliss with God.

So far all the Hindus are agreed. This is the common religion of all the sects of India; but, then, perfection is absolute, and the absolute cannot be two or three. It cannot have any qualities. It cannot be an individual. And so when a soul becomes perfect and absolute, it must become one with Brahman, and it would only realise the Lord as the perfection, the reality, of its own nature and existence, the existence absolute, knowledge absolute, and bliss absolute. We have often and often read this called the losing of individuality and becoming a stock or a stone. "He jests at scars that never felt a wound."

I tell you it is nothing of the kind. If it is happiness to enjoy the consciousness of this small body, it must be greater happiness to enjoy the consciousness of two bodies, the measure of happiness increasing with the consciousness of an increasing number of bodies, the aim, the ultimate of happiness being reached when it would become a universal consciousness.

Therefore, to gain this infinite universal individuality, this miserable little prisonindividuality must go. Then alone can death cease when I am one with life, then alone can misery cease when I am one with happiness itself, then alone can all errors cease when I am one with knowledge itself; and this is the necessary scientific conclusion. Science has proved to me that physical individuality is a delusion, that really my body is one little continuously changing body in an unbroken ocean of matter; and Advaita (unity) is the necessary conclusion with my other counterpart, soul.

Science is nothing but the finding of unity. As soon as science would reach perfect unity, it would stop from further progress, because it would reach the goal. Thus Chemistry could not progress farther when it would discover one element out of which all others could be made. Physics would stop when it would be able to fulfill its services in discovering one energy of which all the others are but manifestations, and the science of religion becomes perfect when it would discover Him who is the one life in a universe of death, Him who is the constant basis of an ever-changing world. One who is the only Soul of which all souls are but delusive manifestations? Thus is it, through multiplicity and duality, that the ultimate unity is reached. Religion can go no farther. This is the goal of all science.

All science is bound to come to this conclusion in the long run. Manifestation, and not creation, is the word of science today, and the Hindu is only glad that what he has been cherishing in his bosom for ages is going to be taught in more forcible language and with further light from the latest conclusions of science.

Descend we now from the aspirations of philosophy to the religion of the ignorant. At the very outset, I may tell you that there is no polytheism in India. In every temple, if one stands by and listens, one will find the worshippers applying all the attributes of God, including omnipresence, to the images. It is not polytheism, nor would the name henotheism explain the situation. "The rose called by any other name would smell as sweet." Names are not explanations.

I remember, as a boy, hearing a Christian missionary preach to a crowd in India. Among other sweet things he was telling them was that if he gave a blow to their idol with his stick, what could it do? One of his hearers sharply answered, "If I abuse your God, what can He do?" "You would be punished," said the preacher, "when you die." "So my idol will punish you when you die," retorted the Hindu.

The tree is known by its fruits. When I have seen amongst them that are called idolaters, men, the like of whom in morality and spirituality and love I have never seen anywhere, I stop and ask myself, "Can sin beget holiness?"

Superstition is a great enemy of man, but bigotry is worse. Why does a Christian go to church? Why is the cross holy? Why is the face turned toward the sky in prayer? Why are there so many images in the Catholic Church? Why are there so many images in the minds of Protestants when they pray? My brethren, we can no more think about anything without a mental image than we can live without breathing. By the law of association, the material image calls up the mental idea and vice versa. This is why the Hindu uses an external symbol when he worships. He will tell you, it helps to keep his mind fixed on the Being to whom he prays. He knows as well as you do that the image is not God, is not omnipresent. After all, how much does omnipresence mean to almost the whole world? It stands merely as a word, a symbol. Has God superficial area? If not, when we repeat that word "omnipresent", we think of the extended sky or of space, that is all. As we find that somehow or other, by the laws of our mental constitution, we have to associate our ideas of infinity with the image of the blue sky, or of the sea, so we naturally connect our idea of holiness with the image of a church, a mosque, or a cross. The Hindus have associated the idea of holiness, purity, truth, omnipresence, and such other ideas with different images and forms. But with this difference that while some people devote their whole lives to their idol of a church and never rise higher, because with them religion means an intellectual assent to certain doctrines and doing good to their fellows, the whole religion of the Hindu is centred in realisation. Man is to become divine by realising the divine. Idols or temples or churches or books are only the supports, the helps, of his spiritual childhood: but on and on he must progress.

He must not stop anywhere. "External worship, material worship," say the scriptures, "is the lowest stage; struggling to rise high, mental prayer is the next stage, but the highest stage is when the Lord has been realised." Mark, the same earnest man who is kneeling before the idol tells you,"Him the sun cannot express, nor the moon, nor the stars, the lightning cannot express Him, nor what we speak of as fire; through Him they shine." But he does not abuse any one's idol or call its worship sin. He recognises in it a necessary stage of life."The child is father of the man." Would it be right for an old man to say that childhood is a sin or youth a sin?

If a man can realise his divine nature with the help of an image would it be right to call that a sin? Nor even when he has passed that stage, should he call it an error. To the Hindu, man is not travelling from error to truth, but from truth to truth, from lower to higher truth. To him all the religions, from the lowest fetishism to the highest absolutism, mean so many attempts of the human soul to grasp and realise the Infinite, each determined by the conditions of its birth and association, and each of these marks a stage of progress; and every soul is a young eagle soaring higher and higher, gathering more and more strength, till it reaches the Glorious Sun.

Unity in variety is the plan of nature, and the Hindu has recognised it. Every other religion lays down certain fixed dogmas, and tries to force society to adopt them. It places before society only one coat which must fit Jack and John and Henry, all alike. If it does not fit John or Henry, he must go without a coat to cover his body. The Hindus have discovered that the absolute can only be realised, or thought of, or stated, through the relative, and the images, crosses, and crescents are simply so many symbols–so many pegs to hang the spiritual ideas on. It is not that this help is necessary for every one, but those that do not need it have no right to say that it is wrong. Nor is it compulsory in Hinduism. One thing I must tell you. Idolatry in India does not mean anything horrible. It is not the mother of harlots. On the other hand, it is the attempt of undeveloped minds to grasp high spiritual truths. The Hindus have their faults, they sometimes have their exceptions; but mark this, they are always for punishing their own bodies, and never for cutting the throats of their neighbours. If the Hindu fanatic burns himself on the pyre, he never lights the fire of Inquisition. And even this cannot be laid at the door of his religion any more than the burning of witches can be laid at the door of Christianity.

To the Hindu, then, the whole world of religions is only a travelling, a coming up, of different men and women, through various conditions and circumstances, to the same goal. Every religion is only evolving a God out of the material man, and the same God is the inspirer of all of them. Why, then, are there so many contradictions? They are only apparent, says the Hindu. The contradictions come from the same truth adapting itself to the varying circumstances of different natures.

It is the same light coming through glasses of different colours. And these little variations are necessary for purposes of adaptation. But in the heart of everything the same truth reigns. The Lord has declared to the Hindu in His incarnation as Krishna, "I am in every religion as the thread through a string of pearls. Wherever thou seest extraordinary holiness and extraordinary power raising and purifying humanity, know thou that I am there." And what has been the result? I challenge the world to find, throughout the whole system of Sanskrit philosophy, any such expression as that the Hindu alone will be saved and not others. Says Vyasa, "We find perfect men even beyond the pale of our caste and creed." One thing more. How, then, can the Hindu, whose whole fabric of thought centers in God, believe in Buddhism which is agnostic, or in Jainism which is atheistic?

The Buddhists or the Jains do not depend upon God; but the

whole force of their religion is directed to the great central truth in every religion, to evolve a God out of man. They have not seen the Father, but they have seen the Son. And he that hath seen the Son hath seen the Father also. This, brethren, is a short sketch of the religious ideas of the Hindus. The Hindu may have failed to carry out all his plans, but if there is ever to be a universal religion, it must be one which will have no location in place or time; which will be infinite like the God it will preach, and whose sun will shine upon the followers of Krishna and of Christ, on saints and sinners alike; which will not be Brahminic or Buddhistic, Christian or Mohammedan, but the sum total of all these, and still have infinite space for development; which in its catholicity will embrace in its infinite arms, and find a place for, every human being, from the lowest groveling savage not far removed from the brute, to the highest man towering by the virtues of his head and heart almost above humanity, making society stand in awe of him and doubt his human nature. It will be a religion which will have no place for persecution or intolerance in its polity, which will recognise divinity in every man and woman, and whose whole scope, whose whole force, will be created in aiding humanity to realise its own true, divine nature.

Offer such a religion, and all the nations will follow you. Asoka's council was a council of the Buddhist faith. Akbar's, though more to the purpose, was only a parlour-meeting. It was reserved for America to proclaim to all quarters of the globe that the Lord is in every religion. May He who is the Brahman of the Hindus, the Ahura-Mazda of the Zoroastrians, the Buddha of the Buddhists, the Jehovah of the Jews, the Father in Heaven of the Christians, give strength to you to carry out your noble idea! The star arose in the East; it travelled steadily towards the West, sometimes dimmed and sometimes effulgent, till it made a circuit of the world; and now it is again rising on the very horizon of the East, the borders of the Sanpo, a thousand fold more effulgent than it ever was before. Hail, Columbia, motherland of liberty! It has been given to thee, who never dipped her hand in her neighbour's blood, who never found out that the shortest way of becoming rich was by robbing one's neighbours, it has been given to thee to march at the vanguard of civilisation with the flag of harmony.

Religion not the crying need of India

(20th September, 1893)

[On 19th September 1893, Vivekananda's speech veered towards anti-Christian expressions. On 20th September, before Vivekananda started his impromptu speech (as other speakers had not turned up), Prof. Isaac T. Headland, a missionary who worked in China, had presented a paper on "Religion in Peking." This prompted Swamiji to react to this paper and observe that as poverty was prevailing in China it would be advisable for the missionaries to help in alleviating this problem by setting up camps, rather than persuading them to convert to Christianity. In his speech Swamiji in the same context then presented his theme "Religion not the crying need of India" admonishing Christians for their missionary activity in India. This speech was his fourth lecture at the parliament. Vivekananda was not scheduled to speak that day. After the end of Mr. Headland's speech, Dr. Momerie announced that the other speaker for that evening was absent. The audience saw Vivekananda in the gallery and asked him to deliver a lecture. Vivekananda assented to the request and started his speech.]

Christians must always be ready for good criticism, and I hardly think that you will mind if I make a little criticism. You Christians, who are so fond of sending out missionaries to save the soul of the heathen–why do you not try to save their bodies from starvation? In India, during the terrible famines, thousands died from hunger, yet you Christians did nothing. You erect churches all through India, but the crying evil in the East is not religion– they have religion enough–but it is bread that the suffering millions of burning India cry out for with parched throats. They ask us for bread, but we give them stones. It is an insult to a starving people to offer them religion; it is an insult to a starving man to teach him metaphysics. In India a priest that preached for money would lose caste and be spat upon by the people. I came here to seek aid for my impoverished people, and I fully realised how difficult it was to get help for heathens from Christians in a Christian land.

Buddhism, the fulfillment of Hinduism

(26th September, 1893)

[Swami Vivekananda, also known as 'neo-Vedanti', in his lecture at the Parliament, highlighted the fact that the Buddha is worshipped as one of the incarnations of God where as in China, Japan and Ceylon (Sri Lanka) Buddhism is the religious practice. He particularly said that Buddhism was a rebel child of Hinduism. Buddha's teachings were a "Gift to the World" and could be traced to Christianity. He stated that the two religious practices—Hinduism, a Vedic religion, and Buddhism of the Shakyamuni, a Hindu who "expanded on the truths from the hidden Vedas"—are mutually inclusive. The teachings of Buddha were not new but were rooted in Vedic scriptures and he was the first monk who initiated the proselytisation of his ethos all over the world; the other religious preachers came much later. However, one distinction he pointed out in his lecture was a comparison with other religions of the world such as Christianity in which Jews who opposed Jesus Christ crucified him, while in India in contrast Buddha was worshipped as God. He was also critical of the way Buddhism was practised in the world now.

Swamiji elaborated on the reasons for the near total elimination of the Buddhist religion (Mahayana Buddhism) from India. This was due to the fact that Buddha's philosophy clashed with the "eternal rocks of the Vedas" to which people, Brahmin's in particular, was wedded and did not want to accept change. Thus Buddhism could not survive in India. Swamiji also stated that Buddhism should not be confused with Vedanta, in the same way as the Salvation Army is not to be confused with Christianity. Swamiji also opined that Buddhism was the "fulfillment of Hinduism" and thus Buddhists were wedded to the "brains and philosophy of the Brahmins" and similarly the Buddhists were the heart of the Hinduism.]

I am not a Buddhist, as you have heard, and yet I am. If China, or Japan, or Ceylon follow the teachings of the Great Master, India worships him as God incarnate on earth. You have just now heard that I am going to criticise Buddhism, but by that I wish you to understand only this. Far be it from me to criticise him whom I worship as God incarnate on earth. But our views about Buddha are that he was not understood properly by his disciples. The relation between Hinduism (by Hinduism, I mean the religion of the Vedas) and what is called Buddhism at the present day is nearly the same as between Judaism and Christianity. Jesus Christ was a Jew, and Shakya Muni was a Hindu. The Jews rejected Jesus Christ, nay, crucified him, and the Hindus have accepted Shakya Muni as God and worship him. But the real difference that we Hindus want to show between modern Buddhism and what we should understand as the teachings of Lord Buddha lies principally in this: Shakya Muni came to preach nothing new. He also, like Jesus, came to fulfil and not to destroy. Only, in the case of Jesus, it was the old people, the Jews, who did not understand him, while in the case of Buddha, it was his own followers who did not realise the import of this teachings. As the Jew did not understand the fulfilment of the Old Testament, so the Buddhist did not understand the fulfilment of the truths of the Hindu religion. Again, I repeat, Shakya Muni came not to destroy, but he was the fulfilment, the logical conclusion, the logical development of the religion of the Hindus.

The religion of the Hindus is divided into two parts: the ceremonial and the spiritual. The spiritual portion is specially studied by the monks. In that there is no caste. A man from the highest caste and a man from the lowest may become a monk in India, and the two castes become equal. In religion there is no caste; caste is simply a social institution. Shakya Muni himself was a monk, and it was his glory that he had the large-heartedness to bring out the truths from the hidden Vedas and throw them broadcast all over the world. He was the first being in the world who brought missionarising into practice–nay, he was the first to conceive the idea of proselytising.

The great glory of the Master lay in his wonderful sympathy for everybody, especially for the ignorant and the poor. Some of his disciples were Brahmins. When Buddha was teaching, Sanskrit was no more the spoken language in India. It was then only in the books of the learned. Some of Buddha's Brahmin disciples wanted to translate his teachings into Sanskrit, but he distinctly told them, "I am for the poor, for the people; let me speak in the tongue of the people." And so to this day the great bulk of his teachings are in the vernacular of that day in India. Whatever may be the position of philosophy, whatever may be the position of metaphysics, so long as there is such a thing as death in the world, so long as there is such a thing as weakness in the human heart, so long as there is a cry going out of the heart of man in his very weakness, there shall be a faith in God.

On the philosophic side the disciples of the Great Master dashed themselves against the eternal rocks of the Vedas and could not crush them, and on the other side they took away from the nation that eternal God to which every one, man or woman, clings so fondly. And the result was that Buddhism had to die a natural death in India. At the present day there is not one who calls oneself a Buddhist in India, the land of its birth.

But at the same time, Brahminism lost something–that reforming zeal, that wonderful sympathy and charity for everybody, that wonderful leaven which Buddhism had brought to the masses and which had rendered Indian society so great that a Greek historian who wrote about India of that time was led to say that no Hindu was known to tell an untruth and no Hindu woman was known to be unchaste.

Hinduism cannot live without Buddhism, nor Buddhism without Hinduism. Then realise what the separation has shown to us that the Buddhists cannot stand without the brain and philosophy of the Brahmins, nor the Brahmin without the heart of the Buddhist. This separation between the Buddhists and the Brahmins is the cause of the downfall of India. That is why India is populated by three hundred millions of beggars, and that is why India has been the slave of conquerors for the last thousand years. Let us then join the wonderful intellect of the Brahmins with the heart, the noble soul, the wonderful humanising power of the Great Master.

Address at the Final Session

(27th September, 1893)

The World's Parliament of Religions has become an accomplished fact, and the merciful Father has helped those who laboured to bring it into existence, and crowned with success their most unselfish labour. My thanks to those noble souls whose large hearts and love of truth first dreamed this wonderful dream and then realised it. My thanks to the shower of liberal sentiments that has overflowed this platform. My thanks to this enlightened audience for their uniform kindness to me and for their appreciation of every thought that tends to smooth the friction of religions. A few jarring notes were heard from time to time in this harmony. My special thanks to them, for they have, by their striking contrast, made general harmony the sweeter.

Much has been said of the common ground of religious unity. I am not going just now to venture my own theory. But if anyone here hopes that this unity will come by the triumph of any one of the religions and the destruction of the other, to him I say, "Brother, yours is an impossible hope." Do I wish that the Christian would become Hindu? God forbid. Do I wish that the Hindu or Buddhist would become Christian? God forbid. The seed is put in the ground, and earth and air and water are placed around it. Does the seed become the earth, or the air, or the water? No. It becomes a plant, it develops after the law of its own growth assimilates the air, the earth, and the water, converts them into plant substance, and grows into a plant.

Similar is the case with religion. The Christian is not to become a Hindu or a Buddhist, nor a Hindu or a Buddhist to become a Christian. But each must assimilate the spirit of the others and yet preserve his individuality and grow according to his own law of growth. If the Parliament of Religions has shown anything to the world it is this: It has proved to the world that holiness, purity and charity are not the exclusive possessions of any church in the world, and that every system has produced men and women of the most exalted character. In the face of this evidence, if anybody dreams of the exclusive survival of his own religion and the destruction of the others, I pity him from the bottom of my heart, and point out to him that upon the banner of every religion will soon be written, in spite of resistance: "Help and not Fight," "Assimilation and not Destruction," "Harmony and Peace and not Dissension."

□

The Vedanta Philosophy*

—Swami Vivekananda

The Vedanta philosophy, as it is generally called at the present day, really comprises all the various sects that now exist in India. Thus there have been various interpretations, and to my mind they have been progressive, beginning with the dualistic or Dvaita and ending with the non-dualistic or Advaita. The word Vedanta literally means the end of the Vedas–the Vedas being the scriptures of the Hindus. Sometimes in the West by the Vedas are meant only the hymns and rituals of the Vedas. But at the present time these parts have almost gone out of use, and usually by the word Vedas in India, the Vedanta is meant. All our commentators, when they want to quote a passage from the scriptures, as a rule, quote from the Vedanta, which has another technical name with the commentators–the Shrutis. Now, all the books known by the name of the Vedanta were not entirely written after the ritualistic portions of the Vedas. For instance, one of them–the Isha Upanishad–forms the fortieth chapter of the Yajur-veda, that being one of the oldest parts of the Vedas. There are other Upanishads which form portions of the Brahmanas or ritualistic writings; and the rest of the Upanishads are independent, not comprised in any of the Brahmanas or other parts of the Vedas; but there is no reason to suppose that they were entirely independent of other parts, for, as we well know, many of these have been lost

* *Philosophy Department, Harvard University, Boston (USA), 25th March, 1996*

entirely and many of the Brahmanas have become extinct. So it is quite possible that the independent Upanishads belonged to some Brahmanas, which in course of time fell into disuse, while the Upanishads remained. These Upanishads are also called Forest Books or Aranyakas.

The Vedanta, then, practically forms the scriptures of the Hindus, and all systems of philosophy that are orthodox have to take it as their foundation. Even the Buddhists and Jains, when it suits their purpose, will quote a passage from the Vedanta as authority. All schools of philosophy in India, although they claim to have been based upon the Vedas, took different names for their systems. The last one, the system of Vyasa, took its stand upon the doctrines of the Vedas more than the previous systems did, and made an attempt to harmonise the preceding philosophies, such as the Sankhya and the Nyaya, with the doctrines of the Vedanta. So it is especially called the Vedanta philosophy; and the Sutras or aphorisms of Vyasa are, in modern India, the basis of the Vedanta philosophy. Again, these Sutras of Vyasa have been variously explained by different commentators. In general there are three sorts of commentator in India now; from their interpretations have arisen three systems of philosophy and sects. One is dualistic, or Dvaita; a second is the qualified non-dualistic, or Vishishtadvaita; and a third is the non-dualistic, or Advaita. Of these the dualistic and the qualified non-dualistic include the largest number of the Indian people. The non-dualists are comparatively few in number. Now I will try to lay before you the ideas that are contained in all these three sects; but before going on, I will make one remark–that these different Vedanta systems have one common psychology, and that is, the psychology of the Sankhya system. The Sankhya psychology is very much like the psychologies of the Nyaya and Vaisheshika systems, differing only in minor particulars.

All the Vedantists agree on three points. They believe in God, in the Vedas as revealed, and in cycles. We have already considered the Vedas. The belief about cycles is as follows: All matter throughout the universe is the outcome of one primal matter called Akasha; and all force, whether gravitation, attraction or repulsion, or life, is the outcome of one primal force called Prana.

Prana acting on Akasha is creating or projectin the universe. At the beginning of a cycle, Akasha is motionless, unmanifested. Then Prana begins to act, more and more, creating grosser and grosser forms out of Akasha–plants, animals, men, stars, and so on. After an incalculable time this evolution ceases and involution begins, everything being resolved back through finer and finer forms into the original Akasha and Prana, when a new cycle follows. Now there is something beyond Akasha and Prana. Both can be resolved into a third thing called Mahat–the Cosmic Mind. This Cosmic Mind does not create Akasha and Prana, but changes itself into them.

We will now take up the beliefs about mind, soul, and God. According to the universally accepted Sankhya psychology, in perception–in the case of vision, for instance–there are, first of all, the instruments of vision, the eyes. Behind the instruments–the eyes–is the organ of vision or Indriya–the optic nerve and its centres–which is not the external instrument, but without which the eyes will not see. More still is needed for perception. The mind or Manas must come and attach itself to the organ. And besides this, the sensation must be carried to the intellect or Buddhi–the determinative, reactive state of the mind. When the reaction comes from Buddhi, along with it flashes the external world and egoism. Here then is the will; but everything is not complete. Just as every picture, being composed of successive impulses of light, must be united on something stationary to form a whole, so all the ideas in the mind must be gathered and projected on something that is stationary–relatively to the body and mind–that is, on what is called the Soul or Purusha or Atman.

According to the Sankhya philosophy, the reactive state of the mind called Buddhi or intellect is the outcome, the change, or a certain manifestation of the Mahat or Cosmic Mind. The Mahat becomes changed into vibrating thought; and that becomes in one part changed into the organs, and in the other part into the fine particles of matter. Out of the combination of all these, the whole of this universe is produced. Behind even Mahat, the Sankhya conceives of a certain state which is called Avyakta or unmanifested, where even the manifestation of mind is not present, but only the causes exists. It is also called Prakriti. Beyond this Prakriti, and eternally separate from it, is the Purusha, the soul of the Sankhya which is without attributes and omnipresent. The Purusha is not the doer but the witness. The illustration of the crystal is used to explain the Purusha. The latter is said to be like a crystal without any colour, before which different colours are placed, and then it seems to be coloured by the colours before it, but in reality it is not. The Vedantists reject the Sankhya ideas of the soul and nature. They claim that between them there is a huge gulf to be bridged over. On the one hand the Sankhya system comes to nature, and then at once it has to jump over to the other side and come to the soul, which is entirely separate from nature. How can these different colours, as Sankhya called them, be able to act on that soul which by its nature is colourless? So the Vedantists, from the very first, affirm that this soul and this nature are one.

Vedantists admit that the Atman or God is not only the efficient cause of this universe, but also the material cause. But they only say so in so many words. They do not really mean it, for they try to escape from their conclusions, in this way: They say there are three existences in this universe–God, soul, and nature. Nature and soul are, as it were, the body of God, and in this sense it may be said that God and the whole universe are one. But this nature and all these various souls remain different from each other through all eternity. Only at the beginning of a cycle do they become manifest; and when the cycle ends, they become fine, and remain in a fine state. The Advaita Vedantists–the non-dualists–reject this theory of the soul, and, having nearly the whole range of the Upanishads in their favour, build their philosophy entirely upon them. All the books contained in the Upanishads have one subject, one task before them–to prove the following theme: "Just as by the knowledge of one lump of clay we have the knowledge of all the clay in the universe, so what is that, knowing which we know everything in the universe?" The idea of the Advaitists is to generalise the whole universe into one–that something which is really the whole of this universe. And they claim that this whole universe is one, that it is one Being manifesting itself in all these various forms. They admit that what the Sankhya calls nature exists, but say that nature is God. It is this Being, the Sat, which has become converted into all this–the universe, man, soul, and everything that exists. Mind and Mahat are but the manifestations of that one Sat. But then the difficulty arises that this would be pantheism. How came that Sat which is unchangeable, as they admit (for that which is absolute is unchangeable), to be changed into that which is changeable, and perishable? The Advaitists here have a theory which they call Vivarta Vada or apparent manifestation. According to the dualists and the Sankyas, the whole of this universe is the evolution of primal nature. According to some of the Advaitists and some of the dualists, the whole of this universe is evolved from God. And according to the Advaitists proper, the followers of Shankaracharya, the whole universe is the apparent evolution of God. God is the material cause of this universe, but not really, only apparently. The celebrated illustration used is that of the rope and the snake, where the rope appeared to be the snake, but was not really so. The rope did not really change into the snake. Even so this whole universe as it exists is that Being. It is unchanged, and all the changes we see in it are only apparent. These changes are caused by Desha, Kala, and Nimitta (space, time, and causation), or, according to a higher psychological generalisation, by Nama and Rupa (name and form). It is by name and form that one thing is differentiated from another. The name and form alone cause the difference. In reality they are one and the same. Again, it is not, the Vedantists say, that there is something as phenomenon and something as noumenon. The rope is changed into the snake apparently only; and when the delusion ceases, the snake vanishes. When one is in ignorance, he sees the phenomenon and does not see God. When he sees God, this universe vanishes entirely for him. Ignorance or Maya, as it is called, is the cause of all this phenomenon–the Absolute, the Unchangeable, being taken as this manifested universe. This Maya is not absolute zero, nor non-existence. It is defined as neither existence nor non-existence. It is not existence, because that can be said only of the Absolute, the Unchangeable, and in this sense, Maya is non-existence. Again, it cannot be said it is non-existence; for if it were, it could never produce the phenomenon. So it is something which is neither; and in the Vedanta philosophy it is called Anirvachaniya or inexpressible. Maya, then, is the real cause of this universe. Maya gives the name and form to what Brahman or God gives the material; and the latter seems to have been transformed into all this. The Advaitists, then have no place for the individual soul. They say individual souls are created by Maya. In reality they cannot exist. If there were only one existence throughout, how could it be that I am one, and you are one, and so forth? We are all one, and the cause of evil is the perception of duality. As soon as I begin to feel that I am separate from this universe, then first comes fear, and then comes misery. "Where one hears another, one sees another, that is small. Where one does not see another, where one does not hear another, that is the greatest, that is God. In that greatest is perfect happiness. In small things there is no happiness."

According to the Advaita philosophy, then, this differentiation of matter, these phenomena, are, as it were, for a time, hiding the real nature of man; but the latter really has not been changed at all. In the lowest worm, as well as in the highest human being, the same divine nature is present. The worm form is the lower form in which the divinity has been more overshadowed by Maya; that is the highest form in which it has been least overshadowed. Behind everything the same divinity is existing, and out of this comes the basis of morality. Do not injure another. Love everyone as your own self, because the whole universe is one. In injuring another, I am injuring myself; in loving another, I am loving myself. From this also springs that principle of Advaita morality which has been summed up in one word–self-abnegation. The Advaitist says, this little personalised self is the cause of all my misery. This individualised self, which makes me different from all other beings brings hatred and jealousy and misery, struggle and all other evils. And when this idea has been got rid of, all struggle will cease, all misery vanish. So this is to be given up. We must always hold ourselves ready, even to give up our lives for the lowest beings. When a man has become ready even to give up his life for a little insect, he has reached the perfection which the Advaitist wants to attain; and at that moment when he has become thus ready, the veil of ignorance falls away from him, and he will feel his own nature. Even in this life, he will feel that he is one with the universe. For a time, as it were, the whole of this phenomenal world will disappear for him, and he will realise what he is. But so long as the Karma of this body remains, he will have to live. This state, when the veil has vanished and yet the body remains for some time, is what the Vedantists call the Jivanmukti, the living freedom. If a man is deluded by a mirage for some time, and one day the mirage disappears–if it comes back again the next day, or at some future time, he will not be deluded. Before the mirage first broke, the man could not distinguish between the reality and the deception. But when it has once broken, as long as he has organs and eyes to work with, he will see the image, but will no more be deluded. That fine distinction between the actual world and the mirage he has caught, and the latter cannot delude him any more. So when the Vedantist has realised his own nature, the whole world has vanished for him. It will come back again, but no more the same world of misery. The prison of misery has become changed into Sat, Chit, Ananda–Existence Absolute, Knowledge Absolute, Bliss Absolute–and the attainment of this is the goal of the Advaita Philosophy.

□

Unity In Diversity*

—Swami Vivekananda

[During his second visit to England in May 1896 Vivekananda met Max Müller, a noted Indologist from Oxford University who wrote Ramakrishna's first biography in the West. From England, Vivekananda visited other European countries. In Germany he met Paul Deussen, another Indologist. Vivekananda was offered academic positions in two American universities (one the chair in Eastern Philosophy at Harvard University and a similar position at Columbia University); he declined both, since his duties would conflict with his commitment as a monk.]

"The Self-existent One projected the senses outwards and, therefore; a man looks outward, not within himself. A certain wise one, desiring immortality, with inverted senses, perceived the Self within." As I have already said, the first inquiry that we find in the Vedas was concerning outward things, and then a new idea came that the reality of things is not to be found in the external world; not by looking outwards, but by turning the eyes, as it is literally expressed, inwards. And the word used for the Soul is very significant: it is He who has gone inward, the innermost reality of our being, the heart centre, the core, from

* *39 Victoria Street, Greycoat Gardens, London (England), 3rd November, 1896*

which, as it were, everything comes out; the central sun of which the mind, the body, the sense-organs, and everything else we have are but rays going outwards. "Men of childish intellect, ignorant persons, run after desires which are external, and enter the trap of far-reaching death, but the wise, understanding immortality, never seek for the Eternal in this life of finite things." The same idea is here made clear that in this external world, which is full of finite things, it is impossible to see and find the Infinite. The Infinite must be sought in that alone which is infinite, and the only thing infinite about us is that which is within us, our own soul. Neither the body, nor the mind, nor even our thoughts, nor the world we see around us, are infinite. The Seer, He to whom they all belong, the Soul of man, He who is awake in the internal man, alone is infinite, and to seek for the Infinite Cause of this whole universe we must go there. In the Infinite Soul alone we can find it. What is here is there too, and what is there is here also. He who sees the manifold goes from death to death." We have seen how at first there was the desire to go to heaven. When these ancient Aryans became dissatisfied with the world around them, they naturally thought that after death they would go to some place where there would be all happiness without any misery; these places they multiplied and called Svargas–the word may be translated as heavens–where there would be joy for ever, the body would become perfect, and also the mind, and there they would live with their forefathers. But as soon as philosophy came, men found that this was impossible and absurd. The very idea of an infinite in place would be a contradiction in terms, as a place must begin and continue in time. Therefore they had to give up this idea. They found out that the gods who lived in these heavens had once been human beings on earth, who through their good works had become gods, and the godhoods, as they call them, were different states, different positions; none of the gods spoken of in the Vedas are permanent individuals.

For instance, Indra and Varuna are not the names of certain persons, but the names of positions as governors and so on. The Indra who had lived before is not the same person as the Indra of the present day; he has passed away, and another man from earth has filled his place. So with all the other gods. These are certain positions, which are filled successively by human souls who have raised themselves to the condition of gods, and yet even they die. In the old Rig-Veda we find the word "immortality" used with regard to these gods, but later on it is dropped entirely, for they found that immortality which is beyond time and space cannot be spoken of with regard to any physical form, however subtle it may be. However fine it may be, it must have a beginning in time and space, for the necessary factors that enter into the make-up of form are in space. Try to think of a form without space; it is impossible. Space is one of the materials, as it were, which make up the form, and this is continually changing. Space and time are in Maya, and this idea is expressed in the line–"What is here, that is there too." If there are these gods, they must be bound by the same laws that apply here, and all laws involved destruction and renewal again and again. These laws are moulding matter into different forms, and crushing them out again. Everything born must die; and so, if there are heavens, the same laws must hold good there.

In this world we find that all happiness is followed by misery as its shadow. Life has its shadow, death. They must go together, because they are not contradictory, not two separate existences, but different manifestations of the same unit, life and death, sorrow and happiness, good and evil. The dualistic conception that good and evil are two separate entities, and that they are both going on eternally, is absurd on the face of it. They are the diverse manifestations of one and the same fact, one time appearing as bad, and at another time as good. The difference does not exist in kind, but only in degree. They differ from each other in degree of intensity. We find as a fact that the same nerve systems carry good and bad sensations alike, and when the nerves are injured, neither sensation comes to us. If a certain nerve is paralysed, we do not get the pleasurable feelings that used to come along the wire; and at the same time we do not get the painful feelings either. They are never two, but the same. Again, the same thing produces pleasure and pain at different times of life. The same phenomenon will produce pleasure in one, and pain in another. The eating of meat produces pleasure to a man, but pain to the animal which is eaten. There has never been anything which gives pleasure to all alike. Some are pleased, other displeased. So on it will go. Therefore, this duality of existence is denied. And what follows? I told you in my last lecture that we can never have ultimately everything good on this earth and nothing bad. It may have disappointed and frightened some of you, but I cannot help it, and I am open to conviction when I am shown to the contrary; but until that can be proved to me, and I can find that it is true, I cannot say so.

The general argument against my statement, and apparently a very convincing one, is this that in the course of evolution, all that is evil in what we see around us is gradually being eliminated, and the result is that if this elimination continues for millions of years, a time will come when all the evil will have been extirpated, and the good alone will remain. This is apparently a very sound argument. Would to God it were true! But there is a fallacy in it. and it is this that it takes for granted that both good and evil are things that are eternally fixed. It takes for granted that there is a definite mass of evil, which may be represented by a hundred, and likewise of good, and that this mass of evil is being diminished every day, leaving only the good. But is this so? The history of the world shows that evil is a continuously increasing quantity, as well as good. Take the lowest man; he lives in a forest. His sense of enjoyment is very small, and so also is his power to suffer. His misery is entirely on the sense-plane. If he does not get plenty of food, he is miserable; but give him plenty of food and freedom to rove and to hunt, and he is perfectly happy. His happiness consists only in the senses, and so does his misery also. But if that man increases in knowledge, his happiness will increase, the intellect will open to him, and his sense-enjoyment will evolve into intellectual enjoyment. He will feel pleasure in reading a beautiful poem, and a mathematical problem will be of absorbing interest to him. But, with these, the finer nerves will become more and more susceptible to miseries of mental pain, of which the savage does not think. Take a very simple illustration. In Tibet there is no marriage, and there is no jealousy, yet we know that marriage is a much higher state. The Tibetans have not known the wonderful enjoyment, the blessing of chastity, the happiness of having a chaste, virtuous wife, or a chaste, virtuous husband. These people cannot feel that. And similarly they do not feel the intense jealousy of the chaste wife or husband, or the misery caused by unfaithfulness on either side, with all the heart-burnings and sorrows which believers in chastity experience. On one side, the latter gain happiness, but on the other, they suffer misery too.

Take your country which is the richest in the world, and which is more luxurious than any other, and see how intense in the misery, how many more lunatics you have, compared with other races, only because the desires are so keen. A man must keep up a high standard of living, and the amount of money he spends in one year would be a fortune to a man in India. You cannot preach to him of simple living because society demands so much of him. The wheel of society is rolling on; it stops not for the widow's tears or orphans' wails. This is the state of things everywhere. Your sense of enjoyment is developed, your society is very much more beautiful than some others. You have so many more things to enjoy. But those who have fewer have much less misery. You can argue thus throughout, the higher the ideal you have in the brain, the greater is your enjoyment, and the more profound your misery. One is like the shadow of the other. That the evils are being eliminated may be true, but if so, the good also must be dying out. But are not evils multiplying fast, and good diminishing, if I may so put it? If good increases in arithmetical progression, evil increases in geometrical progression. And this is Maya. This is neither optimism nor pessimism. Vedanta does not take the position that this world is only a miserable one. That would be untrue. At the same time, it is a mistake to say that this world is full of happiness and blessings.

So it is useless to tell children that this world is all good, all flowers, all milk and honey. That is what we have all dreamt. At the same time it is erroneous to think, because one man has suffered more than another, that all is evil. It is this duality, this play of good and evil that makes our world of experiences. At the same time the Vedanta says, "Do not think that good and evil are two, are two separate essences, for they are one and the same thing, appearing in different degrees and in different guises and producing differences of feeling in the same mind." So, the first thought of the Vedanta is the finding of unity in the external; the One Existence manifesting Itself, however different It may appear in manifestation. Think of the old crude theory of the Persians–two gods creating this world, the good god doing everything that is good, and the bad one, everything bad. On the very face of it, you see the absurdity, for if it be carried out, every law of nature must have two parts, one of which is manipulated by one god, and then he goes away and the other god manipulates the other part. There the difficulty comes that both are working in the same world, and these two gods keep themselves in harmony by injuring one portion and doing good to another. This is a crude case, of course, the crudest way of expressing the duality of existence. But, take the more advanced, the more abstract theory that this world is partly good and partly bad. This also is absurd, arguing from the same standpoint. It is the law of unity that gives us our food, and it is the same law that kills many through accidents or misadventure.

We find, then, that this world is neither optimistic nor pessimistic; it is a mixture of both, and as we go on we shall find that the whole blame is taken away from nature and put upon our shoulders. At the same time the Vedanta shows the way out, but not by denial of evil, because it analyses boldly the fact as it is and does not seek to conceal anything. It is not hopeless; it is not agnostic. It finds out a remedy, but it wants to place that remedy on adamantine foundations; not by shutting the child's mouth and blinding its eyes with something which is untrue, and which the child will find out in a few days. I remember when I was young, a young man's father died and left him poorly off, with a large family to support, and he found that his father's friends were unwilling to help him. He had a conversation with a clergyman who offered this consolation, "Oh, it is all good, all is sent for our good." That is the old method of trying to put a piece of gold leaf on an old sore. It is a confession of weakness, or absurdity. The young man went away, and six months afterwards a son was born to the clergyman, and he gave a thanksgiving party to which the young man was invited. The clergyman prayed, "Thank God for His mercies." And the young man stood up and said, "Stop, this is all misery." The clergyman asked, "What?" "Because when my father died you said it was good, though apparently evil; so now, this is apparently good, but really evil." Is this the way to cure the misery of the world? Be good and have mercy on those who suffer. Do not try to patch it up, nothing will cure this world; go beyond it.

This is a world of good and evil. Wherever there is good, evil follows, but beyond and behind all these manifestations, all these contradictions, the Vedanta finds out that Unity. It says, "Give up what is evil and give up what is good." What remains then? Behind good and evil stands something which is yours, the real you, beyond every evil, and beyond every good too, and it is that which is manifesting itself as good and bad. Know that first, and then and then alone you will be a true optimist, and not before; for then you will be able to control everything. Control these manifestations and you will be at liberty to manifest the real "you". First be master of yourself, stand up and be free, go beyond the pale of these laws, for these laws do not absolutely govern you, they are only part of your being. First find out that you are not the slave of nature, never were and never will be; that this nature, infinite as you may think it, is only finite, a drop in the ocean, and your Soul is the ocean; you are beyond the stars, the sun, and the moon. They are like mere bubbles compared with your infinite being. Know that, and you will control both good and evil. Then alone the whole vision will change and you will stand up and say, "How beautiful is good and how wonderful is evil!"

That is what the Vedanta teaches. It does not propose any slipshod remedy by covering wounds with gold leaf and the more the wound festers, putting on more gold leaf. This life is a hard fact; work your way through it boldly, though it may be adamantine; no matter, the soul is stronger. It lays no responsibility on little gods; for you are the makers of your own fortunes. You make yourselves suffer, you make good and evil, and it is you who put your hands before your eyes and say it is dark. Take your hands away and see the light; you are effulgent, you are perfect already, from the very beginning. We now understand the verse: "He goes from death to death who sees the many here." See that One and be free.

How are we to see it? This mind, so deluded, so weak, so easily led, even this mind can be strong and may catch a glimpse of that knowledge, that Oneness, which saves us from dying again and again. As rain falling upon a mountain flows in various streams down the sides of the mountain, so all the energies which you see here are from that one Unit. It has become manifold falling upon Maya. Do not run after the manifold; go towards the One. "He is in all that moves; He is in all that is pure; He fills the universe; He is in the sacrifice; He is the guest in the house; He is in man, in water, in animals, in truth; He is the Great One. As fire coming into this world is manifesting itself in various forms, even so, that one Soul of the universe is manifesting Himself in all these various forms. As air coming into this universe manifests itself in various forms, even so, the One Soul of all souls, of all beings, is manifesting Himself in all forms." This is true for you when you have understood this Unity, and not before. Then is all optimism, because He is seen everywhere. The question is that if all this be true that that Pure One–the Self, the Infinite–has entered all this, how is it that He suffers, how is it that He becomes miserable, impure? He does not, says the Upanishad. "As the sun is the cause of the eyesight of every being, yet is not made defective by the defect in any eye, even so the Self of all is not affected by the miseries of the body, or by any misery that is around you." I may have some disease and see everything yellow, but the sun is not affected by it. "He is the One, the Creator of all, the Ruler of all, the Internal Soul of every being–He who makes His Oneness manifold. Thus sages who realise Him as the Soul of their souls, unto them belongs eternal peace; unto none else, unto none else. He who in this world of evanescence finds Him who never changes, he who in this universe of death finds that One Life, he who in this manifold finds that Oneness, and all those who realise Him as the Soul of their souls, to them belongs eternal peace; unto none else, unto none else. Where to find Him in the external world, where to find Him in the suns, and moons, and stars? There the sun cannot illumine, nor the moon, nor the stars, the flash of lightning cannot illumine the place; what to speak of this mortal fire? He shining, everything else shines. It is His light that they have borrowed, and He is shining through them." Here is another beautiful simile. Those of you who have been in India and have seen how the banyan tree comes from one root and spreads itself far around, will understand this. He is that banyan tree; He is the root of all and has branched out until He has become this universe, and however far He extends, every one of these trunks and branches is connected.

Various heavens are spoken of in the Brahmana portion of the Vedas, but the philosophical teaching of the Upanishads gives up the idea of going to heaven. Happiness is not in this heaven or in that heaven, it is in the soul; places do not signify anything. Here is another passage which shows the different states of realisation. "In the heaven of the forefathers, as a man sees things in a dream, so the Real Truth is seen." As in dreams we see things hazy and not so distinct, so we see the Reality there. There is another heaven called the Gandharva, in which it is still less clear; as a man sees his own reflection in the water, so is the Reality seen there. The highest heaven, of which the Hindus conceive is called the Brahmaloka; and in this, the Truth is seen much more clearly, like light and shade, but not yet quite distinctly. But as a man sees his own face in a mirror, perfect, distinct, and clear, so is the Truth shining in the soul of man. The highest heaven, therefore, is in our own souls; the greatest temple of worship is the human soul, greater than all heavens, says the Vedanta; for in no heaven anywhere, can we understand the reality as distinctly and clearly as in this life, in our own soul. Changing places does not help one much. I thought while I was in India that the cave would give me clearer vision. I found it was not so. Then I thought the forest would do so, then, Varanasi. But the same difficulty existed everywhere, because we make our own worlds. If I am evil, the whole world is evil to me. That is what the Upanishad says. And the same thing applies to all worlds. If I die and go to heaven, I should find the same, for until I am pure it is no use going to caves, or forests, or to Varanasi, or to heaven, and if I have polished my mirror, it does not matter where I live, I get the Reality just as It is.

So it is useless, running hither and thither, and spending energy in vain, which should be spent only in polishing the mirror. The same idea is expressed again: "None sees Him, none sees His form with the eyes. It is in the mind, in the pure mind, that He is seen, and thus immortality is gained."

Those who were at the summer lectures on Raja-Yoga will be interested to know that what was taught then was a different kind of Yoga. The Yoga which we are now considering consists chiefly in controlling the senses. When the senses are held as slaves by the human soul, when they can no longer disturb the mind, then the Yogi has reached the goal. "When all vain desires of the heart have been given up, then this very mortal becomes immortal, then he becomes one with God even here. When all the knots of the heart are cut asunder, then the mortal becomes immortal, and he enjoys Brahman here." Here, on earth, nowhere else.

A few words ought to be said here. You will generally hear that this Vedanta, this philosophy and other Eastern systems, look only to something beyond, letting go the enjoyments and struggle of this life. This idea is entirely wrong. It is only ignorant people who do not know anything of Eastern thought, and never had brain enough to understand anything of its real teaching, that tell you so. On the contrary, we read in our scriptures that our philosophers do not want to go to other worlds, but depreciate them as places where people weep and laugh for a little while only, and then die. As long as we are weak we shall have to go through these experiences; but whatever is true, is here, and that is the human soul. And this also is insisted upon, that by committing suicide, we cannot escape the inevitable; we cannot evade it. But the right path is hard to find. The Hindu is just as practical as the Western, only we differ in our views of life. The one says, build a good house, let us have good clothes and food, intellectual culture, and so on, for this is the whole of life; and in that he is immensely practical. But the Hindu says, true knowledge of the world means knowledge of the soul, metaphysics; and he wants to enjoy that life. In America there was a great agnostic, a very noble man, a very good man, and a very fine speaker. He lectured on religion, which he said was of no use; why bother our heads about other worlds? He employed this simile; we have an orange here, and we want to squeeze all the juice out of it. I met him once and said, "I agree with you entirely. I have some fruit, and I too want to squeeze out the juice. Our difference lies in the choice of the fruit. You want an orange, and I prefer a mango. You think it is enough to live here and eat and drink and have a little scientific knowledge; but you have no right to say that that will suit all tastes. Such a conception is nothing to me. If I had only to learn how an apple falls to the ground, or how an electric current shakes my nerves, I would commit suicide. I want to understand the heart of things, the very kernel itself. Your study is the manifestation of life, mine is the life itself. My philosophy says you must know that and drive out from your mind all thoughts of heaven and hell and all other superstitions, even though they exist in the same sense that this world exists. I must know the heart of this life, its very essence, what it is, not only how it works and what are its manifestations. I want the why of everything. I leave the how to children. As one of your countrymen said, 'While I am smoking a cigarette, if I were to write a book, it would be the science of the cigarette.' It is good and great to be scientific, God bless them in their search; but when a man says that is all, he is talking foolishly, not caring to know the raison d'tre of life, never studying existence itself. I may argue that all your knowledge is nonsense, without a basis. You are studying the manifestations of life, and when I ask you what life is, you say you do not know. You are welcome to your study, but leave me to mine."

I am practical, very practical, in my own way. So your idea that only the West is practical is nonsense. You are practical in your way, and I in another. There are different types of men and minds. If in the East a man is told that he will find the truth by standing on one leg all his life, he will pursue that method. If in the West men hear that there is a gold mine somewhere in an uncivilised country, thousands will face the dangers there, in the hope of getting the gold; and, perhaps, only one succeeds. The same men have heard that they have souls but are content to leave the care of them to the church. The first man will not go near the savages, he says it may be dangerous. But if we tell him that on the top of a high mountain lives a wonderful sage who can give him knowledge of the soul, he tries to climb up to him, even if he be killed in the attempt. Both types of men are practical, but the

The objective of the Satyagraha was to secure religious and cultural liberty for the Hindus who at that time constituted 86% of total population of Hyderabad State. Many notable people like Senapati Bapat, V.G. Deshpande, Prabhakar Balwant Dani, Madhavrao Mule, took part in it. The Arya Samaj also sent around 10000 civil resisters. At last, on 19th July, 1939, the Nizam government announced some political reforms. In the new dispensation, 50% seats were left for non-Muslims. Although Hindus were the majority in the state and Muslims were in minority, Hindu Mahasabha accepted this proposal. They withdrew the movement despite the fact that these reforms for partial reforms. Indian National Congress did not support this movement and called it 'communal' and 'anti-national'.

Savarkar was an outspoken critic of Mahatma Gandhi. He considered him 'a sissy', who was willing to cooperate with Britishers. He criticized Gandhi for being a hypocrite as he supported use of violence by Britishers against Germany. He also criticized his utopian views of Hindu-Muslim Unity and his appeasement of Muslims at the time of Khilafat Movement. In articles from the 1920s to the 1940s Savarkar considered Gandhi as a naive leader, and was of the view that Gandhi happened to babble about compassion, forgiveness, yet notwithstanding his sublime and broad heart, he has a very narrow and immature head.

The All-India Muslim League adopted the Lahore Resolution, also known as the Pakistan Resolution, on the occasion of its three-day general session in Lahore during 22nd to 24th March, 1940. Based on the Two-Nation Theory, it called for the creation of 'independent states' for Muslims in north-western and eastern British India. The constituent units of these states were to be autonomous and sovereign. The resolution was presented by A. K. Fazlul Huq, the Prime Minister of Bengal. It was later interpreted as a demand for a separate and single Muslim state called Pakistan. 23rd March is a national holiday to be celebrated as 'Pakistan Day' in Pakistan to commemorate both Lahore Resolution

(1940) and the Republic Day (1956); the country became the first Islamic Republic in the world. But it was invoked in the Six point movement of the Awami League in 1966, which eventually led to the creation of Bangladesh in 1971.

Savarkar was totally against the Lahore Resolution. It was the backdrop, in December 1940 presidential address at the Twenty-second Session of the Akhil Bharatiya Hindu Mahasabha at Madurai, Savarkar criticised Gandhi's various renderings of absolute nonviolence unsparingly, and termed Gandhi's act as "The Dangerous Cult of Absolute Non-violence." That became a landmark speech in the revival of Hindu Cultural Nationalism during last phase of Independence Movement in India. Savarkar's views in that speech were allegedly the ideological inspiration for Nathuram Godse who became his protégé. Although so called secular Congress and other parties leaders tried hard to establish a direct link between Savarkar's views and those of Godse as a put forward in his trial speech, but none was found be true in the trial court.]

Relative nonviolence on the whole, is doubtless a virtue so preeminently contributing to human good as to form one of the fundamentals on which human life whether individual or social can take its stand and evolve all social amenities. But absolute nonviolence, i.e. nonviolence under all circumstances and even when instead of helping human life, whether individual or national, it causes an incalculable harm to humanity as a whole and ought to be condemned as a moral perversity. It is on the whole condemned likewise by those very religious and moral schools which lauded relative nonviolence as the first and foremost human virtue.

It should be noted in particular that the ahimsa preached by Buddhism or Jainism is directly opposed to the absolute ahimsa or the absolute nonviolence as Gandhiji interprets it, condemning all armed resistance under all circumstances. The very fact that the Jains reared up kingdoms, produced heroes and heroines who fought armed battles and Jain commanders-in-chief leading

Jain armies without being ostracized by the Jain acharyas, prove the point to the hilt that the ahimsa of the Jains cannot be the rabid ahimsa of the Gandhist school. The Jain scriptures openly assert that armed resistance to incorrigible aggression is not only justifiable but imperative. Lord Buddha also gave the same ruling when questioned by the leaders of a clan as to whether they should take to armed resistance as soldiers against the armed aggression of another clan. 'Soldiers may fight against armed aggression,' said Lord Buddha, 'without committing a sin if but they fight with arms in defence of a righteous cause.'

Call it a law of nature or the will of God as you like, the hard fact remains that there is no room for absolute nonviolence in nature. Man could not have saved himself from utter extinction and nor could he have led the precarious and wretched life of a coward had he not succeeded in adding the strength of artificial arms to his natural arms. Throughout the paleolethic and neolethic periods, the bronze age and the iron age man could maintain himself, multiply and master this earth chiefly through his armed strength. In all honesty, the 'defensive sword was the first saviour of man'.

You may perhaps add something new to history but you cannot add to or take away a syllable from the iron law of nature itself. Even today if man hands over a blank cheque to a wolf or a tiger to be filled in, with a human pledge of absolute nonviolence, no killing of a living being, no armed force to be used, even then the wolves and the tigers will lay waste your mandirs (temples) and mosques, culture and cultivation and ashrams. In face of such an iron law of nature can anything be more immoral and sinful than to preach a principle so antihuman as that of absolute nonviolence condemning all armed resistance even to aggression? Yet it is curious to find that even those who condemn this doctrine of absolute nonviolence as impracticable, still seem to believe that though it is impracticable for us worldly men, this doctrine is nevertheless highly moral and evince some mahatmaic excellence, some superhuman sanctity. This apologetic tone must be changed. It raises these prophets of this eccentric doctrine in their own estimation and makes them feel they had really invented some moral law raising human politics to some divine level. Seeing that, even their opponents on practical grounds attribute to them a superhuman saintliness. Owing to the very eccentricity of their doctrine, they grow, perhaps unconsciously all the more eccentric and have the insane temerity to preach in all seriousness to the Indian public that even the taking up of a lathi (stick) is sinful. The best means of freeing India from the foreign yoke is the spinning-wheel.

Not only that, but even after India becomes independent there would not be any necessity of maintaining a single armed soldier or a single warship to protect her frontiers. If but India believes and acts in the spirit of such absolute nonviolence maintaining no army, no navy or no air force, no nation in the world shall invade her and even if some armed nations did so they could be easily persuaded to fall back as soon as they are confronted by the unarmed army of our 'desha sevikas' (caretakers of the country) singing to the tune of the spinning-wheel, appealing to the conscience of the invading forces. When things have come to such a pass that such quixotic souls are sent as accredited spokesmen by the credulous crowd to the Round Table Conferences and even in foreign lands, such senseless proposals are seriously advanced by them in the name of the Indian nation to the great amusement of the foreign statesmen and the general public in Europe and America. The time has surely come to take this doctrinal plague quite seriously and to counteract it as quickly as possible. We must tell them, in no apologetic language but in firm accents, that your doctrine of absolute nonviolence is not only absolutely impracticable but absolutely immoral. It is not an outcome of any saintliness but of insanity. It requires no ingenuity on your part to tell us that if all men observe absolute nonviolence, there will be no war in the world and no necessity of any armed forces. Just as it requires no extraordinary insight to maintain that if but men learn to live forever, mankind would be free from death.

[Following the assassination of Gandhi on 30th January, 1948, police arrested the assassin Nathuram Godse and his alleged accomplices and conspirators. Godse claimed full responsibility for planning and carrying out the assassination.

He was a member of the Hindu Mahasabha and of the Rashtriya Swayamsevak Sangh. Savarkar, now the former president of the Hindu Mahasabha, was arrested on 5th February, 1948, from his house in Shivaji Park, and kept under detention in the Arthur Road Prison, Mumbai. He was charged with murder, conspiracy to murder and abetment to murder. A day before his arrest, Savarkar in a public written statement, as reported in The Times of India, Mumbai dated 7th February, 1948, termed Gandhi's assassination a fratricidal crime, endangering India's existence as a nascent nation.

However, according to the Approver Digamber Badge, on 17th January, 1948, Nathuram Godse went to have a last darshan (audience) with Savarkar in Bombay before the assassination. While Badge and Shankar Kistaiya waited outside, Nathuram and Narayan Apte went in. On coming out Apte told Badge that Savarkar blessed them 'Yashasvi houn ya' (be successful and return). Apte also said that Savarkar predicted that Gandhi's 100 years were over and there was no doubt that the task would be successfully finished. However Badge's testimony was not accepted as the approver's evidence lacked independent corroboration and hence Savarkar was acquitted.

Actually, when the Congress launched the Quit India movement in 1942, Savarkar criticised it and asked Hindus to stay active in the war effort and not disobey the government, he urged the Hindus to enlist in the armed forces to learn the 'arts of war'. Hindu Mahasabha activists protested Gandhi's initiative to hold talks with Jinnah in 1944, which Savarkar denounced as 'appeasement.' He assailed the British proposals for transfer of power, attacking both the Congress and the British for making concessions to Muslim separatists. So, after Gandhi's assassination, the Congress led India Government's attitudes towards Savarkar was clearly revengeful.

After he was acquitted of the allegations related to Gandhi's assassination and released from jail, Savarkar was arrested by the Congress government, for making "militant Hindu nationalist speeches", he was released after agreeing to give up political activities. He continued addressing social and cultural elements of Hindutva. He resumed political activism after the ban on it was lifted, it was however limited until his death because of ill health. His followers bestowed upon him honours and financial awards when he was alive. His demise on 26th February, 1966 was unique, for he died through Prayopaveshan, death bv his own wish. Two thousand RSS workers gave his funeral procession a guard of honour.

But Savarkar never died in the minds of millions of Indian, particularly of Hindu Cultural Nationalism supporters of RSS backed organizations and is being remembered as 'Swatantryaveer' (Freedom Hero). In his death, he was a man who had seen most of his life mission fulfilled Physically, he took the last bow on the worlds stage, but his thoughts, the philosophy which he so intensely propounded and untiringly propagated, are immortal and continue to be a beacon to the beleaguered Hindu society. Savarkar's 'The Dangerous Cult of Absolute Non-violence' speech still haunts the so called secularist political commentators.]

□□□